CW01640863

·stening, Speaking ·ritical Thinking 3

UNLOCK

STUDENT'S BOOK WITH DIGITAL PACK

THIRD EDITION

Greg Archer, Nancy Jordan,
Sabina Ostrowska, with Chris Sowton

CAMBRIDGE
UNIVERSITY PRESS

CAMBRIDGE
UNIVERSITY PRESS & ASSESSMENT

Shaftesbury Road, Cambridge CB2 8EA, United Kingdom

One Liberty Plaza, 20th Floor, New York, NY 10006, USA

477 Williamstown Road, Port Melbourne, VIC 3207, Australia

314–321, 3rd Floor, Plot 3, Splendor Forum, Jasola District Centre, New Delhi – 110025, India

103 Penang Road, #05–06/07, Visioncrest Commercial, Singapore 238467

Cambridge University Press & Assessment is a department of the University of Cambridge.

We share the University's mission to contribute to society through the pursuit of education, learning and research at the highest international levels of excellence.

www.cambridge.org
Information on this title: www.cambridge.org/9781009797559

First published 2014
Second Edition 2019
Second Edition update published 2021
Third Edition 2025

20 19 18 17 16 15 14 13 12 11 10 9 8 7 6 5 4 3

Printed in the Netherlands by Wilco BV

A catalogue record for this publication is available from the British Library

ISBN 978-1-009-79755-9 Listening, Speaking and Critical Thinking Student's Book with Digital Pack 3
ISBN 978-1-009-54407-8 Listening, Speaking and Critical Thinking Student's eBook with Digital Pack 3

CONTENTS

MAP OF THE BOOK

UNIT	VIDEO	LISTENING	VOCABULARY
1 ANIMALS Listening 1: A debate about using animals for work (Biology / Zoology) Listening 2: A presentation about human threats to the African forest elephant (Biology / Zoology / Environmental science)	The mental skills of chimpanzees	***Key listening skills:*** Taking notes Listening for contrasting ideas Listening for signposting language ***Additional skills:*** Understanding key vocabulary Using your knowledge Predicting content using visuals Listening for main ideas Listening for text organization Listening for detail Synthesizing ***Pronunciation for listening:*** Intonation of lists	Word families
2 THE ENVIRONMENT Listening 1: A lecture about hydroponic agriculture (Ecology / Environmental science) Listening 2: A debate about nuclear power (Environmental science / Political science)	Blowing in the wind: offshore wind farms	***Key listening skills:*** Listening for explanations Listening for counter-arguments ***Additional skills:*** Understanding key vocabulary Predicting content using visuals Using your knowledge Listening for main ideas Listening for detail Listening for text organization Identifying for and against arguments Synthesizing ***Pronunciation for listening:*** Connected speech: linking sounds	Negative prefixes
3 TRANSPORT Listening 1: A podcast about traffic in cities (Sociology / Civil engineering) Listening 2: A presentation about cycling to work (Sociology / Civil engineering)	Sustainable transport	***Key listening skill:*** Listening for rhetorical questions ***Additional skills:*** Understanding key vocabulary Using your knowledge Listening for main ideas Taking notes on detail Listening for detail Listening for text organization Synthesizing ***Pronunciation for listening:*** Word stress	Talking about problems and solutions
4 CUSTOMS AND TRADITIONS Listening 1: A podcast about changing customs in the modern world (Anthropology) Listening 2: A discussion about gift-giving (Sociology)	Chinese moon cakes	***Key listening skills:*** Identifying cause and effect Listening for opinion ***Additional skills:*** Understanding key vocabulary Using your knowledge Listening for main ideas Taking notes on detail Synthesizing ***Pronunciation for listening:*** Connected speech: /t/ and /d/ at the end of words	Suffixes

GRAMMAR	CRITICAL THINKING	SPEAKING
Modals for obligation, prohibition and advice	Creating a talk for a specific audience	*Preparation for speaking:* Using signposting language Introducing examples Expressing general beliefs *Pronunciation for speaking:* Signposting a presentation *Speaking task:* Give a two-minute presentation about the human threats to an endangered species.
Modal verbs to express future possibility	Making counter-arguments	*Preparation for speaking:* Linking ideas with transition words and phrases Talking about advantages and disadvantages Giving counter-arguments *Speaking task:* Take part in a debate about allowing a new wind farm near your town.
Comparative and superlative adjectives	Evaluating problems and proposing solutions	*Preparation for speaking:* Giving recommendations Expanding on an idea *Speaking task:* Give a presentation on a transport problem and suggest solutions to solve the problem.
Present perfect	Creating a convincing argument	*Preparation for speaking:* Being polite in a discussion Using adverbs for emphasis Phrases with *that* *Pronunciation for speaking:* Stress patterns in phrases for agreeing and disagreeing *Speaking task:* Take part in a discussion about whether special occasions have become too commercial.

UNIT	VIDEO	LISTENING	VOCABULARY
5 HEALTH AND FITNESS Listening 1: A podcast about why some people live a long life (Health Science) Listening 2: Four presentations about programmes to improve your health (taekwondo, team sports, cycling, acupuncture) (Health Science / Sports management)	Brain health	*Key listening skills:* Listening for attitude Identifying references to common knowledge *Additional skills* Understanding key vocabulary Using your knowledge Listening for main ideas Taking notes on detail Synthesizing *Pronunciation for listening:* Attitude and emotion	Adjectives to describe well-being
6 DISCOVERY AND INVENTION Listening 1: A museum tour about inventions from the Middle Ages (History) Listening 2: A lecture about the history of smartphone apps (Art and design)	A career as a research scientist	*Key listening skills:* Understanding references to earlier ideas Understanding lecture organization *Additional skills:* Understanding key vocabulary Using your knowledge Listening for main ideas Predicting content using context Taking notes: jigsaw reading Listening for detail Synthesizing *Pronunciation for listening:* Weak and strong forms	Uses of the verb *make*
7 FASHION Listening 1: A discussion about fast fashion (Fashion design / Business) Listening 2: An interview with a fashion designer (Fashion design / Business / Marketing)	Interview with College of Art graduate Christopher Raeburn	*Key listening skills:* Taking notes on main ideas and details Auxiliary verbs for emphasis *Additional skills:* Understanding key vocabulary Predicting content using visuals Taking notes on detail Using your knowledge Listening for main ideas Making inferences Synthesizing *Pronunciation for listening:* Vowel omission	Talking about recent events and actions
8 ECONOMICS Listening 1: A podcast about millionaire lifestyles (Sociology / Economics / Business) Listening 2: A discussion about whether university students should be paid for good grades (Sociology / Economics)	Money management	*Key listening skill:* Understanding paraphrases *Additional skills:* Understanding key vocabulary Using your knowledge Listening for main ideas Taking notes on detail Listening for detail Listening for opinion Synthesizing *Pronunciation for listening:* Silent letters	Collocations with *pay* and *money*

GRAMMAR	CRITICAL THINKING	SPEAKING
Phrasal verbs	Brainstorming and evaluating ideas using an ideas map	*Preparation for speaking:* Problem–solution organization Presenting persuasively *Speaking task:* Give a presentation to a group of students about an idea for a health product or programme.
Passive verb forms	Summarizing information using *Wh-* questions	*Preparation for speaking:* Previewing a topic Organizing ideas Explaining how something is used *Speaking task:* Give a presentation about an invention or a discovery which has changed our lives.
Adverbs *already*, *just*, *yet* and *still* Predictions and expectations about the future	Creating a purpose statement Evaluating interview questions	*Preparation for speaking:* Asking for opinions and checking information Asking follow-up questions *Speaking task:* Take part in an interview to find out attitudes about uniforms and dress codes.
Conditional sentences	Evaluating arguments	*Preparation for speaking:* Using gerunds as subjects to talk about actions Presenting reasons and evidence to support an argument Using paraphrases *Speaking task:* Take part in a discussion about whether young people should be allowed to have credit cards.

YOUR GUIDE TO UNLOCK

UNLOCK YOUR ACADEMIC POTENTIAL

Unlock Third Edition is a six-level, academic-light English course created to build the skills and language students need for their studies (CEFR Pre-A1 to C1). It develops students' ability to think critically in an academic context right from the start of their language learning. Every level has inspiring videos on a range of academic topics.

CRITICAL THINKING

Unlock Third Edition includes the right mix of lower- and higher-order thinking skills development in every unit, with clear learning objectives. Students are better prepared for their academic studies and have the confidence to apply the critical thinking skills they have developed. Critical thinking in *Unlock* Third Edition:

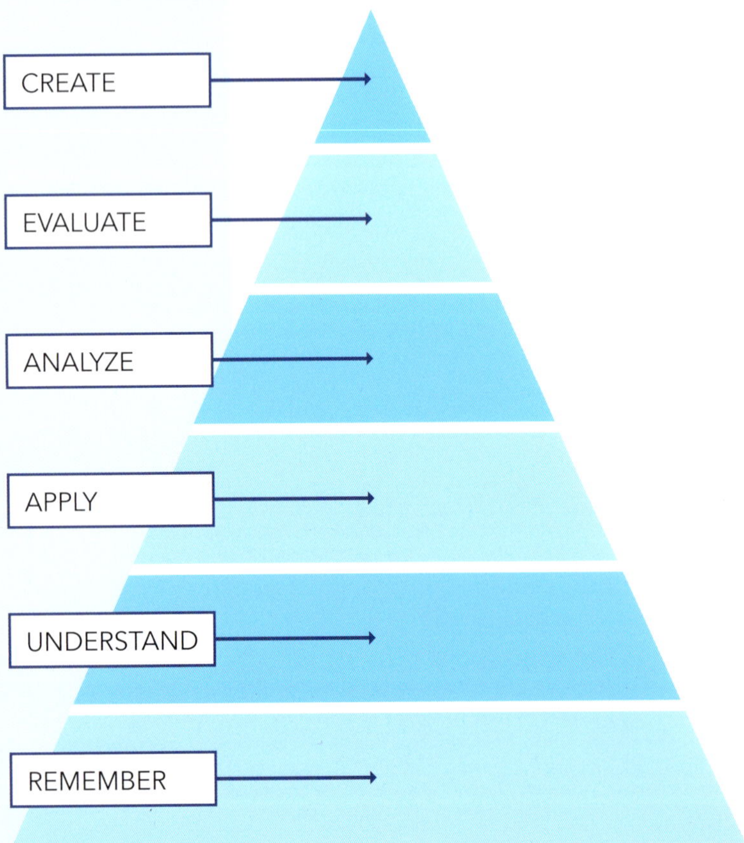

- is **informed** by a range of academic research from Bloom in the 1950s, to Krathwohl and Anderson in the 2000s, to more recent considerations relating to 21st Century Skills
- has a **refined** syllabus with a better mix of higher- and lower-order critical thinking skills
- is **measurable**, with objectives and self-evaluation so students can track their critical thinking progress
- is **transparent** so teachers and students know when and why they're developing critical thinking skills
- is **supported** with professional development material for teachers so teachers can teach with confidence

TEACHER RESOURCES

We've carried out research with teachers across the world to understand their needs and how we can better meet them with *Unlock*. All teacher resources can be accessed on our learning platform, Cambridge One cambridge.org/one.

- Fully interactive presentation software, **Presentation Plus**, with pop-up activities to type or automatically display answers.
- Downloadable **Model Answer Booklet** with model answers for all end-of-unit productive activities and example answers for all 'Answers may vary' activity types in the Student's Book.
- **Variations of unit tests, mid- and end-of-course tests** give teachers options when assessing student understanding and progress.
- **Teacher Manual and Development Pack** supports your teaching with flexible lesson plans with timings for every unit.
- **Digital Workbook with videos** to assign additional practice for your students whenever you see this symbol UNLOCK DIGITAL WORKBOOK

RESEARCH

Unlock Third Edition is informed by consulting with a global advisory panel and comprehensive review of the material so you can be assured of the quality of every lesson.

- **extensive market research** with teachers and students to fully understand their needs throughout the course's development
- consulting **academic research** into critical thinking
- refined vocabulary syllabus using our **exclusive Corpus research**

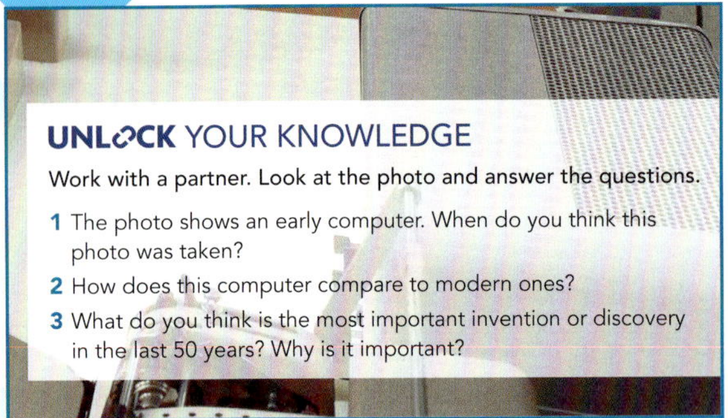

UNLOCK YOUR KNOWLEDGE

Work with a partner. Look at the photo and answer the questions.

1 The photo shows an early computer. When do you think this photo was taken?
2 How does this computer compare to modern ones?
3 What do you think is the most important invention or discovery in the last 50 years? Why is it important?

Unlock your knowledge

Encourages discussion around the themes of the unit with inspiration from interesting questions and striking images.

WATCH AND LISTEN

ACTIVATING YOUR KNOWLEDGE

PREPARING TO WATCH

1 Work with a partner and answer the questions.
1 What are the four 'STEM' subjects?
a Science, Technology, Engineering, Mechanics

Watch and listen

Features an engaging and motivating video which generates interest in the topic and develops listening skills.

LISTENING

LISTENING 1

PREPARING TO LISTEN

1 Work in groups. Look at the photos and discuss the questions.
1 Which of these inventions do you think is the oldest?
2 Which do you think is the newest?
3 Which do you think has been the most useful?
4 Where in the world do you think they were invented?

Listening 1

Provides information about the topic and practises pre-listening, while-listening and post-listening skills. This section may also include a focus on pronunciation which will further enhance listening comprehension.

LANGUAGE DEVELOPMENT

USES OF THE VERB *MAKE*

VOCABULARY

The verb *make* has three main meanings: *force*, *cause* or *produce*.
Force: *My boss* ***made*** *me work late last night.*
Cause: *Water and weights* ***make*** *the mechanical clocks work.*
Produce: *The first fountain pen was* ***made*** *in 953.*

1 Work with a partner. Discuss the meaning of *make* in each sentence. Write *C* (cause), *F* (force) or *P* (produce).
1 Gunpowder was first **made** in China. *P*
2 My professor **made** me rewrite my assignment because there were too many mistakes. ____
3 Social media **makes** it easy for people to stay in touch. ____

Language development

Practises the vocabulary and grammar from Listening 1 and pre-teaches the vocabulary and grammar for Listening 2.

LISTENING 2

PREDICTING CONTENT USING CONTEXT

PREPARING TO LISTEN

1 Read the introduction to a lecture about an invention. Answer the questions.
1 Can you guess the name of the invention? ____
2 What two words are used to refer to it? ____ and ____

In today's lecture, I want to discuss an invention which has changed our lives. This product has made a huge difference in the way we work, travel, communicate and socialize with friends. Can you guess what it is? I'm talking here about mobile phone [redacted] *The word* [redacted] *comes from* [redacted] *Traditionally,* [redacted] *were used in computers to help them perform better. However, with the invention of smartphones, the word* [redacted] *is used to refer to phone* [redacted] *In this lecture, we'll start by discussing the very first* [redacted] *and their development. We will then discuss how* [redacted] *have changed our lives. Finally, we'll focus on some of the most popular* [redacted] *used by people today.*

Listening 2

Presents a second listening text on the topic, often in a different format, and serves as a model for the speaking task.

3 How will you find your way to your destination? What will you do if you get lost?
4 Where are the address and phone numbers of the hotels where you want to stay?

LISTENING FOR MAIN IDEAS

6 6.5 Listen to the lecture. Are your answers to the questions in Exercise 5 similar to the speaker's? Check your notes and add ideas.

7 Work in groups of three students, A, B and C. Your teacher is going to give a text to each student in the group. Read your text and underline the key information in it. Then make notes about it.

8 Work in your group from Exercise 7. Use your notes to tell each other about the key information in your text.

9 Work in your groups again. Use your notes to underline eight mistakes in the notes. Write the correct words or numbers in gaps 1–8 on page 138.

TAKING NOTES: JIGSAW READING

first apps used for:	*second generation apps:*	*another effect of apps:*	*negative effects of apps:*

QR codes

Allows students to easily access the audio of the listening passages and activities.

SPEAKING

CRITICAL THINKING

At the end of this unit, you will do the speaking task below.

Give a presentation about an invention or a discovery which has changed our lives.

Summarizing information using *Wh-* questions

SKILLS

When you do research on a topic, try asking yourself the following questions: *Who? What? When? Where? Why?* Many researchers add *How?* to this list. Then search for the answers to these questions. To organize your research, it is helpful to make an ideas map like the one in Exercise 1. This is a quick and easy way to focus on the key details of a topic.

1 Choose one of the inventions from Listening 1 or one of the apps from Listening 2. Write this in the Topic box below. Complete the ideas map for the invention or app. Use information from your notes on page 130 or 137. Try answering some of these questions:

UNDERSTAND

1 When was the last time you used this thing?
2 What are its uses?
3 What would life be like without it?
4 How has it affected our lives?

Critical thinking

Develops the lower- and higher-order thinking skills required for the speaking task.

PREPARATION FOR SPEAKING

PREVIEWING A TOPIC

SKILLS

In the introduction to a presentation, give a preview of what you will talk about. This helps your audience follow your talk. Here are some examples of language you can use to preview a topic:
I'd like to begin my talk by looking at …
After that, I'm going to explain …
Then, I'll discuss …
Finally, I'll explore …

1 6.6 Listen to an introduction to a presentation which previews what the speaker will talk about. Circle the things that the speaker does.

1 mentions the invention's name in the first sentence
2 gives a description of the invention
3 says how you can use it
4 gives specific details of how it was invented
5 explains what will happen next in the presentation

2 Work with a partner. Practise giving an introduction about a simple

Preparation for speaking

Presents and practises functional language, pronunciation and speaking strategies for the speaking task.

SPEAKING TASK

Give a presentation about an invention or a discovery which has changed our lives.

PREPARE

1 Look at the ideas map you created in Exercise 4 in the Critical thinking section. Add any new information. Decide in what order you will answer the *Wh-* questions and write them below.

1 ________
2 ________
3 ________
4 ________
5 ________
6 ________

2 Make notes about the language you will use. Use language like this:

To preview your topic	To explain how something is used
I'd like to start by talking about …	_____ *helps people to …*
Then, I'll discuss …	*Without* _____, *…*
Finally, I'll explore …	_____ *makes it* _____ *to …*
Passive verbs	References to earlier ideas

Speaking task

Uses the skills and language learned throughout the unit to support students in producing a presentational or interactional speaking task. This is the unit's main learning objective.

OBJECTIVES REVIEW

1 Check your learning objectives for this unit. Write *3*, *2* or *1* for each objective.

3 = very well 2 = well 1 = not so well

I can …

watch and understand a video about research scientists.	___
understand references to earlier ideas.	___
understand lecture organization.	___
summarize information using *Wh-* questions.	___
use passive verb forms.	___
preview a topic.	___
organize ideas.	___
explain how something is used.	___
give a presentation about an invention or a discovery which has changed our lives.	___

Objectives review

Allows learners to evaluate how well they have mastered the skills covered in the unit.

WORDLIST

access (v) ⊙	make a comparison (v phr)	make attempts (v phr)
allow (v) ⊙	make a contribution (v phr)	make improvements (v phr)
app (n)	make a decision (v phr)	make public (v phr)
contribution (n) ⊙	make a difference (v phr)	outcome (n) ⊙
create (v) ⊙	make an investment (v phr)	product (n) ⊙
device (n) ⊙		scholar (n) ⊙
diagram (n) ⊙		technology (n) ⊙
discovery (n) ⊙		user (n) ⊙
industry (n) ⊙		weapon (n) ⊙
install (v)		

⊙ = high-frequency words in the Cambridge Academic Corpus

Wordlist

Lists the key vocabulary from the unit. The most frequent words used at this level in an academic context are highlighted with this icon ⊙

COMPONENTS

Unlock offers 70–90 hours per Student's Book, which is extendable with the Digital Pack, and other additional activities in the Teacher's Manual and Development Pack.

Unlock is a paired-skills course with two separate Student's Books per level. For levels 1–5 (CEFR A1 – C1), these are ***Reading, Writing and Critical Thinking*** and ***Listening, Speaking and Critical Thinking***. They share the same unit topics so you have access to a wide range of material at each level. Each Student's Book includes access to the Digital Pack.

Unlock Basic has been developed for pre-A1 learners. ***Unlock Basic Skills*** integrates reading, writing, listening, speaking and critical thinking in one book to provide students with an effective and manageable learning experience. ***Unlock Basic Literacy*** develops and builds confidence in literacy. The Basic books also share the same unit topics and so can be used together or separately, and ***Unlock Basic Literacy*** can be used for self-study.

STUDENT COMPONENTS

All material in the Student's Digital Pack (Levels 1–5) can be accessed on Cambridge One, our learning platform using the unique code printed on the inside front cover of the Student's Book.

Resource	Description
Student's Book with Digital Pack	• 8 units per level (Levels 1–4); 10 units (Level 5) • QR codes for students to easily access the Class Audio • Levels 1–5 includes access to the Digital Pack: – Interactive eBook with videos – Digital Workbook – Downloadable audio for listening activities and pronunciation (Listening and Speaking strand) – Downloadable audio for reading passages (Reading and Writing strand) • *Unlock Basic Skills* comes with downloadable audio and video (11 units) • *Unlock Basic Literacy* comes with downloadable audio (11 units)
Interactive eBook with videos	• Levels 1–5 • Digital version of the Student's Book with auto-graded activities • Student's Book videos for students to watch on their own
Digital Workbook with videos	• Levels 1–5 • Extension activities to further practise the language and skills learned • Additional video comprehension and extension activities that are different from the activities in the Student's Book.

TEACHER COMPONENTS

All teacher components can be accessed on Cambridge One, our learning platform. Teachers can access the Digital Workbook with videos by creating an account. To access the Teacher's Resources and Presentation Plus, please request an access code from your local Cambridge representative.

Resource	Description
Audio	• Downloadable audio for listening activities and pronunciation (Listening and Speaking strand) • Downloadable audio for reading passages (Reading and Writing strand)
Teacher's Manual and Development Pack	• Flexible lesson plans with timings, lesson objectives and lesson observation templates • Downloadable Model Answer Booklet with model and example answers for productive skills • Supplementary classroom materials for Levels 1–4 • Common student errors • *Developing critical thinking skills in your students*, a teacher development material with clear objectives, in-practice activities and opportunities for review and self-evaluation.
Teacher Development Resources	Additional materials which can be used for professional development: • Peer-to-peer training workshop materials with PowerPoint presentations • In-session worksheets, trainer's notes • Pre- and post- workshop quizzes
Presentation Plus	• Fully interactive presentation software, with pop-up activities to type or automatically display answers • Embedded audio and video for easy access to play in class
Tests	• Unit, mid- and end-of-course tests for the assessment of student understanding and progress

TEACHING WITH UNLOCK THIRD EDITION

This online training course gives you a thorough knowledge of how *Unlock* works, what it includes and acquaints teachers with the methodological principles behind the course.

UNIT 1

ANIMALS

LEARNING OBJECTIVES

Watch and listen
Watch and understand a video about the mental skills of chimpanzees.

Listening skills
Take notes; listen for contrasting ideas; listen for signposting language.

Critical thinking
Create a talk for a specific audience; organize information for a presentation.

Grammar
Use modals for obligation, prohibition and advice.

Speaking skills
Use signposting language; introduce examples; express general beliefs.

Speaking task
Give a presentation about threats to an endangered species.

UNIT 1 ANIMALS

UNLOCK YOUR KNOWLEDGE

Work with a partner. Look at the photo and answer the questions.

1 What work are the animals doing?

2 Do people use animals for work in your country? If yes, what work do they do?

3 What other types of work can animals do?

WATCH AND LISTEN

ACTIVATING YOUR KNOWLEDGE

PREDICTING CONTENT USING VISUALS

PREPARING TO WATCH

1 Work with a partner and answer the questions.

1 Can animals solve problems? Give examples.
2 How do animals play? Do you think they like puzzles or games? Why / Why not?

2 You are going to watch a video about the mental skills of chimpanzees. Before you watch, look at the photos from the video. Discuss the questions with your partner.

1 What is the goal of a game like a maze?
2 In your opinion, is the chimpanzee thinking? Why / Why not?
3 Do you think the chimpanzee and the man are happy or angry?

GLOSSARY

mental (adj) relating to the mind
maze (n) a type of puzzle with a series of paths from entrance to exit
in the wild (phr) in nature, not in a zoo, on a farm or as a pet
reflect upon (phr v) to think about in a serious and careful way

UNDERSTANDING MAIN IDEAS

WHILE WATCHING

3 Watch the video. Circle the correct answer.

1 The scientists wanted to find out if chimpanzees could …
  a look for food.
  b plan ahead.
  c protect themselves.
2 The chimpanzee is able to …
  a use a computer.
  b ask for food.
  c listen to commands.

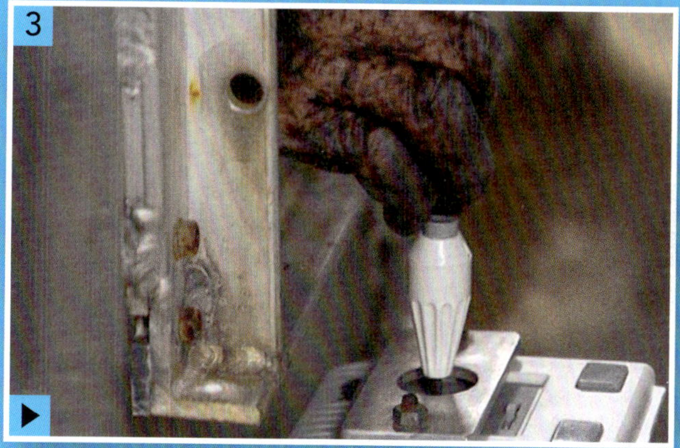

3 The goal of the game is to …
  a climb the stairs.
  b eat the cherries.
  c find the exit.

4 Sometimes Panzee, the chimpanzee, is able to solve a maze more quickly than …
  a a human.
  b a computer.
  c the scientist.

5 According to the professor, chimpanzees are able to …
  a communicate.
  b make plans.
  c think faster than people.

UNDERSTANDING DETAIL

4 Watch again. Write *T* (true), *F* (false) or *DNS* (does not say) next to the statements below. Then correct the false statements.

_____ 1 In the wild, chimpanzees have to look for friends.
_____ 2 Panzee can often complete mazes which she has never seen before.
_____ 3 Planning before acting is just a human skill.
_____ 4 The scientist says that chimpanzees reflect upon the past.
_____ 5 Chimpanzees can plan ahead for centuries.

DISCUSSION

5 Discuss the questions below in a small group. Then compare your answers with another group.

1 Make a list of five animals which are very intelligent.
2 For each animal you chose, give an example of its intelligence.
3 Do you think animals remember things? Give reasons and examples for your answer.

LISTENING

LISTENING 1

PREPARING TO LISTEN

UNDERSTANDING KEY VOCABULARY

1 You are going to listen to a debate about using animals for work. Before you listen, read the definitions below. Complete the sentences with the words in bold.

abuse (n) violent or unfair treatment of somebody
conditions (n pl) the situation in which somebody lives or works
cruel (adj) not kind
issue (n) a topic or problem which causes concern and discussion
protect (v) to keep safe from danger
suffer (v) to feel pain or unhappiness
survive (v) to continue to live, in spite of danger and difficulty
welfare (n) somebody's or something's health and happiness

1 Everybody should give more money to organizations that ________ animals which are in danger.
2 People who let animals go hungry are ________ and should be punished for their actions.
3 Animals living in cages in zoos ________ for no good reason.
4 There are too many laws which defend the ________ of animals.
5 The use of animals in scientific experiments is a hugely important ________ that everybody should care about.
6 People must make big changes to the way they live to make sure animals can ________ in the future.
7 If zoo animals live in good ________ with plenty of space, scientists can learn a lot from their behaviour.
8 The ________ of circus animals should not be permitted.

2 Compare your answers to Exercise 1 with a partner. Which words are new for you?

3 Work with a partner. Discuss your opinions on the statements in Exercise 1.

I agree with number 1 because … What do you think?

USING YOUR KNOWLEDGE

4 Discuss the questions below in a small group.

1 It's said that using animals for work is an essential part of human development. What reasons can you think of to support this idea?
2 What is your opinion of buying and selling animals?

WHILE LISTENING

LISTENING FOR MAIN IDEAS

5 1.1 Listen to a debate on using animals for work and complete the table. What are the animals used for?

	protection	building	transport	war
dogs	✔			
horses				
elephants				
camels				

SKILLS

Taking notes

Taking notes while listening will make you a more active listener. There are many ways to take notes while listening. One way to take notes is by using a T-chart. T-charts can help you organize information into two aspects of a topic, such as pros and cons, or facts and opinions. Remember, notes should be short. Only write the most important words. You do not need to write complete sentences.

Using Animals for Work

cons (against)	pros (for)
live in difficult conditions	*keep us safe*

TAKING NOTES ON DETAIL

6 1.1 Listen to the debate again. Complete the student's notes about the pros and cons of using animals for work. Write a word you hear from the recording in each gap.

cons (Ms Johnson's ideas)	*pros (Dr Kuryan's ideas)*
suffering of working animals (e.g. horses, dogs, elephants) rarely recognized	*humans lack skills and strength for some jobs*
(1) ______ available today can replace work animals	*(4) working animals necessary part of life for ______ people*
(2) not enough people who represent animals or ______ their rights	*(5) use of animals for work not always ______*
(3) old-fashioned and ______ to use animals for work	*(6) domesticated animals wouldn't have been able to ______ without humans*

POST-LISTENING

SKILLS

Listening for contrasting ideas

Speakers use certain words and phrases to signal a contrast, or difference, between two ideas. To identify contrasting ideas, listen for these transition words and phrases: *yet, but, on the contrary, even though, however.*

Animals, like elephants and horses, were used to build amazing structures, like the pyramids in Egypt. ***Yet/But*** *their hard work and suffering are hardly ever recognized.*

Not all animal use is abuse. ***On the contrary***, *without humans, these domesticated animals would not have been able to survive.*

Even though *animals work hard for us, they are often abandoned when they get sick or too old to work.*

These animals work long hours and live in difficult conditions. ***However***, *they get very little reward.*

Use *even though* to connect two contrasting ideas in the same sentence. It is followed by a subject and verb.

Use *however* and *on the contrary* followed by a comma to add a contrasting idea in a new sentence.

You can use *yet/but* to start a new sentence. Do not put a comma after *yet/but*.

LISTENING FOR TEXT ORGANIZATION

7 **Circle the correct contrasting transition words and phrases. Use the examples from the Skills box above to help you.**

1 *Even though / However* I love animals, I don't think people should keep them in their homes.
2 Some people think the reason I became a vegetarian is because I love animals. *Even though / On the contrary*, I am a vegetarian for health reasons and not because I care about animal rights.
3 Many people are against animal testing. *Even though / Yet* without such tests, we would not have developed new medicines.
4 *Even though / Yet* people claim that animal rights aren't protected, there are many organizations which focus on this issue.
5 Many people eat meat. *Yet / On the contrary* humans don't need animal protein to stay healthy.

8 Work with a partner. Discuss whether the words and phrases in bold are used correctly. Suggest how you could correct them.

1 People talk a lot about protecting animals, **on the contrary** they often don't do anything to help the animals.
2 Zoos are fun places for children to visit. **But,** some zoos do not provide good living conditions for their animals.
3 **However** I like animals, I wouldn't want to be a vet.
4 Animal charities are doing a huge amount of work to save endangered animals. **Yet** this may not be enough to save some species.
5 Most people aren't cruel to animals. **Even though**, they care a lot about animal welfare.

DISCUSSION

9 Read the statements. Do you agree or disagree with them? Work alone and make notes. Think of reasons for your opinion.

1 In the modern world, there is no longer any need to use animals for work. We have developed technology which can replace them.
2 People often spend too much time and money on improving animal welfare.

10 Work in a group of three. Discuss your opinions on the statements in Exercise 9. Use language from the Skills box for contrasting ideas.

> In my opinion, replacing working animals with technology isn't always possible. On the contrary …

> Even though animal charities receive huge amounts of money every year …

11 Choose one of the statements from Exercise 9. Write around 100 words to explain the reasons for your opinion(s).

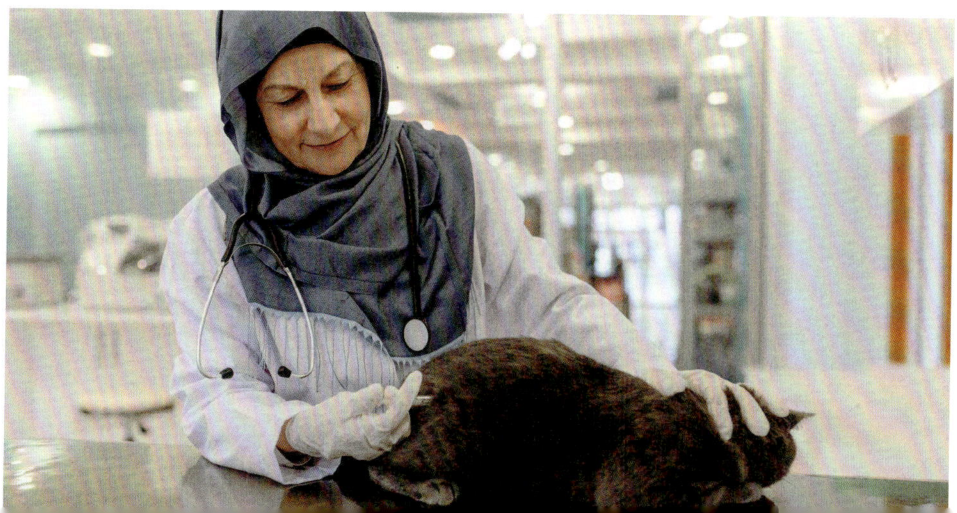

LANGUAGE DEVELOPMENT

WORD FAMILIES

VOCABULARY

You can develop your academic vocabulary by learning about word families. Word families often start the same and end differently, depending on the form (noun, verb, adjective or adverb). When you write down a new word, make sure to write down any other forms from its word family. If you don't know a word, you may be able to guess it from another form of the word.

1 Complete the table. In some items, more than one answer is possible. Use a dictionary to help you.

noun	verb	adjective	adverb
abandonment			
	abuse		abusively
analysis	analyze	analytical	analytically
communication			communicatively
	connect		
		damaged	
	debate		
environment			
		involved	
	lose		
protection			protectively
	support		supportively
survivor / survival			

2 Work with a partner. Cover the verb, adjective and adverb columns in the table. Say the nouns. Can you remember the words related to each one?

3 Work with a partner. Student A: Read sentences 1–5. Pause to show the gap and tell your partner the word in brackets. Student B: Say the correct form of the word to complete the sentence. Then change roles for sentences 6–10.

There is a … between the cost of food and animal welfare. Connect.

Connection!

Student A

1 The __________ of the blood sample showed that the horse was healthy. (analyze)

2 Domesticated animals may find it very hard to __________ in the wild. (survival)

3 Owners sometimes __________ their animals when they can no longer care for them. (abandonment)

4 She has always been very __________ of animal rights. (supporter)

5 Using __________ damaging chemicals on farms can endanger wild animals as well as plants. (environment)

Student B

6 Scientists are exploring how birds __________ with each other by using different sounds. (communicative)

7 She has had a lot of __________ in animal rights for the last 25 years. (involved)

8 Many people are very __________ towards animals and they want to care for them. (protection)

9 I listened to a __________ about animal rights. (debated)

10 Many people who are __________ to animals aren't that way on purpose. (abuse)

MODALS FOR OBLIGATION, PROHIBITION AND ADVICE

GRAMMAR

Use *have to, have got to, need to* or *must* before a verb to say that something is an obligation. In other words, that it is necessary.

*Animals **have to** / **have got to** / **need to** / **must** find food, water and a safe place to live in order to survive.*

Use *don't have to* or *don't need to* to say that there is a choice whether or not to do something.

*You **don't have to** / **don't need to** feed the chickens now. I can do it when I get home.*

Or that it is not necessary to do something.

*Humans **don't have to** / **don't need to** eat meat all the time to stay healthy.*

Use *mustn't* to say that something is prohibited, or not allowed.

*Visitors to the zoo **mustn't** touch the animals.*

Use *should* or *ought to* to give advice that you are sure about.

*You **should** / **ought to** give some money to that animal rights organization. It does good work.*

Use *might* or *could* to give advice when you are not sure.

*It **might** be a good idea to volunteer at the animal shelter.*

*You **could** volunteer at the animal shelter.*

4 Read the sentences and the underlined modals. What does each sentence express? Write *O* (obligation), *P* (prohibition) or *A* (advice) next to each sentence.

_____ 1 You have to love animals to be a vet.
_____ 2 You mustn't give human food to animals.
_____ 3 If you want to work with animals, you could become a vet.
_____ 4 We must do more as a society to prevent animal cruelty.
_____ 5 What courses do you need to complete to get a veterinary degree?
_____ 6 You ought to visit the San Diego Zoo. It has some great animals.
_____ 7 We should be kind to animals. They have feelings, too.
_____ 8 It might be a good idea to help out on a farm if you are interested in working with animals.

5 Circle the sentence which best matches each picture.

1 a She has to wear a uniform to work.
b She shouldn't wear a uniform to work.

2 a You mustn't put your hand into the cage.
b You don't have to put your hand into the cage.

3 a I've got to go to work on Saturdays.
b I don't need to go to work on Saturdays.

4 a You should call your grandparents to say 'thank you'.
b You don't have to call your grandparents to say 'thank you'.

6 Work in groups. Make a list of advice you would give to a child who is going to the zoo for the first time. Use each of the modals for obligation, prohibition and advice from the Grammar box on page 23 at least once.

You mustn't touch the animals.

LISTENING 2

PREPARING TO LISTEN

UNDERSTANDING KEY VOCABULARY

1 You are going to listen to a presentation about human threats to African forest elephants. Before you listen, read the sentences. Which definitions for the words in bold are correct? Write your own definitions if they are not correct. Use a dictionary to help you.

1 The vets at the zoo are treating a **critically** ill tiger.
Definition: in a way that is very bad or serious

____

2 There is concern that the giant panda will soon become **extinct**.
Definition: at risk of no longer existing

____

3 Polar bears **depend on** sea ice for survival. Without it, it's difficult for them to hunt seals.
Definition: to need

____

4 Most people have only seen lions in an animal park and not in their own **habitat** in Africa.
Definition: a building where animals live in a zoo

____

5 There are two **species** of elephants: Asian and African.
Definition: a group of plants or animals which share similar features

____

6 Gorillas are **endangered**. If we don't do something to save them, they will probably disappear.
Definition: dangerous to humans

____

7 Because of what the **poachers** did to her mother, the baby orangutan was left alone in the forest.
Definition: somebody who catches and kills animals even when it is against the law

____

8 The greatest human **threat** to the environment is climate change.
Definition: the possibility of trouble, danger or disaster

____

9 It is **illegal** to keep wild animals, like tigers, as pets.
Definition: only possible if you have a licence

____

2 Compare your answers with a partner. Then use a dictionary to check. Which words are new for you?

PREDICTING CONTENT USING VISUALS

3 Look at the photos below and answer the questions.

1 Can you explain what is happening in the photos?
2 What threats do you think the speaker will talk about?
3 Can you think of any other threats to African elephants?

4 1.2 Listen to the presentation. Were your ideas mentioned?

WHILE LISTENING

GLOSSARY

ban (v) to refuse to allow something by law

fence (n) a structure around a house or piece of land; similar to a wall but made of wood

tusks (n, pl) the two long, pointed teeth of some animals, such as elephants

TAKING NOTES ON MAIN IDEAS

5 1.2 Listen to the presentation again and complete the notes. Remember, you do not need to write complete sentences.

human threats to African forest elephants	*what people should/must do to help African forest elephants*
1 hunting by poachers	*4*
2	*5*
3	*6*

LISTENING FOR DETAIL

6 Write *T* (true), *F* (false) or *DNS* (does not say) next to the statements below. Then listen again to check your answers.

_____ 1 Today, the number of African elephants has probably fallen below 50,000.
_____ 2 A ban on the international trade of ivory was introduced in 1989.
_____ 3 Humans destroy forest areas where elephants live to create areas for farming.

_____ 4 Elephants are often killed because they damage the tracks people use to transport food.

_____ 5 It is the responsibility of police officers working in local towns to find poachers.

_____ 6 To keep elephants away, local communities should put up fences.

POST-LISTENING

Listening for signposting language

SKILLS

When you listen to a presentation, listen for signposting phrases (*first, second, to summarize*). These phrases are like road signs – they help you know when a speaker is moving to a new point or section.

First, overfishing of the coastal waters has reduced the seabirds' food supply.
Second, habitat destruction has reduced the amount of land on which the birds can nest.
To summarize, the actions of people are pushing the local seabird population towards extinction.

7 1.3 Listen to extracts from the presentation and write the signposting phrases you hear.

LISTENING FOR TEXT ORGANIZATION

1 _______________ , there needs to be an increase in the number of specially trained guards who work in the rainforests to catch the poachers.

2 _______________ , governments must introduce an immediate and complete ban on anyone buying or selling ivory, even between countries sharing a border.

3 So, _______________ , as well as habitat loss and human contact, the main threat to forest elephants comes from poaching.

PRONUNCIATION FOR LISTENING

Intonation of lists

SKILLS

Speakers often list examples of what they are talking about. Giving a list of examples can help persuade the audience. These lists have their own intonation patterns. Speakers pause between each example in the list and stress each word.

If the list is complete, the last example in the list has falling intonation, like this:

1.4 *… they see this as the only way to protect themselves ↗, their families ↗, their food ↗ and their homes ↘.*

Perhaps words like: intelligent ↗, majestic ↗, powerful ↘.

SKILLS

If the list is not complete, the last example has rising intonation, like this:

1.5 *As we all know, there are many animals which are disappearing from our planet: rhinos ↗, orangutans ↗, sea turtles ↗ …*

When you are taking notes, it is important to listen for this intonation so you know that the list isn't complete yet.

8 1.6 Listen to the lists. Is each list complete or not complete? Write *C* (complete) or *NC* (not complete).

1 large, white, strong ____
2 pandas, sea turtles, chimpanzees, tigers ____
3 poachers, loss of habitat, human contact ____
4 more guards, a ban on selling ivory, building fences ____

9 1.6 Listen to the lists again. Practise saying one with rising and falling intonation.

10 Work with a partner. Use the lists from Exercise 8 to create sentences. Then read them out to your partner using correct intonation.

Polar bears are large ↗, white ↗, strong ↘ creatures that live in the Arctic.

DISCUSSION

SYNTHESIZING

11 Work in small groups. Use ideas from Listening 1 and Listening 2 to answer the following questions.

1 Do you think humans should be responsible for protecting animals? Why / Why not?
2 There are about 8.7 million species on Earth. Does it matter if some of them become extinct? Why / Why not?

In my opinion, all humans should feel responsible for protecting animals …

I don't agree because …

SPEAKING

CRITICAL THINKING

At the end of this unit, you are going to do the speaking task below.

Give a two-minute presentation about the human threats to an endangered species.

SKILLS

Creating a talk for a specific audience

When you are preparing to give a presentation, it is important to think about who your audience will be. If the audience is already familiar with the topic, you may not need to explain certain ideas. However, if the audience does not know much about the topic, you will need to explain your ideas so they understand what you are talking about. You will also need to use language of an appropriate level for the audience.

ANALYZE

1 Read the introductions to three different talks about African forest elephants. Who is the audience for each talk? Write *A* (young children), *B* (secondary school students) or *C* (scientists).

1 Today, I'm going to talk about human threats to African forest elephants. The biggest threat comes from the actions of poachers. First, can anybody tell me what a poacher is, and what they might be doing to the elephants?
Audience: ______

2 Today, we're going to review the latest research regarding the substantial impacts of human activity on the habitat of the African forest elephant and discuss ways in which technological innovations can contribute to reducing these threats.
Audience: ______

3 Today, I'm going to tell you all about African forest elephants. African forest elephants are very big creatures that live in the jungle in Africa. Put your hand up if you know what colour elephants are.
Audience: ______

REMEMBER

2 **Think about Listening 2 and circle the correct answer.**

1 Who is the audience? Who is the speaker talking to?
  a scientists
  b university students
  c work colleagues
2 What is the speaker's most important objective or purpose?
  a to inform the audience about human threats to the African forest elephant
  b to teach the audience about African forest elephants' habits
  c to explain about the effects of the illegal ivory trade

3 **The speaker in Listening 2 used this table to plan her presentation. Complete the table. Use information from your notes on page 26.**

main idea	____________________ are threatened by humans.
supporting details	Threats: • • • What people should/must do to help: • • •
conclusion / summary	

APPLY

4 Choose an endangered species to talk about. Use one of the species from the box or choose another. Decide who your audience will be (young children / secondary school students / people at a professional conference / people in your community). Complete the planning table for your presentation. You can do an internet search for information.

gorilla	polar bear	rhino	sea turtle	tiger	whale

Species: ______________________________

Audience: ______________________________

main idea	
supporting details	Threats: • • • What people should/must do to help: • • •
conclusion / summary	

EVALUATE

5 Look at your notes in the planning table. Imagine you are doing a presentation on the same topic for a different audience. What changes would you make to your presentation? Share your ideas with a partner.

PREPARATION FOR SPEAKING

SIGNPOSTING A PRESENTATION

1 1.7 Listen to a presentation about using animals for entertainment. Write answers to the questions.

1 What is the speaker's opinion about using animals for entertainment?
2 What points does the speaker make?
3 What examples does the speaker give to support each point?
4 What advice does the speaker give at the end of the presentation?

SKILLS

Using signposting language

Use signposting phrases to help your audience follow your presentation.

To introduce the first point	To add another idea	To introduce a conclusion
First,	*Furthermore,*	*To sum up,*
First of all,	*Second,*	*In conclusion,*
	Another point is that …	*To summarize,*
	Finally,	*In short,*

2 Circle the correct signposting phrase for each sentence.

1 ________ , I'd like to remind you that you can make a difference. Thank you so much for coming today. You've been a great audience!
a Another point is that b First of all c To conclude
2 There are several issues with producing oil in the Arctic. First, it's expensive. ________ , it's bad for the environment.
a In short b Furthermore c To summarize
3 Today I'm going to talk about endangered species and what we can do to help them. ________ , we can give money to environmental organizations.
a First b To sum up c Second

SKILLS

Introducing examples

Speakers also use signposting phrases (*for instance*, *for example*, *such as*) to introduce examples. The speaker will usually pause briefly at a comma before they continue with the sentence.

Another point is that zoos have an important educational role. ***For instance****, children can see animals up close.*

Keeping animals in zoos helps protect them. ***For example****, many species,* ***such as*** *the giant panda and the snow leopard, are endangered.*

3 Work with a partner. Add your own examples to these points. Use a signposting phrase to introduce your ideas.

1 I think that zoos are sometimes good for animals. ____.

2 You can see many exotic animals in zoos, ____.

3 Animals are sometimes unhappy in zoos. ____.

Expressing general beliefs

SKILLS

In a presentation, use phrases like *It's believed that* … to talk about what most people think or believe. This shows that the idea is not only your idea.

It's often said that it's cruel to use animals for entertainment.
It's believed that there are fewer than 500,000 African elephants.
It's widely known that tusks are made of ivory.

4 Complete the sentences with your own ideas. Then think of reasons 'for and against' each idea.

1 It's often said that ____.
2 It's believed that ____.
3 It's widely known that ____.

It's often said that we should not use animals in medical testing. We have the technology to do scientific research without being cruel to animals.

5 Work with a partner. Take turns reading your sentences in Exercise 4. Do you agree with your partner's ideas? Why / Why not?

PRONUNCIATION FOR SPEAKING

6 1.8 Listen to the extracts. Notice how the signposting phrases in bold are pronounced as one complete phrase. Underline the stressed word in each phrase.

1 **First of all**, keeping animals in zoos helps protect them.
2 **For example**, many species, such as the giant panda and the snow leopard, are endangered in the wild.
3 **Another point is that** zoos have an important educational role.
4 **To summarize**, zoos help protect animals and educate us.

7 Work with a partner. Practise using the signposting phrases from Exercise 6 to discuss and develop your ideas from Exercise 4. Check your partner is stressing the phrases correctly.

SPEAKING TASK

Give a two-minute presentation about the human threats to an endangered species.

PREPARE

1 Look at the plan you created in Exercise 4 in the Critical thinking section. Review your notes and add any new information.

2 Prepare how to introduce your animal to the audience. Consider using a rhetorical question, e.g. What do you think of when you hear *'African elephant'*?

3 For each supporting detail in your plan, make notes about the language you will use. Try to include language for signposting, giving examples and expressing general beliefs.

4 Prepare a concluding statement. Say what you believe people must or mustn't do, or should or shouldn't do, to save the species.

5 Refer to the Task checklist below as you prepare your presentation.

TASK CHECKLIST	✔
Use transition words and phrases to contrast ideas.	
Use modals for obligation, prohibition and advice.	
Use appropriate intonation in lists.	
Use examples to support your points and express beliefs.	
Use appropriate signposting language.	

PRACTISE

6 Work in a group of three. Take turns practising your presentations. Discuss the questions below. Take notes during the discussion.

1 Did the speaker clearly identify each threat to the species?
2 Did the speaker use signposting phrases to help the listener?
3 Did the speaker use examples to support points?
4 How could the speaker improve the presentation?

PRESENT

7 Take turns giving your presentations to the class.

OBJECTIVES REVIEW

1 Check your learning objectives for this unit. Write *3*, *2* or *1* for each objective.

3 = very well   2 = well   1 = not so well

I can …

watch and understand a video about the mental skills of chimpanzees.	_____
take notes.	_____
listen for contrasting ideas.	_____
listen for signposting language.	_____
create a talk for a specific audience.	_____
organize information for a presentation.	_____
use modals for obligation, prohibition and advice.	_____
use signposting language.	_____
introduce examples.	_____
express general beliefs.	_____
give a two-minute presentation about the human threats to an endangered species.	_____

2 Use the *Unlock* Digital Workbook for more practice with this unit's learning objectives.

UNLOCK DIGITAL WORKBOOK

WORDLIST

abandon (v) ⊙
abuse (n) ⊙
abuse (v) ⊙
analyze (v) ⊙
communicate (v) ⊙
conditions (n pl) ⊙
connect (v) ⊙
critically (adv) ⊙
cruel (adj)
damage (v) ⊙
debate (v) ⊙
depend on (phr v)
endangered (adj)
environment (n) ⊙
extinct (adj)
habitat (n) ⊙
illegal (adj) ⊙
involve (v) ⊙
issue (n) ⊙
loss (n) ⊙
poacher (n)
protect (v) ⊙
species (n) ⊙
suffer (v) ⊙
support (v) ⊙
survive (v) ⊙
threat (n) ⊙
welfare (n)

⊙ = high-frequency words in the Cambridge Academic Corpus

UNIT 2

THE ENVIRONMENT

LEARNING OBJECTIVES

Watch and listen
Watch and understand a video about offshore wind farms.

Listening skills
Listen for explanations; listen for counter-arguments.

Critical thinking
Make counter-arguments.

Grammar
Use modal verbs to express future possibility.

Speaking skills
Link ideas with transition words and phrases; talk about advantages and disadvantages; give counter-arguments.

Speaking task
Take part in a debate about allowing a new wind farm near your town.

UNLOCK YOUR KNOWLEDGE

Work with a partner. Look at the photo and answer the questions.

1 Look at the photo of solar panels. What do you know about this energy source?

2 What are some other sources of energy?

3 Are these energy sources common in your country? If not, what sources are common? Why?

WATCH AND LISTEN

1

2

PREPARING TO WATCH

GLOSSARY

run out (phr v) to use all of something so that there is none left

alternative energy (n phr) power which comes from natural resources, like the sun or wind

turbine (n) a type of machine which uses air or water to produce power

assemble (v) to build something by putting parts together

ACTIVATING YOUR KNOWLEDGE

1 Work with a partner and answer the questions.

1 Why do people build wind turbines?
2 Are there wind turbines where you live? Where? Describe them.

PREDICTING CONTENT USING VISUALS

2 You are going to watch a video about offshore wind farms. Before you watch, look at the photos from the video. Discuss the questions with your partner.

1 How big do you think wind turbines are? Compare them to a building you know.
2 Why would people put a wind turbine in the ocean?
3 Why might a ship have 'legs'?

WHILE WATCHING

UNDERSTANDING MAIN IDEAS

3 Watch the video. Write *T* (true) or *F* (false) next to the statements below. Then correct the false statements.

_____ 1 People are using wind as a source of energy these days.

____

_____ 2 The ship made it possible to build the turbines in the middle of London.

____

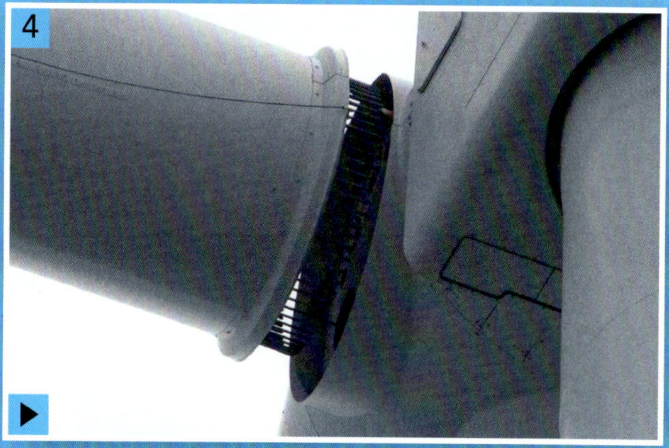

_____ 3 The turbines can get energy even from light winds.
____

_____ 4 It was difficult to build the turbines in sunny weather.
____

_____ 5 One turbine can provide energy for thousands of homes.
____

4 ▶ Watch again. Complete the sentences with the numbers from the box.

UNDERSTANDING DETAIL

12	120	175	3,000	500,000

1 The wind farm is about _______ miles from the coast of England.
2 There are _______ turbines in the London Array.
3 Each of the turbines is about _______ metres across.
4 Each turbine can provide electricity for _______ homes.
5 The London Array provides electricity to more than _______ homes.

DISCUSSION

5 Discuss the questions below with a partner.

1 Do you agree or disagree with the following statement?
The government of my country should build more sources of alternative energy, like wind turbines.
Give reasons and examples for your answer.
2 What could you do in your home to use less energy?

LISTENING

LISTENING 1

PREPARING TO LISTEN

UNDERSTANDING KEY VOCABULARY

1 You are going to listen to a lecture. Before you listen, circle the best word to complete each sentence. Then compare your answers with a partner.

1 Fossil fuels are a … source of energy. Some scientists predict that they will be gone by the end of this century.
   a reduced   b limited   c saved
2 Wind can … people with energy which is cheap and clean.
   a provide   b arrange   c send
3 One … to the problem of climate change is to use public transport.
   a explanation   b solution   c suggestion
4 We should use fewer fossil fuels and more … forms of energy, such as solar and wind power.
   a unusual   b special   c alternative
5 Climate change is the world's biggest … issue. It is having serious effects on the planet.
   a natural   b environmental   c geographical
6 Scientists have developed a new … for growing food. It involves using solar energy to grow food in the desert.
   a arrangement   b organization   c system
7 Water is the world's most important … , so it's important to protect it.
   a resource   b equipment   c material
8 It hasn't rained for six months, so our area is experiencing a water …
   a difficulty   b crisis   c lack

2 Work in a group of three. Look at the photo and the picture and answer the questions.

1 What do you think will be the topic of the lecture?

____

2 What do you think is happening in the photo and the picture?

____

3 What sources of energy are used on this farm?

____

PREDICTING CONTENT USING VISUALS

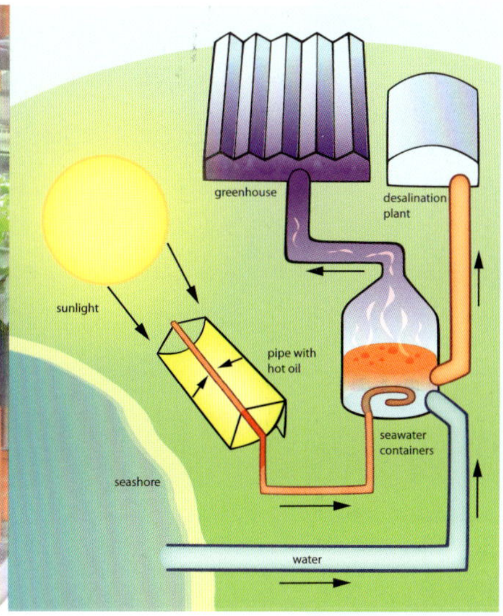

PRONUNCIATION FOR LISTENING

Connected speech: linking sounds

When people speak fluently, there is often an extra linking sound between words when the first word ends with a vowel sound and the second word starts with a vowel sound. Common linking sounds are /j/ and /w/.

This type of farming could solve some of the environmental problems we‿/j/‿are now facing.
The rest of the heated water goes to‿/w/‿a desalination plant.

SKILLS

3 2.1 Listen to the sentences. What linking sound do you hear between the words in bold? Write *j* or *w* next to each sentence.

1 Today I want **to explain** some alternative solutions. ____
2 As **we all** know, in order to grow plants we need water and sunlight. ____
3 I think that desert farms might **be a** very interesting way to farm in the future. ____
4 If **you add** the nutrients to water, you can grow fruit and vegetables in water. ____

4 Work with a partner. Take turns reading the sentences below. Pay attention to the /j/ and /w/ sounds as you speak.

1 If you'd like **to ask** any questions at **the end** of the lecture, please raise your hand.
2 This technology might **be available** within the next five years **to all** farmers around the world.

WHILE LISTENING

LISTENING FOR MAIN IDEAS

5 2.2 Listen to the lecture and circle the main ideas that the speaker mentions.

1 Growing food in the desert
2 Using solar panels on farms
3 Combining farming technology and solar energy
4 Farming in extreme climates
5 Growing plants in different seasons
6 Using different types of water in farming

LISTENING FOR DETAIL

6 2.3 Listen to part of the lecture again. Number the photos (a–f) in the order you hear them (1–6).

HYDROPONICS PROCESS

a seawater in special containers

b desalination plant

c tomatoes on sale in the supermarket

d mirrors for reflecting heat

e plants growing in the greenhouse

f pipe with hot oil inside

7 2.3 Listen again to part of the lecture and complete the summary.

Sundrop Farms, Australia: Hydroponics process

- *The farm is* (1)____________________ *metres from the sea.*
- *Heat is reflected from the* (2)____________________ *onto a pipe which has oil inside.*
- *The hot oil heats up the* (3)____________________ .
- *When the seawater is at a temperature of* (4)____________________ *°C, the steam heats the greenhouse.*
- *The desalination plant produces up to* (5)____________________ *litres of fresh water every day.*
- *No pesticides are used during the process.*
- *This type of farming has a minimal effect on the* (6)____________________ .

POST-LISTENING

Listening for explanations

SKILLS

In a lecture, speakers often explain difficult or new words. They do this by:

- using certain phrases to introduce a definition of the word, or an explanation of a process.
- giving more context to the word (e.g. what it is similar to – or different from – or what group of things it belongs to).

Hydroponics means growing plants in water, without using soil.

Hydroponics is a system for growing vegetables and plants which is different to traditional methods.

LISTENING FOR TEXT ORGANIZATION

8 Match the extracts from the lecture (1–4) to the ways of explaining difficult or new words (a–d). Use the words in bold to help you.

1 Scientists have combined solar energy with a farming technology called hydroponics. **Hydroponics means growing plants in water.** ____
2 ... they do need nutrients to help them grow. **Nutrients are like food for the plants.** ____
3 The rest of the heated water goes to a desalination plant. **Desalination is when we remove the salt from seawater to create drinkable water.** ____
4 Many supermarkets are interested in buying these vegetables because they're grown without pesticides **or other chemicals.** ____

The lecturer ...
a gives a simple example of what these things are similar to.
b says what group of things this belongs to.
c gives a simple explanation of a process.
d explains what the word means.

9 Look back at the vocabulary from Unit 1, and Unit 2 Listening 1. Choose six words that you can explain and write a definition for each one.

Limited means that there isn't enough of something to use.
Endangered is when ...

10 Work in groups. Read your explanations without saying the word you are describing. Guess the word each person is explaining.

Student A: *It means that there isn't enough of something to use.*
Student B: *Limited.*

DISCUSSION

11 Discuss the questions below in a small group.

1 Do you know how the food you eat is grown? Is this important to you? Why / Why not?
2 Would you mind paying a lot more money for food if you knew it was produced in an environmentally friendly way? Why / Why not?
3 What do you think might be some problems with hydroponics?

No, I don't know very much and it isn't important to me because ...
I wouldn't mind paying more, especially knowing that ...
Although hydroponics is an interesting system for growing vegetables, ...

12 Write an email to a food supermarket near to where you live. Explain that you would like it to start selling more food that is grown on hydroponic farms. Give reasons why. Use ideas from your discussion in Exercise 11 to help you. Write around 150 words.

LANGUAGE DEVELOPMENT

NEGATIVE PREFIXES

1 A prefix is a group of letters which goes at the start of a word to make a new word with a different meaning. All the prefixes in the table below mean *not*. Match the words from the box to the prefixes in the table and write the word with its prefix. Use a dictionary to help you.

advantage	~~necessary~~	correct	responsible	possible

prefix	example
un-	*unnecessary*
in-	
ir-	
dis-	
im-	

2 Write the correct prefix from Exercise 1 to complete the words.

1 Using nuclear power is ____responsible. It's just too dangerous.
2 Of course, the future of hydroponics is ____known. But I think it's going to become very common.
3 I ____agree that nuclear power is the best kind of energy. Solar power is much safer.
4 Solar power is cheap, clean and ____expensive. It costs much less than fossil fuels.
5 We are ____able to feed the world's population by traditional farming methods alone. Many people don't have enough food.
6 I don't think it's ____possible to end world hunger. Hydroponic farming could help.
7 That information is ____correct. Would you like me to give you the right information?
8 One ____advantage of wind power is that some people think the wind turbines are ugly.
9 Solar power is cheap, clean and ____limited. There will always be enough of it.
10 I ____approve of using chemicals to grow food. It's bad for the environment and it's bad for people's health.

MODAL VERBS TO EXPRESS FUTURE POSSIBILITY

GRAMMAR

Use *will* (or *won't*) to say that you are certain about the future.

If there is an accident, then it ***will*** *be huge and it* ***will*** *have long-term effects on the environment.*

Use *could*, *might* or *may* to say that you are uncertain about the future.

We'll briefly discuss how this type of farming ***could/might/may*** *solve some of the environmental problems we are now facing.*

Use *might not* or *may not*, but NOT *could not*, to say that you are uncertain about the future.

It ***might not / may not*** *ever be possible to change people's eating habits completely.*

Might and *could* are more common than *may* in conversation. *May* sounds more formal.

Use an infinitive without 'to' after the modal verb.

I think that desert farms ***could/might become*** *a very important source of food in the future.*

3 Write the correct modal verb in the correct place in the sentences. You may also need to change the main verb. In some items, more than one answer is possible.

1 Farming in the desert solves the problem of food crisis. (uncertainty in the future)
Farming in the desert ***might*** *solve the problem of food crisis.*

2 Not using fossil fuels reduces climate change. (uncertainty in the future)
____

3 Taxing fossil fuels reduces the use of cars. (certainty in the future)
____

4 Using solar energy does not lead to any environmental disasters. (certainty in the future)
____

4 Work with a partner. Look again at the statements in Exercise 3. Do you agree or disagree with them? Discuss your opinions.

I do worry that there could be a risk of a food crisis, but …
Even if we stop using fossil fuels, there might not be enough time to reverse the effects of climate change …

LISTENING 2

PREPARING TO LISTEN

UNDERSTANDING KEY VOCABULARY

1 Read the blog post about wind power. Then discuss the meaning of the words in bold with a partner. Use a dictionary to check your answers.

The benefits and risks of wind power

Many people think wind power has a lot of **benefits**. First, it's very clean and it doesn't **pollute** the environment. Also, there are very few **risks** connected to wind power. Unlike coal mines and nuclear power plants, it is unlikely to cause accidents and it never leads to **disasters**. Most importantly, this source of energy is **affordable**. It's much cheaper than fossil fuels. However, not everybody thinks that wind power is a good idea. **Opponents** of wind power argue that the wind turbines can have a negative effect on the environment, and that turbines take up a lot of space. Opponents also say that the wind turbines aren't a **long-term** source of energy because, unlike nuclear power plants, the turbines need to be replaced after 10–15 years.

USING YOUR KNOWLEDGE

2 Discuss the questions below in a small group.

1. What advantages of wind power are mentioned in the blog post? Do you agree with them? Why / Why not?
2. What disadvantages of wind power are mentioned? Do you agree with them? Why / Why not?
3. What environmentally friendly sources of energy do you know about? Which ones are used in your country?
4. What are some advantages of nuclear power plants?
5. What are some disadvantages of nuclear power plants?

WHILE LISTENING

GLOSSARY

sustainable (adj) causing little or no damage to the environment, and therefore able to continue for a long time

low-income (adj) not having or making much money

RUNNING DICTATION

3 Your teacher is going to provide a text for you to do a running dictation. The text is the introduction to a debate about nuclear power. Before you start, read the instructions below. Then work in teams of two or three. Use a piece of paper and a pen/pencil.

- In each team, one or two people are the **writers**. One person is the **runner**.
- The **runner** walks or runs to the text. They read and memorize a sentence. Then they come back to their team and dictate the sentence to the **writers**. The writers write the sentence, focusing on spelling and punctuation. The runner is not allowed to write!
- The runner and writers change roles after each sentence.
- When team members finish the task, they listen to the debate introduction and check their writing.

IDENTIFYING FOR AND AGAINST ARGUMENTS

4 2.4 Listen to the debate about nuclear power. For each topic, circle the person who talks about it: Emma, Jack or both.

1 Nuclear power in low-income countries	Emma / Jack / both
2 Possible effects of a nuclear plant on food supplies	Emma / Jack / both
3 Nuclear plants causing air pollution	Emma / Jack / both
4 Length of time to build a nuclear plant	Emma / Jack / both
5 Size of a nuclear plant compared to other sources of power	Emma / Jack / both
6 Financial benefits of nuclear power	Emma / Jack / both
7 Cost of building a nuclear plant	Emma / Jack / both

5 2.4 Listen to the debate again. Underline eight mistakes in the notes. Then compare your answers with a partner.

TAKING NOTES ON DETAIL

For nuclear power	*Against nuclear power*
• *only two major nuclear accidents in the last 30 years – many more people die working with coal, natural gas and hydropower*	• *accidents have short-term effects on the environment, e.g., the Fukushima nuclear disaster in Japan*
• *the most environmentally friendly and the most sustainable source of energy*	• *people had to leave their homes because of the possibility of radiation*
• *does not pollute the soil*	• *the radioactive material spread to the water and air*
• *relatively cheap*	• *the plant was dangerous for months*
• *can provide a huge amount of electricity to factories*	• *people won't be able to live in the area for the next 20 years*
• *building nuclear power plants is expensive but the cost of the production of energy is very high*	• *irresponsible to build nuclear power plants near schools*
• *low-income countries can sell the electricity to their neighbours and improve their environment*	• *takes years to build a nuclear power plant – hundreds of machines work day and night and pollute the air*
• *nuclear energy makes countries less dependent on oil and gas*	• *there are safer and more environmentally friendly sources, e.g., solar and hydropower energy*
• *solar panels and wind turbines take up a lot of space*	• *solar and wind energy are more affordable for most countries*
• *solar panels and wind turbines are cheap and don't last as long as a nuclear power plant*	• *nuclear power plants are not a solution for low-income countries*

6 2.4 Listen again and write the correct words on the lines below. Then compare your answers with a partner.

1 ______________________________
2 ______________________________
3 ______________________________
4 ______________________________
5 ______________________________
6 ______________________________
7 ______________________________
8 ______________________________

POST-LISTENING

SKILLS

Listening for counter-arguments

In a debate or a discussion, speakers often use counter-arguments to say why they disagree with a viewpoint. Speakers sometimes introduce a counter-argument with words or phrases like *and*, *yet* or *but*.

Some people think that nuclear power is an environmentally friendly source of energy because it creates less pollution than traditional power plants. But opponents of nuclear energy believe that it has more dangers than benefits.

7 Read these extracts from the debate. What idea is the speaker arguing against in each extract?

1 Some people are worried that nuclear power is a big risk. And yet, there are hundreds of nuclear power plants all over the world and there have only been three major nuclear accidents in the last 30 years.

The speaker is arguing against the idea that ____________________ ____.

2 Some people say that nuclear energy doesn't pollute the air, but that's not completely true. It takes many years to build a nuclear power plant. During this time, hundreds of machines work day and night and pollute the air in the area.

The speaker is arguing against the idea that ____________________ ____.

DISCUSSION

SYNTHESIZING

8 Work in small groups. Use ideas from Listening 1 and Listening 2 to discuss the following questions.

1 What are some of the similarities between hydroponics and nuclear energy? What are some of the differences?
2 Do you think nuclear power is a good energy solution? Why / Why not?
3 What do you think is the best form of energy? Why?

Hydroponics is similar to nuclear power because both are …
Although hydroponics provides us with a safe source of energy, …
Nuclear power is a good energy solution because …
In my opinion, … is the best form of energy because …

SPEAKING

CRITICAL THINKING

At the end of this unit, you are going to do the speaking task below.

Take part in a debate about allowing a new wind farm near your town. You are a member of a town council. Some members of the council want a wind farm to be built. Argue for or against building a wind farm near your town.

Making counter-arguments

SKILLS

Use counter-arguments to help make your point stronger. To make an effective counter-argument, first show that you understand the opposing viewpoint.

Some people think that solar and wind energy are greener than nuclear energy.

Then, explain the weaknesses of the opposing viewpoint.

But I don't think that's accurate. Wind turbines are not exactly friendly for birds, not to mention that solar panels and wind turbines take up a lot of space.

UNDERSTAND

1 Complete the table. Make notes about the opinions of the speakers in Listening 2. Use the notes from Exercise 5 on page 49 to help you.

	for / against nuclear power	arguments	counter-arguments
Emma			
Jack			

2 Work with a partner. Compare your tables. Add or change any information as necessary. Tell your partner whether you agree more with Emma or Jack. Do you agree with your partner? Why / Why not?

EVALUATE

3 Work in a small group. Think of some of the advantages and disadvantages of building a wind farm near your town, on a large empty piece of land. Write your ideas in the table. Then decide whether you are for or against the wind farm.

advantages of a wind farm	disadvantages of a wind farm
Will bring jobs to the local area.	*Lack of wind in my region at any point in the year.*

Overall, I am for / against building a wind farm near our town.

APPLY

4 Write your best ideas from Exercise 3 in the *arguments* column. Remember, your arguments must relate to your opinion, so include advantages OR disadvantages – not both.

arguments	counter-arguments

5 Look at your ideas in Exercise 3 which support the opposite viewpoint. Think of what you will say in response to those arguments to make your argument stronger. Write your ideas in the *counter-arguments* column in the table in Exercise 4.

PREPARATION FOR SPEAKING

LINKING IDEAS WITH TRANSITION WORDS AND PHRASES

SKILLS

Speakers use transition words and phrases to link ideas. Different words and phrases are used for different purposes.

to explain a sequence of ideas	to compare and contrast ideas	to add another idea	to summarize ideas
first of all	and yet	and	all in all
first	though	also	to sum up
to begin with	but	on top of that	overall
second	on the other hand	in addition	in short
next	in comparison	plus	
finally		not to mention (that)	

There are numerous benefits of wind power. ***First of all****, it is a clean source of energy.*

Governments tell us that nuclear power is clean and safe ***and yet*** *there have been a number of serious incidents around the world.*

Burning fossil fuels causes serious pollution problems, ***not to mention*** *the environmental damage caused by things like oil spills.*

All in all*, I think wind and solar power are the best ways to meet our country's energy needs.*

1 Circle the correct answer. Think about the purpose of the words to help you.

1 In my opinion, nuclear energy is safe. *Also / Though*, it's cheap and clean.
2 Solar energy is an unlimited source of energy. *On the other hand / On top of that*, it's safe and environmentally friendly.
3 Wind turbines produce clean energy and create many jobs *plus / and yet* many people are still unhappy to see them close to their homes.
4 There are many reasons why we should build a solar power plant. *In addition / First of all*, solar energy is affordable and safe.
5 I think that nuclear power plants look ugly and destroy the landscape. *In addition / Finally*, they don't always provide jobs for local people.

2 Read extracts from a discussion about building a new nuclear power plant near a city. Complete the extracts with words and phrases from the box.

addition	~~begin~~	comparison	first of all
and yet	overall	second	the other hand

A: I would like to say that I completely disagree with the idea of building a nuclear power plant so close to the city. To (1) ___begin___ with, I understand that modern nuclear power plants are safer than they used to be and that the plant would be far from our homes. (2) ________ I worry about my children. If there is a nuclear disaster, our children will be exposed to radiation.

B: I have to agree with this. I worry about the nuclear waste. There are two big questions here. (3) ________ , how can we make sure that it doesn't leak into our water supply or soil? (4) ________ , where are we going to get rid of the nuclear waste? I don't think the government should go ahead with this project. Instead, we could build a solar power plant. It would be cleaner. So, (5) ________ , I think that solar energy would be the best option.

C: I don't think it's completely true that solar panels are better than nuclear energy. Solar power is very expensive to set up and then what? In (6) ________ , a nuclear power plant would be cheaper in the long term. And it would create more jobs.

D: I agree that our city needs more jobs. In (7) ________ , we need cheap, affordable energy. On the one hand, it's clear that a nuclear power plant will solve both these problems. On (8) ________ , I worry about the plant being so close to our homes. I suggest that we build it as far from the city as possible.

TALKING ABOUT ADVANTAGES AND DISADVANTAGES

3 Read the extracts from a debate about solar energy. Do the words and phrases in bold refer to advantages or disadvantages? Write *A* (advantage) or *D* (disadvantage).

1 In my opinion, there are many **pros** of solar energy. ____
2 Personally, I think that solar energy **has a negative effect on** our wildlife. ____
3 **The good thing about** solar energy is that it's cheap. ____
4 The main **benefit** of solar energy is that it's environmentally friendly. ____
5 There are several **cons** of using solar energy. ____
6 The second **drawback** of solar energy is that solar farms are unattractive. ____

4 Complete the sentences with your own ideas.

1 The biggest drawback of nuclear energy is that *there is a risk of a nuclear accident.*

2 There are many benefits of electric cars. For example, ______________________.

3 There are many pros and cons of using wind power. For instance, ______________________.

5 Work in a group of three. Discuss the sentences in Exercises 3 and 4. Develop and link the ideas with transition words and phrases.

The biggest drawback of nuclear energy is that there is a risk of a nuclear accident, though this is extremely rare.

GIVING COUNTER-ARGUMENTS

6 Write a counter-argument for each argument below. Use a word or phrase from the box and then add your own ideas.

yet ~~but~~ that's completely true

1 People often say that nuclear energy is dangerous, *but there have been very few nuclear power accidents.*

2 Some people say that solar power is the best kind of energy. I'm not sure ______________________.

3 It may be true that fossil fuels have a negative effect on the environment. And ______________________.

7 Work with a partner. Look at the sentences in Exercise 6. Discuss which of the statements you agree with, and which you disagree with. Give reasons.

You say that our societies will suffer if we stop using fossil fuels, but I'm not sure …

SPEAKING TASK

Take part in a debate about allowing a new wind farm near your town. You are a member of a town council. Some members want a wind farm to be built. Argue for or against building the wind farm.

PREPARE

1 Look at the tables you created in Exercises 3–5 in the Critical thinking section. Review your notes with a partner who has the same opinion about the wind farm as you.

2 Refer to the Task checklist below as you prepare your arguments. You can use language like this:

In my opinion, there are many pros/cons …

The main benefit/drawback is …

To sum up, …

3 Prepare some notes about your counter-arguments.

It may be true that … *But …* *And yet …*

4 Complete the sentences with the best modal verb: *may* / *might* / *could* / *will*. In some items, more than one answer is possible. Use the examples to plan how to include modal verbs in your arguments.

1 An accident at a nuclear power station ________ happen in the future, but I think it is unlikely.
2 Building a wind farm ________ definitely have a negative effect on the local area.

5 Add the correct negative prefix to each word in brackets and complete the sentences with the words. Then plan how you will use negative prefixes in the debate.

1 I believe it is ________ (responsible) behaviour to continue using fossil fuels in the way that we do.
2 There are a lot of people who ________ (approve) of building wind farms. And yet, what alternatives do we have?
3 I think that it will be ________ (possible) to prevent terrible damage to the environment if we don't act soon.

TASK CHECKLIST	✔
Use clear arguments and counter-arguments.	
Link ideas effectively with transition words and phrases.	
Explain advantages and disadvantages in a clear way.	
Use modals to express future possibility.	
Use negative prefixes correctly, where appropriate.	

PRACTISE

6 Work in a group of three with people who have the same opinion as you. Practise explaining why you are for or against the wind farm.

7 Think about your arguments. Discuss ways to improve them.

DISCUSS

8 Work in a group of four. Your group should have two people with each viewpoint. Discuss your ideas and together decide whether the town would be better with a wind farm.

9 Present your group's decision to the class and explain your reasons.

OBJECTIVES REVIEW

1 Check your learning objectives for this unit. Write *3*, *2* or *1* for each objective.

3 = very well   2 = well   1 = not so well

I can …

watch and understand a video about offshore wind farms.	_____
listen for explanations.	_____
listen for counter-arguments.	_____
make counter-arguments.	_____
use modals to express future possibility.	_____
link ideas with transition words and phrases.	_____
talk about advantages and disadvantages.	_____
give counter-arguments.	_____
take part in a debate about allowing a new wind farm near my town.	_____

2 Use the *Unlock* Digital Workbook for more practice with this unit's learning objectives.

UNLOCK DIGITAL WORKBOOK

WORDLIST

affordable (adj)
alternative (adj) ʘ
benefit (n) ʘ
crisis (n) ʘ
disaster (n) ʘ
environmental (adj) ʘ
limited (adj) ʘ
long-term (adj) ʘ
opponent (n) ʘ
pollute (v)
provide (v) ʘ
resource (n) ʘ
risk (n) ʘ
solution (n) ʘ
system (n) ʘ

ʘ = high-frequency words in the Cambridge Academic Corpus

UNIT 3

TRANSPORT

LEARNING OBJECTIVES

Watch and listen
Watch and understand a video about sustainable transport.

Listening skills
Listen for rhetorical questions.

Critical thinking
Evaluate problems and propose solutions.

Grammar
Use comparative and superlative adjectives.

Speaking skills
Give recommendations; expand on an idea.

Speaking task
Give a presentation on a transport problem and suggest solutions to solve the problem.

UNIT 3 TRANSPORT

UNLOCK YOUR KNOWLEDGE

Work with a partner. Look at the photo and answer the questions.

1 What are some problems with modern forms of transport?
2 What are some of the major changes in transport over the last 50 years?
3 What do you think is the future of transport? How will it be different in 50 years?

WATCH AND LISTEN

1

2

PREPARING TO WATCH

ACTIVATING YOUR KNOWLEDGE

1 Work with a partner and answer the questions.

1 Which types of transport do you frequently use? Why?
2 In your country, what is the most common type of transport that people use? How environmentally-friendly is it?

PREDICTING CONTENT USING VISUALS

2 You are going to watch a video about sustainable transport. Before you watch, look at the photos from the video. Discuss the questions with your partner.

1 What parts of the world can you see in the photos? What forms of transport are shown? What do you think the video will tell you about them?
2 Which of these forms of transport is the most/least environmentally-friendly?
3 How can people make their travel less damaging to the environment?

GLOSSARY

congestion (n) a situation in which a place has too much traffic, and movement is difficult

electromagnet (n) wire that has electricity passing through it, creating the effect of a magnet (able to attract iron and steel objects)

emission (n) an amount of gas, heat, light, etc. that is produced and sent out into the air which is damaging to the environment

sustainable (adj) causing little or no damage to the environment and therefore able to continue for a long time

registration number (n) the series of letters and numbers on the front and back of a vehicle that identify it

WHILE WATCHING

SUMMARIZING

3 Work with a partner. Read the paragraph and try to predict the words you will hear. Then watch the video and complete the gaps.

Heavy transport use around the world is a cause of (1)__________ . Carbon emissions create pollution as a result of people using (2)__________ to power their vehicles. Many cities are trying to find ways to make (3)__________ more environmentally-friendly. This can include limiting the amount of transport in a (4)__________ , or encouraging people to take advantage of (5)__________ – an increasingly safe and popular option. It is more difficult to control the damage that (6)__________ do to the environment.

UNDERSTANDING DETAIL

4 Watch again. Complete each sentence with two words from the box.

cable	car	congestion	electric	~~road~~
tram	scooter	systems	~~vehicles~~	zone

1 Three-quarters of all transport emissions are created by *road vehicles* .
2 London is a city with a __________ . Drivers pay a charge to enter.
3 Millions of people now go to work by __________ , not by car.
4 In Batumi, people often travel up hills by electric __________ .
5 Older forms of transport, such as the __________ in Prague and Melbourne, can be environmentally-friendly.

DISCUSSION

5 Discuss the questions below in a small group.

1 Which of the forms of transport would you like to travel on? Why?
2 Which is the better option to reduce carbon emissions in city centres: congestion zones or no-drive days? Why?

LISTENING

LISTENING 1

PRONUNCIATION FOR LISTENING

SKILLS

Word stress

Some words have the same form whether they are a noun or a verb.

Over the past century, there's been a huge ***increase*** *in the traffic that moves through our cities.* (increase = noun)

What will we do when the amount of traffic ***increases*** *even more?* (increase = verb)

However, the pronunciation may not be the same. In many two-syllable words, nouns are stressed on the first syllable and verbs on the second syllable.

increase (= noun) *increase* (= verb)

Note that not all words follow this pattern.

control (= noun) *control* (= verb)

1 3.1 **Underline the stressed syllable in each of the words in bold. Then listen and check.**

1 There has been a **decrease** in the number of bus passengers this year.
2 The traffic will **decrease** after they have finished repairing the road.
3 Most cities don't **permit** cyclists to ride on the pavement.
4 You need a special **permit** to park in the city centre.

2 **Work with a partner. Take turns reading the sentences below to each other. Stress what you think is the correct syllable in each of the words in bold.**

1 The town hall keeps a **record** of how many vehicles use this road.
2 His mum bought him a new car as a **present** for passing his exams.
3 I went back to the shop to get a **refund** on my bus pass.
4 Each year, the taxi company **presents** an award to its most careful driver.
5 Will you **promise** me that you'll call as soon as your flight lands?
6 The train company are going to **refund** the cost of my ticket because of the delays.
7 We want to **record** the traffic noise around the city to see how high it actually is.
8 This car is the most comfortable you will ever drive. That's a **promise**!

3 3.2 **Listen to the sentences. Check your answers and underline the correct stressed syllables. Then practise saying them again to your partner.**

PREPARING TO LISTEN

UNDERSTANDING KEY VOCABULARY

4 You are going to listen to a podcast about traffic in cities. Before you listen, complete the sentences with the words from the box.

avoid	block	cope	crash	extreme	management	measure	primary

1 Airline companies ________ how many people use their service at different times of the year.
2 They're going to ________ this road next week so they can repair it. You won't be able to drive on it.
3 There was a big ________ on the motorway this morning. Fortunately, nobody was hurt.
4 I try to ________ driving to work because the traffic is terrible. I usually take the underground.
5 I don't know how the taxi drivers in this city ________ – their job seems so stressful.
6 The weather was so ________ this morning that I had to wait in my car for forty minutes before I could get out!
7 My ________ aim as minister for transport is to improve the quality of our public transport systems.
8 The quality of our bus routes has suffered after several years of bad ________ .

5 Write the words from Exercise 4 next to the correct definitions.

1 ________ (v) to stay away from something or not allow yourself to do something
2 ________ (v) to prevent movement through or past something
3 ________ (n) an accident in which a vehicle hits something
4 ________ (v) deal successfully with a difficult situation
5 ________ (adj) very severe or bad
6 ________ (v) to discover the exact amount or size of something
7 ________ (n) the control and organization of something
8 ________ (adj) more important than anything else

USING YOUR KNOWLEDGE

6 Discuss the questions below in a small group.

1 Which of these forms of transport do you think is the best for getting around a city? Why?

bus	private car	motorbike	walking	underground	bicycle

2 Which of the forms of transport is most popular in your city or town?

WHILE LISTENING

GLOSSARY

drone (n) – an aircraft that is controlled by somebody (or by a computer) on the ground

junction (n) – a place where roads come together

steering wheel (n) – the wheel that a driver turns to make a vehicle go in a particular direction

traffic signals (n pl) – a set of lights that control the movement of vehicles

LISTENING FOR MAIN IDEAS

7 3.3 Listen to the first part of a podcast and circle the correct answer.

1 In the introduction, what does the host say the podcast is about?
  a Differences in traffic in cities around the world.
  b The problem of traffic in cities around the world.
  c How traffic has changed in cities around the world.
2 What does Mark say causes extreme levels of traffic in cities?
  a The lack of public transport available.
  b The low cost of owning a private vehicle.
  c The small number of people who travel together.
3 What does Mark say next?
  a Vehicle crashes in cities happen too frequently.
  b Even brief events can cause long delays.
  c Parking rules should be changed immediately.
4 What comment does Mark make about traditional traffic lights?
  a They can cause traffic problems all day long.
  b They are only suitable for use in smaller cities.
  c They change colour too quickly at certain times.

8 3.4 Listen to the second part of the podcast. Complete the notes using the words you hear.

TAKING NOTES ON DETAIL

Modern traffic signals: improved (1) __________ helps keep the traffic flowing, or register crashes. They record information and send it to a control (2) __________ . This is a big improvement on old signals, which constantly had the same timings on the (3) __________ .
Drones: these can be used instead of road vehicles for checking (4) __________ lines or delivering small (5) __________ , which means there are fewer vehicles in our cities.
Anybody who chooses to drive should think about their (6) __________ , and act more responsibly. When they drive, people often become less (7) __________ to others. In particular, everybody should pay more attention to drivers in the (8) __________ lane.

POST-LISTENING

Listening for rhetorical questions

SKILLS

Rhetorical questions are an unusual type of question. Their purpose is to bring the listener's attention to a topic or an idea. The speaker does not expect an answer to the question.

When you ask **regular questions**, you stop speaking and wait for an answer.

When you ask **rhetorical questions**, you continue speaking.

A: *Is the amount of traffic in our cities worse than ever?*
(regular question, the speaker expects an answer)

B: *Yes, I firmly believe that it is.*

Speaker: *Is the amount of traffic in our cities worse than ever? I don't believe so, but others would disagree.*
(rhetorical question, the speaker does not expect an answer)

9 3.3 Listen to the first part of the podcast again. Which questions are rhetorical questions? Which are regular questions? Write *RH* (rhetorical) or *REG* (regular).

LISTENING FOR TEXT ORGANIZATION

1 Do you live, study or work in a large city? ______
2 Are the traffic problems so serious they often cause you to be late? ______
3 What will we do when the amount of traffic increases even more? ______
4 How will we cope? ______
5 Mark, what's happening in our cities? ______
6 What other factors influence how well traffic flows? ______
7 Should we blame car drivers for all this, then? ______

DISCUSSION

10 Discuss the questions below in a small group.

1 What transport problems does your city or town have?
2 What other methods of reducing traffic in cities can you think of? Which method do you think would work the best?
3 Why is it important for local and national governments to try to reduce the amount of traffic in cities?

11 You read the message below from your teacher on your class's online discussion board. Write an answer to the task.

> Hi, everybody,
> Great discussion in class today! Your homework is to write a summary of each of the main points we talked about (aim for 50–60 words for each point):
> - transport problems in our city;
> - methods for reducing traffic;
> - why it is important for governments to reduce traffic in cities.
>
> Email it to me or bring it to our next lesson.
>
> 7 Likes Comments Share

LANGUAGE DEVELOPMENT

TALKING ABOUT PROBLEMS AND SOLUTIONS

1 Work with a partner. Discuss the meanings of the words and phrases from the box. Use a dictionary to help you. Do you use them in your speaking or writing?

control figure out fixed impact influence serious trouble

2 Write each definition from the box below next to the correct word. There are two definitions you do not need.

effect problems important or bad to limit something unusual or different to research a problem not able to be changed to affect how somebody acts or thinks to remove something

1 impact ______
2 trouble ______
3 serious ______
4 control ______
5 fixed ______
6 influence ______
7 figure out ______

3 Complete the sentences with the words from Exercise 1.

1 Can we do anything to ______ the amount of traffic on our roads?
2 Are the traffic problems so ______ they often cause you to be late?
3 A badly-parked vehicle can cause real ______ for everybody behind it.
4 A crash on a busy road can have a huge ______ on all of the roads close by.
5 The traffic controllers can ______ the best way to keep everything moving.
6 They don't have to follow the same, ______ timings for the lights all day long.
7 What other factors ______ how well traffic flows?

4 Which words have the same pronunciation for both the verb and the noun? Use a dictionary to check.

5 Work with a partner and answer the questions.

1 Who has (or had) the most **influence** on your life?

2 What happened the last time you were in **trouble** with somebody?

My first boss had a huge influence on my life because …

When I was fifteen, I was in trouble with my parents because …

COMPARATIVE AND SUPERLATIVE ADJECTIVES

GRAMMAR

Comparative adjectives say how two people, things or ideas are different.
Superlative adjectives compare a person, thing or idea to all others.

Spelling of comparative and superlative adjectives

One-syllable adjectives	Add *-er* or *-r* / *-est*	fast → fast**er** → the fast**est** large → large**r** → the large**st**
One-syllable adjectives ending with one vowel and one consonant (Do not double the consonant *w*)	Double the consonant and add *-er* / *-est*	big → bi**gger** → the bi**ggest** (low → low**er** → the low**est**)
Two-syllable adjectives ending in *-y*	Remove the *-y* and add *-ier* / *-iest*	scar**y** → scar**ier** → the scar**iest**
Most adjectives with two or more syllables	Use *more* / *less* or *the most* / *the least*	serious → **more/less** serious → **the most/least** serious
Irregular comparative and superlative adjectives		good → **better** → the **best** bad → **worse** → the **worst**

Comparatives are most commonly used with *than* and can be followed by:

a noun *Drones are smaller than vans.*

subject + verb *Everybody's journey becomes more difficult than **they expected**.*

an object pronoun *If that doesn't annoy you as well, you're a better person than **me**!*

an *-ing* verb *It's better than **doing** nothing.*

Superlatives are most commonly introduced with *the*: *It's **the** most annoying thing in the world!*

A superlative is followed by a noun: *It's the most efficient **way** to travel.*

We use adverbials with comparatives and superlatives to make them stronger:

*Although it's expensive to put in these signals across a whole city, it's **far** better than doing nothing.*

Adverbials to use with comparatives	Adverbials to use with superlatives
a lot, considerably, far, (so) much	*easily, by far*

You can also use adverbials such as **definitely** and **absolutely** with comparatives and superlatives to indicate certainty.

*Cycling is **definitely** more environmentally-friendly than driving.*

Stress the adverbials in the correct place when you speak.

I think everybody needs to be a lot more responsible as drivers.

6 Work with a partner. Student A: Complete the purple parts of the table. Student B: Complete the white parts of the table.

Adjective	Comparative form	Superlative form
fast		
safe		
comfortable		
healthy		
cheap		
bad		
thin		
slow		
relaxing		
noisy		
dangerous		
dirty		

7 Compare your answers and complete the whole table together. Correct each other's answers where necessary.

8 Complete the sentences with the correct form (comparative or superlative) of the adjectives in brackets.

1 The ________________ route to my office is not always the fastest, because there is often a lot of traffic. (direct)
2 I'm always ________________ in a car than in a plane. (calm)
3 Using mobile phones while driving is the ________________ driving safety issue. (serious)
4 Driving your own car is the ________________ way to travel. (comfortable)
5 If you are in a hurry, it is often ________________ to cycle than to drive a car. (fast)
6 Buying a monthly pass for public transport is ________________ than paying for every trip. (affordable)
7 In many countries, the ________________ tip for a taxi driver is 20% of the fare. (appropriate)
8 Many people are scared of flying, but flying is a lot ________________ than driving. (safe)

9 Circle the word or syllable in each phrase in bold which has the most stress.

1 The course was **a (lot) more challenging than** I expected.
2 We can see that **by far the most affordable** form of transport is walking.
3 The risks of driving a car are **considerably more significant than** those of flying.
4 For me, flying is **much more comfortable than** travelling by train.
5 Taking a train is **definitely more relaxing than** driving.
6 Using the underground is **a lot faster than** travelling by bus at rush hour.
7 Driving is **considerably more expensive** than walking.
8 Cycling is **absolutely the healthiest** form of transport.

10 3.5 Listen to the sentences from Exercise 9 and check your answers.

11 Work with a partner. Student A: practise saying sentences 1–4 from Exercise 9 to Student B. Student B: practise saying sentences 5–8 from Exercise 9 to Student A. Then change roles. Correct each other's pronunciation where needed.

12 Work in a group of three. Make a list of as many forms of transport as you can think of.

13 Try to connect as many forms of transport from Exercise 12 as you can using comparatives. Each person in the group should make at least two comparisons before you finish with a superlative.

A car is far faster than a bike.

A bike is more environmentally-friendly than a plane.

Travel by plane is so much more expensive than by bus.

A train is by far the easiest way to travel long distances across the country.

LISTENING 2

PREPARING TO LISTEN

UNDERSTANDING KEY VOCABULARY

1 You are going to listen to a presentation about cycling to work. Before you listen, read the sentences (1–8) below. Work with a partner and discuss the meaning of the words in bold.

2 Write each word next to its correct definition (a-h).

1 Did you **injure** your knee when you fell off your bicycle?
2 Drivers should always have **respect** for pedestrians and stop for them.
3 I got a **fine** for driving through a red light. It was over £50.
4 Some people **break the law** by driving without a licence.
5 We can **prevent** accidents by driving within the speed limit.
6 Many accidents happen when drivers **pass** other cars without checking their mirrors.
7 Many people drive cars to work because it's more **convenient** to sit comfortably in your own vehicle.
8 Our city has a lot of traffic problems. To **solve** some of them, we're encouraging people to cycle more and drive less.

a ________ (adj) easy to use or suiting your plans well
b ________ (v) to go past somebody or something
c ________ (v) to hurt or cause physical harm
d ________ (n) polite behaviour towards somebody
e ________ (v) to find a way to fix a problem
f ________ (n) money which has to be paid as a punishment for not obeying a law
g ________ (v) to stop something from happening
h ________ (v phr) to fail to obey the rules of a country, state or city

USING YOUR KNOWLEDGE

3 Work with a partner and discuss the questions.

1 What are some of the reasons that people cycle in a big city?
2 What are some advantages of cycling to work?
3 What are some problems with cycling to work?

People often cycle because it's cheap. It's one of the best forms of transport for …
One advantage of cycling to work is that it's quicker and easier to get through heavy traffic than …
A big problem with cycling to work is that it's dangerous. Drivers can often be …

WHILE LISTENING

LISTENING FOR MAIN IDEAS

4 3.6 Listen to the first part of the presentation and answer the questions.

1 What is the goal of the Wheels to Work group?

____

2 What three main issues with cycling to work does the speaker mention?

a ______________________________

b ______________________________

c ______________________________

LISTENING FOR DETAIL

5 3.6 Listen to the first part of the presentation again. Circle the problems the speaker mentions.

1 Most people don't have bicycles.
2 There's a lot of traffic.
3 There aren't any cycle lanes in the city.
4 The cycle lanes are often too narrow.
5 Cars sometimes drive in the cycle lanes.
6 There's nowhere to put your bicycle while you're working.
7 It's too cold.
8 There's nowhere to shower at work.
9 Some people live far away from work.
10 People don't want to cycle at night.

TAKING NOTES ON DETAIL

6 3.7 Listen to the second part of the presentation. What recommendations does the speaker make? What would be the results of the recommendations? Take notes – remember to write just the main words, not full sentences.

recommendations	*possible results*
1 Fines for driving in cycle lanes	*- drivers avoid hitting cyclists, saves lives*
2	
3	
4	
5	

POST-LISTENING

7 Work with a partner. Look again at sentences 1–10 in Exercise 5. Discuss whether these problems exist in the city or town where you live.

DISCUSSION

8 Work in small groups. Use ideas from Listening 1 and Listening 2 to answer the following questions.

SYNTHESIZING

1 What could the government do to encourage people to travel by bike rather than by car?

2 Do you think the ideas from Listening 2 would work to encourage more cycling in your town or city? If not, what ideas would work? Why?

Perhaps it would be a good idea for governments to provide financial help to people who want to buy a bike but can't afford one …

I'm not sure how well the ideas in Listening 2 would work in my city. The main reason is that …

SPEAKING

CRITICAL THINKING

At the end of this unit, you are going to do the speaking task below.

Give a presentation on a transport problem and suggest solutions to solve the problem.

SKILLS

Evaluating problems and proposing solutions

When you think about a problem, you may be able to identify more than one possible solution. Try to decide which one is the best by predicting the probable results of each solution.

UNDERSTAND

1 Complete the table with the problems, proposed solutions and predicted results from Listening 2. Use information from your notes on page 72.

problems	proposed solutions	predicted results
Cycling is dangerous	*- give fines to drivers who drive in a cycle lane* *- wider cycle lanes* *- add more cycle lanes*	*- drivers avoid hitting cyclists* *- saves lives*

2 Work with a partner. Compare your answers to Exercise 1. Add any necessary information to your table.

REMEMBER

3 Work with a partner. Think about the transport problems in your city or country. Write a list of the problems.

APPLY

4 Choose a transport problem. Write it in the *problems* column of the presentation planning table below. What are some possible solutions to the problem? Write them in the *proposed solutions* column.

problems	proposed solutions	predicted results

ANALYZE

5 What do you predict the results would be of each solution? Write your ideas in the *predicted results* column above. Which solution do you think is best? Circle it.

PREPARATION FOR SPEAKING

GIVING RECOMMENDATIONS

SKILLS

Speakers use certain phrases to give recommendations; that is, ideas about what they think is the best thing to do. Here are some phrases you can use to give recommendations:

I (don't) think the city should have more cycle lanes.
I'd like to see cycle racks on buses.
In my opinion, we should / we ought to do more to keep cyclists safe on the roads.
The best thing would be to have more places in the city to store bicycles.

When a recommendation comes after 'if', the verb is in the past simple:

I'd like it if we had wider cycle lanes.
I think it would be better if there were fines for driving in cycle lanes.

After *I'd suggest*, use a *that* clause (*that* + subject + infinitive + object). In conversation, you can omit *that*:

I'd suggest (that) we put cycle racks on buses.
I'd suggest (that) he buy (not 'buys') a strong lock for his new bike.

1 3.8 Listen to a group discussion about the problem of eating while driving. Circle which speakers believe that eating while driving can be dangerous.

Speaker A Speaker B Speaker C Speaker D

2 Read the extracts. Underline the phrases which introduce a recommendation or proposal.

1 I don't think the government should do anything about it.
2 I think it would be better if they closed drive-through restaurants.
3 I think it would be much better if drivers weren't allowed to eat or drink while they drive.
4 The best thing would be to have more cameras on the roads to record what drivers are doing.
5 I'd suggest that the police give the drivers points on their licence.

EXPANDING ON AN IDEA

SKILLS

When speakers propose an idea or make a recommendation, they often state the idea first and then give more details about it. Details can include reasons and examples from personal experience.

Idea: *I think it would be better if they closed drive-through restaurants.*

Reason: *This is because they only encourage drivers to buy food and eat it while they drive.*

Example from personal experience: *Last week, I bought a sandwich on the way to work.*

3 The speakers in the group discussion expand on their ideas. Match the details (a–d) to the ideas in Exercise 2 (1–5). There is one extra idea.

a From my own experience, I can tell you that it can be very dangerous. *3*

b Personally, I eat fast food in my car a few times a week and I've never had an accident. ____

c The reason for this is the police can check the videos to see who's eating, who's texting and so on. ____

d This is because they only encourage drivers to buy food and eat it while they drive. ____

4 What is your opinion of eating while driving? Discuss your opinion with a partner. Give recommendations and examples from personal experience or knowledge. Do you agree with each other?

Personally, I'd suggest that people pay a fine for eating while driving …

From my own experience, it doesn't cause problems if I'm only eating a small snack …

SPEAKING TASK

Give a presentation on a transport problem and suggest solutions to solve the problem.

PREPARE

1 Look at the table you created in Exercises 4 and 5 in the Critical thinking section. Review your notes and add any new information.

2 Plan the introduction to your presentation.

1 Explain what transport problem you are going to talk about.
2 Suggest why you are interested in this issue.
3 Explain that you will talk about problems first, then solutions.

Hello, everybody. Thank you for being here today.
I'm going to talk about … First, I'll talk about … then I'll suggest …

3 Refer to the Task checklist below as you prepare your presentation. Remember to use language for giving recommendations, like this:

I'd suggest (that) …
I think it would be better if …
In my opinion, we should …
The best thing would be …
I'd like to see …

4 Use comparatives during your talk. Correct the example sentences below to remind yourself how to do this.

1 Getting to work on time is considerably the more difficult than it used to be.

____

2 Many people believe travelling by private car is more convenient then go by bus.

____

5 For each proposed solution, make notes about how you will expand on your idea with reasons and examples from personal experience or knowledge. You can use language like this:

The reason for this is …
This is because …
From my own experience …
Personally, …

TASK CHECKLIST	✔
Use comparatives to compare different options.	
Propose solutions clearly.	
Expand on ideas by giving reasons.	
Talk about personal experiences clearly.	

PRACTISE

6 Work in small groups. Take turns practising your presentations. Take notes during the discussion. Use your notes to give feedback to each other to improve your presentations.

PRESENT

7 Take turns giving your presentation to the class.

OBJECTIVES REVIEW

1 Check your learning objectives for this unit. Write *3*, *2* or *1* for each objective.

3 = very well   2 = well   1 = not so well

I can …

watch and understand a video about sustainable transport.	____
listen for rhetorical questions.	____
evaluate problems and propose solutions.	____
use comparative and superlative adjectives.	____
give recommendations.	____
expand on an idea.	____
give a presentation on a transport problem and suggest solutions to solve the problem.	____

2 Use the *Unlock* Digital Workbook for more practice with this unit's learning objectives.

UNLOCK DIGITAL WORKBOOK

WORDLIST

avoid (v) ⊙	figure out (phr v)	pass (v) ⊙
block (v) ⊙	fine (n) ⊙	prevent (v) ⊙
break the law (v phr)	fixed (adj) ⊙	primary (adj) ⊙
control (v) ⊙	impact (n) ⊙	respect (n) ⊙
convenient (adj) ⊙	influence (v) ⊙	safety (n) ⊙
cope (v) ⊙	injure (v)	serious (adj) ⊙
crash (n)	management (n) ⊙	solve (v) ⊙
extreme (adj) ⊙	measure (v) ⊙	trouble (n) ⊙

⊙ = high-frequency words in the Cambridge Academic Corpus

UNIT 4

CUSTOMS AND TRADITIONS

LEARNING OBJECTIVES

Watch and listen
Watch and understand a video about the Chinese tradition of moon cakes.

Listening skills
Identify cause and effect; listen for opinion.

Critical thinking
Create a convincing argument.

Grammar
Use the present perfect.

Speaking skills
Be polite in a discussion; use adverbs for emphasis; use phrases with *that*.

Speaking task
Take part in a discussion about whether special occasions have become too commercial.

UNIT 4 CUSTOMS AND TRADITIONS

UNLOCK YOUR KNOWLEDGE

Work in small groups. Look at the photo and answer the questions.

1 What country do you think the photo is from? What is the tradition?
2 Do you have any similar traditions in your country?
3 Do you follow all of your country's traditional customs? Why / Why not?

WATCH AND LISTEN

PREPARING TO WATCH

ACTIVATING YOUR KNOWLEDGE

1 Work with a partner and answer the questions.

1. What is a harvest? Is there a harvest festival in your country? If so, when is it and what happens?
2. Are there any events or traditions in your country which are connected to the moon? If so, what are they?
3. At what festivals in your country do people eat particular foods? What are these foods? Do you know why people eat them?

PREDICTING CONTENT USING VISUALS

2 You are going to watch a video about food which people eat at a harvest festival. Before you watch, look at the photos from the video. Discuss the questions with your partner.

1. Look at photo 1. What part or parts of the world do you think this festival takes place in?
2. Look at photo 2. What do you see the chef mixing in the photo?
3. Look at photo 3. What do you think the chef will do in the video?
4. Look at photo 4 and read the glossary. What can you see in this photo?

GLOSSARY

filling (n) food that is put inside things, such as cakes, sandwiches, etc.

paste (n) a soft food which can be used to put on bread, fill cakes, etc.

layer (n) a flat, thin piece of something which covers something else

pastry (n) a food made from flour, butter or oil, and water, cooked and used to cover or hold other food

mould (n) an object that is used to make something in a particular shape

decoration (n) attractive patterns or objects put on something else to make it look nice

WHILE WATCHING

3 Watch the video and check your ideas in Exercise 2. Then answer the questions.

UNDERSTANDING MAIN IDEAS

1 How do people celebrate the Mid-Autumn Festival?

____

2 What is the traditional food of the festival? Why are they given that name?

____

3 Is the traditional food easy to make? Why / Why not?

____

4 Watch again. Correct the mistakes in each sentence.

UNDERSTANDING DETAIL

1 The Mid-Autumn Festival is only celebrated in China.
2 Chinese people like to make moon cakes at home.
3 Moon cakes are filled with black beans and sweet eggs.
4 The decorations on the top of moon cakes are always Chinese letters.
5 After the moon cakes are made, they are left for the pastry to become hard.

DISCUSSION

5 Discuss the questions below in a small group.

1 Which festival foods are usually made at home in your country? Who prepares these in your family? How long does it take? What are the main ingredients?
2 Which foods that people eat at festivals are usually bought from shops? Why? Do you think people buy more festival foods from shops than they used to? Why / Why not?
3 Do you ever give food as a gift? When? What?

LISTENING

LISTENING 1

PREPARING TO LISTEN

UNDERSTANDING KEY VOCABULARY

1 You are going to listen to a podcast about changing customs in the modern world. Before you listen, match the words in bold to the definitions (1–8). Note whether the word is a noun (n), a verb (v), a phrasal verb (phr v) or an adjective (adj). Use a dictionary to help you.

anniversary	________	**interact**	________
celebration	________	**multicultural**	________
die out	________	**political**	________
generation	________	**social**	________

1 relating to the government
2 to become rare and then disappear
3 something to mark a special day or event
4 to communicate and do things with somebody or something
5 all the people of about the same age within a society or a family
6 including people who have many different customs and beliefs
7 the day on which an important event happened in a previous year
8 relating to a large group of people who live together in an organized way

2 Work with a partner. Complete the sentences with the correct form of the words from Exercise 1.

1 My neighbourhood is very ________ . People of many cultures and religions live here.
2 I believe that the tradition of letter writing will soon ________ completely. These days, everybody communicates by social media.
3 Min-Soo ________ with a lot of people all day at work, so when he gets home, he likes to spend time alone.
4 Tomorrow is my tenth work ________ . I can't believe I've had this job for ten years!
5 In the United States, Thanksgiving ________ include getting together with family and friends, enjoying a big meal and watching a football game.
6 A few ________ ago, people listened to the radio at night instead of going online or watching TV.
7 Anna has had an active ________ career. She was on the city council for several years and then she was elected to the national government.
8 ________ anthropologists study the ways in which people live in groups around the world.

USING YOUR KNOWLEDGE

3 Work with a partner and answer the questions.

1 What does *tradition* mean?
2 What are the most important customs and traditions in your country or your family?
3 Why are they important?

WHILE LISTENING

LISTENING FOR MAIN IDEAS

4 4.1 Listen to an advertisement for a podcast. Answer the questions.

1 Who is Dr Kevin Lee?

____

2 What is the main topic of discussion on the podcast?

____

5 Work with a partner. Look at the pictures below. What traditions do you think they show?

6 4.2 Listen to the podcast. Which picture shows a tradition the speaker doesn't mention? _____

a

b

c

d

e

f

TAKING NOTES ON DETAIL

7 4.2 Listen to the podcast again. Write notes in the table.

Effects of modern technology on traditions

	old tradition	*new tradition*
sending cards or messages	*people sent cards*	*people send messages through social networking or by text or email*
preparing holiday food		
recipes		
where people eat holiday meals		

POST-LISTENING

Identifying cause and effect

SKILLS

During a presentation, a speaker sometimes talks about causes and effects.

To identify causes, listen for phrases like: *Due to …* , *The reason for this is …* , *because (of) …* , etc. Use *due to* and *because of* before pronouns, nouns and noun phrases. *The reason for this is (that) …* and *because …* are followed by a clause (subject + verb).

noun phrase

Due to modern kitchens, (cause) *people don't have to spend much time cooking any more.* (effect)

To identify effects, listen for phrases like *That's why …* , *This means …* , etc. These phrases are followed by a clause (subject + verb).

subject verb

You can find any recipe you want on the internet. (cause) ***This means (that)*** *many people don't need cookbooks any more.* (effect)

8 4.3 Listen and complete the extracts from the podcast.

1 Anthropology, in a general sense, is the study of humanity. I know that's not very exact. ________ we have many types of anthropology, like linguistic anthropology and social anthropology.

2 Some traditions die out ________ our way of life changes.

3 Now, ________ developments in technology, people spend more time interacting with other people over the internet.

4 But now we don't have to work so hard. ________ we have modern kitchens and supermarket food.

5 In the United States, at Thanksgiving, which is one of the biggest celebrations, many families go to restaurants ________ they don't want to spend their holiday working in the kitchen.

9 Work with a partner. Underline the cause and circle the effect in each sentence in Exercise 8.

10 Circle the best word or phrase to complete each sentence.

1 *Because / This means that* technology is developing so quickly, most family traditions will die out over the next 20 years.

2 People rarely visit the cinema any more. *The reason for this is that / This means that* it is cheap and easy to watch films on smartphones or at home on TV.

3 *That's why / Because of* how popular social media is today, it is easy to understand why many people socialize online.

11 Work with a partner. Discuss whether you agree or disagree with the statements in Exercise 10. Give reasons for your opinions.

PRONUNCIATION FOR LISTENING

SKILLS

Connected speech: /t/ and /d/ at the end of words

When people speak quickly and naturally, the gaps between words are often not easy to hear and people don't always pronounce all the letters in a word. For example, they don't always pronounce the /t/ or /d/ sounds at the end of words if they are followed directly by a consonant sound.

Listen to this sentence. The letters in dark highlight are not pronounced clearly. The letter in light highlight is pronounced clearly.

4.4 I study different cultures around the world and how social and political changes affect these cultures.

The letter is also pronounced clearly when it is followed by a pause (indicated by a comma).

In Kuwait, and many other countries, you must accept food when somebody offers it to you.

12 4.5 Listen to extracts from the podcast. Circle the /t/ and /d/ sounds which you can hear clearly in the bold words. In one sentence you don't need to circle any sounds.

1 My book is **about** the **effect** of modern technology on traditions **around** the world.
2 People **spent** a **lot** of time **and effort** preparing special meals.
3 Growing up in **different** cultures helps you realize **that** customs and traditions are often local.
4 We still **spend** time interacting with other people, **but** it's **not** always face-to-face.

DISCUSSION

13 Discuss the questions below in a small group.

1 What traditions in your country are different to the way they were 20 years ago? Why have these changes happened?
2 Are there any traditions or customs in other countries which you would like to have in your own country?

14 Write a response to the message board post below. Use your ideas from Exercise 13 to help you. Write between 150–180 words.

Hi, everybody.
I'm going to be spending two months in your country soon. It's my first time there and I want to find out about some important traditions before I go – maybe something I could even experience for myself. Do you have any recommendations?
Luna

Comment Share

LANGUAGE DEVELOPMENT

SUFFIXES

VOCABULARY

A suffix is a group of letters which goes at the end of a word to make a new word. Different suffixes indicate different parts of speech, e.g. words ending with the suffix *-ment* are nouns, words ending with the suffix *-able* are adjectives, and so on.

word	suffix	new word	part of speech
tradition	*-al*	traditional	adjective
end	*-less*	endless	adjective
accept	*-able**	acceptable	adjective
modern	*-ize*	modernize	verb
strength	*-en*	strengthen	verb
develop	*-ment*	development	noun
prevent	*-ion*	prevention	noun
help	*-ful*	helpful	adjective

* If a word ends in a consonant + *y*, change the *y* to *i* and add *-able*: *rely* → *reliable*

1 Look at the suffixes at the end of the words in the box. Which part of speech is each word? Write the words in the correct column in the table.

agreement celebration communication connection
digital digitize excitement frighten hopeful organize
political professional recognize specialize successful
unbelievable unforgettable useless weaken

adjective	verb	noun

2 Work with a partner. Can you think of more words that end in suffixes, as in the language box? Write them in the correct column in the table above. Use a dictionary to help you.

3 Complete the sentences with the correct form of the words in brackets.

1 A lot of people think that it's bad for teenagers to spend so much time on social networking sites, but I think it's __________ (harm) fun!

2 You can find a lot of good, __________ (use) information on the internet. But to be honest, a lot of it is not __________ (rely).

4 Work with a partner. Discuss the sentences in Exercise 3. Do you agree or disagree with each sentence? Why?

PRESENT PERFECT

GRAMMAR

The present perfect connects something that happened in the past with a present result.

It's well known that things such as electricity, the telephone and television ***have changed*** *our lives significantly.* (= these things were invented in the past and still affect our lives in the present)

Use present perfect if you don't know exactly when something happened, or it is not important to say exactly when it happened:

In your book, you discuss how technology ***has changed*** *the way we celebrate important holidays.* (= the change(s) happened in the past, it's not important or certain when, and affect our celebrations in the present)

Or when something happened frequently, or over a period of time:

I ***have noticed*** *that there are often more similarities than differences between people.* (= I noticed this several times in the past and it affects my opinion in the present).

Compare this to the past simple, which describes finished actions that don't affect the present:

As a child, I ***lived*** *in Japan, Spain and Egypt. My parents* ***were*** *English teachers, so we* ***travelled*** *a lot.*

To form the present perfect, we use *have/has* + past participle.

In questions, use *have/has* + *subject* + *past participle*. The past participle can be regular or irregular, e.g.

change (present) / changed (past simple) / ***changed (regular past participle)***

choose (present) / chose (past simple) / ***chosen (irregular past participle).***

Statement forms – positive and negative			
The television	*has*	*changed*	*our lives significantly.*
Mahmood and Nila	*have not*	*understood*	*what they need to do next.*

Question forms (*Wh-* questions and *Yes/No* questions)				
What	*have*	*you*	*decided*	*to wear to the party?*
	Has	*Caroline*	*invited*	*you to her party?*

Certain adverbs are often used with the present perfect:

*I've **never** given somebody a gift they didn't like.* (adverb before the past participle)

*We've been to Oman **before**.* (adverb at the end of the sentence)

*Have you **ever** experienced a celebration in another country?* (adverb before the past participle)

'*Have you ever …?*' questions often require past simple answers:

*Yes, I **went** to Indonesia during Eid last year.*

GRAMMAR

5 Find and correct the present perfect simple errors in the sentences. One sentence is correct. Then compare your answers with a partner.

1 Many people are unhappy with the way technology affected our traditions.
2 Do you think special occasions became less important to people these days?
3 I never understood why some traditions still exist.
4 Have you ever prepared a special meal with your family?
5 My parents invited our whole family to my wedding. I'll be so excited to see them all.

6 Work with a partner. Complete the sentences using the present perfect or past simple form of the verbs in brackets.

1 Tania __________ (ask) me six or seven times if I want to come to her graduation ceremony.
2 __________ ever __________ (try) one of Peng Hui's Moon cakes? You should – they're amazing!
3 Marlon __________ (always want) to learn how to put on a kimono. Last week, Yoshi __________ (show) him.
4 We __________ (visit) Thailand three times. The last time we __________ (be) there, we __________ (go) to the Songkran Festival.

7 Put the words in order to make questions.

1 you / been / what / ever / the / to / is / have / best party?
2 wanted / you / to / live / ever / another country / have / in?
3 have / always / enjoyed / you / special holidays / which?
4 you / they / ever / like / didn't / bought / somebody / have / a gift?
5 in your country, / special days / has / people / changed / technology / celebrate / the / way?

8 Write two questions that begin 'In your country/culture'. Use the present perfect at least once in each question.

9 Work with a partner. Answer the questions from Exercises 7 and 8.

LISTENING 2

PREPARING TO LISTEN

UNDERSTANDING KEY VOCABULARY

1 Work with a partner. Read the questions and discuss the meaning of the words in bold. What part of speech is each word? Use the suffixes to help you and write *n*, *v* or *adj* in the brackets. Then use a dictionary to check your answers.

1 What are some special **events** (____) when people give each other gifts in your country? For example, public holidays, anniversaries, when students **graduate** (____) from college or university.
2 What is the most **thoughtful** (____) and **personal** (____) gift that you have received? What was the **occasion** (____)?
3 Do you enjoy buying gifts for special events or holidays or do you feel it is an unnecessary **obligation** (____)?
4 Do you think that holidays have become too **commercial** (____) nowadays? Are they more about money and less about tradition?
5 Are globalization and modern technology responsible for people's changing **behaviour** (____) and attitudes towards special events and customs?

USING YOUR KNOWLEDGE

2 Work in groups. Discuss the questions from Exercise 1.

In my country, we give people gifts when …
The most thoughtful and personal gift I have ever received was …
Sometimes I feel it is an unnecessary obligation when … but usually …
In my opinion, some celebrations are very commercial, for example … , but …
Modern technology might be responsible for some changes in people's behaviour, like …

WHILE LISTENING

LISTENING FOR MAIN IDEAS

3 4.6 You are going to listen to some students discuss an assignment on how customs are changing in the modern world. Listen to the beginning of their conversation. What specific aspect of the topic will they discuss?

4 4.7 Listen to the rest of the conversation. How many of the students are in favour of giving gifts?

TAKING NOTES ON DETAIL

5 4.8 Listen to the whole conversation and take notes about the speakers' *yes* and *no* arguments. Write the reasons people give for their opinion in the table.

Have special occasions become too commercial?	
yes	no
giving gifts is an obligation	*giving a gift shows you were thinking of somebody*

6 Work with a partner. Compare your answers to Exercise 5. Add information to your own table as necessary.

POST-LISTENING

SKILLS

Listening for opinion

When you listen, it is important to understand a speaker's opinion – that is, what the speaker thinks about a topic. To identify opinion, listen for phrases and expressions like these:

signposting an opinion	agreeing	disagreeing
It seems to me …	I agree.	I'm not convinced.
What about … ?	Yes, that's true.	I disagree.
Why not … ?	That's right.	It's not true.
Personally, I …	It's true.	I'm against …
I think that …	I couldn't agree more.	I don't agree.

LISTENING FOR OPINION

7 4.9 Listen and complete the opinion phrases.

1 I ________________ more.
2 How did this whole gift-giving for every holiday tradition get started, anyway? It ________________ silly to me.
3 I ________________ . I get tired of shopping for gifts.
4 I ________________ . I like giving gifts.
5 But I'm ________________ because then you have to spend money … money which could be spent on more important things.
6 Instead, ________________ write letters of advice for the future? That would be more special.
7 Sorry, I ________________ . I doubt that graduates would be happy if we changed that custom!

DISCUSSION

SYNTHESIZING

8 Work in small groups. Use ideas from Listening 1 and Listening 2 to answer the following questions.

1 Do you think technology has changed gift-giving traditions? If so, how? Are these changes positive or negative?
2 What are your culture's customs for celebrating graduations? What is your opinion of these customs? Can you think of better ways to celebrate graduations?

In my opinion, technology has changed gift-giving because …
One example of a positive change that has happened is …

In my culture, to celebrate graduations, we have a custom of …
What I like about this custom is … but …
One way to make this custom better could be …

SPEAKING

CRITICAL THINKING

At the end of this unit, you are going to do the speaking task below.

Take part in a discussion about whether special occasions have become too commercial.

Creating a convincing argument

SKILLS

A *convincing* argument is one that makes people believe it is right. The best way to make an argument convincing is to provide clear, persuasive reasons to support your point. To check if an argument is convincing, try telling a classmate. Are they convinced? If not, what could you say to be more convincing?

ANALYZE

1 Work with a partner. Look at your notes in the table in Listening 2 on page 93. Write the arguments in the table below. Then write ✓ (I agree) or ✗ (I disagree) next to each argument. Do you agree or disagree with your partner?

	argument	✓ / ✗
Special occasions have become too commercial.		
Special occasions have not become too commercial.		

REMEMBER

2 Work in a small group. Think of ideas for each side of the argument. To help you, consider special occasions in your culture.

1 On which occasions / events do people give gifts?
2 How important is it to give gifts on every special occasion?
3 Do any gifts have a special meaning?
4 How much money should people spend on gifts?

3 Write all of the ideas your group discussed in the table below.

	arguments for the statement
Special occasions have become too commercial.	
Special occasions have not become too commercial.	

EVALUATE

4 Look at the arguments in the two tables. Which side of the debate do you agree with? List the three main reasons for your opinion. Then tell your group.

Reason 1: ______________________________

____

Reason 2: ______________________________

____

Reason 3: ______________________________

____

PREPARATION FOR SPEAKING

BEING POLITE IN A DISCUSSION

SKILLS

To have a good discussion, it is important to say when you agree and disagree with people. When you disagree, show that you understand and respect the other person's opinion first. Then use *but* to introduce your own opinion.

You may be right, but …

I see your point, but …

You should also take turns and ask other people's opinions. You can do this by asking questions.

What do you think?

What's your opinion?

If you want to interrupt somebody because you have a point to make, you can do it politely.

I'm sorry to interrupt, but …

Excuse me for interrupting, but …

Excuse me, can I say something?

1 Read the discussion below. Circle the best options.

A: I think holidays are too commercial. What do you think?

B: (1) *I'm sorry to interrupt / I see your point*, but I think people really enjoy giving and receiving gifts. It's a way to show you care about people.

A: (2) *I agree / You may be right, but* there are better ways to show you care. It can be more thoughtful to spend time with people than to give them gifts.

B: (3) *I understand, but / You misunderstood my point* can't you do both? I mean, there's no reason that you have to choose –

A: (4) *I see your point / I'm sorry to interrupt, but* I actually do feel like it's a choice. Sometimes I'm so busy doing holiday shopping that I don't have enough time to spend with my friends and family.

B: I'm sorry, but (5) *I disagree / I understand.* I think if you plan ahead and maybe shop online, shopping doesn't have to take a lot of time. You can give people nice gifts and also spend time with them.

2 Work with a partner. One of you is Student A and the other is Student B. Read the opinions in the table below. Then choose three expressions from the Skills box on page 96 and use them as you discuss the opinions with your partner.

Student A	Student B
• You think that it's good to relax on holidays. On special days, people should go out to dinner rather than cook. Cooking involves a lot of work and nobody should have to work on holidays.	• You think that traditions are important. People have always made traditional food on special days and they should continue to do that. Cooking is a way to show your family that you care about them.

USING ADVERBS FOR EMPHASIS

SKILLS

We can use adverbs to make a point stronger.

*I **strongly** believe that people spend too much money on gifts.* (= I believe very much.)

*I **really** think that …*

You can use these adverbs when you are sure that you agree or disagree.

*I **totally** agree. (= I agree 100%.)*

*Yes, that's **completely** true.*

*That's **definitely** right.*

*I **strongly** disagree.*

*It's **absolutely not** true.*

The position of *really* in the sentence changes the strength of your disagreement.

*I'm **not really** convinced (= I have some doubts about your point.)*

*I'm **really not** convinced (= I have very big doubts about your point.)*

3 Read the sentences. Circle the sentences that you agree with and change the sentences you disagree with. Add adverbs if you have a strong opinion.

1 It's true that people don't have time to cook on special days any more.

____

2 I'm against spending a lot of money on holidays or celebrations.

____

3 I agree that modern technology has changed the way we interact with each other.

____

4 It's true that travelling to other countries helps us understand other cultures and their traditions.

____

5 I agree that tourists bring bad habits to our country.

____

6 I don't believe that learning English affects local traditions.

____

4 Work with a partner. Compare your ideas from Exercise 3. Say if you agree or disagree with your partner and discuss the reasons why.

It's completely false that people don't have time to cook on special days any more. For one thing, …

I understand why you think that, but …

PRONUNCIATION FOR SPEAKING

SKILLS

Stress patterns in phrases for agreeing and disagreeing

Speakers often stress adverbs for emphasis when they agree or disagree.

4.10 *I **completely** agree that holidays have become too commercial.*

*I **absolutely** disagree that we should stop giving gifts on Mother's Day.*

*I **really** think that we should give fewer gifts.*

5 Work with a partner. Underline the adverbs in the sentences below. Then practise saying the sentences to each other. Remember to stress the adverbs.

1 I strongly believe that we should spend less time using social media.
2 I'm absolutely convinced that buying expensive cars is a waste of money.
3 I really think that we can learn a lot from older people.
4 I completely disagree with that argument.

PHRASES WITH *THAT*

Phrases with *that* can be used to introduce an opinion or an idea.

I think that … ,
I believe that …
Many people believe that …
I doubt that …

SKILLS

6 Write *P* next to the sentences in which the speaker introduces a personal opinion. Write *O* next to the sentences in which the speaker refers to information from other people.

1 **I think that** it shows that you were thinking of somebody. ______
2 **I've heard that** when people receive more than a few gifts, they often can't remember who gave them which gift. ______
3 **I believe that** we should learn about customs and traditions from different places. ______
4 **Many people say that** travel improves the mind. ______
5 **I disagree that** the internet has destroyed local customs and traditions. ______
6 **Everybody knows that** people usually buy gifts because it's an obligation, not because they really want to. ______
7 **I doubt that** graduates would be happy if we changed that custom! ______
8 **It's a well-known fact that** the internet has made it easier to communicate. ______

7 Complete the phrases with your own ideas.

1 I disagree that ______________________________ .
2 I strongly believe that ______________________________ .
3 It's a well-known fact that ______________________________ .
4 Everybody knows that ______________________________ .
5 I've heard that ______________________________ .
6 I doubt that ______________________________ .

8 Work with a partner. Discuss your ideas from Exercise 7.

SPEAKING TASK

Take part in a discussion about whether special occasions have become too commercial.

PREPARE

1 Look at the table you created and your notes in Exercises 3 and 4 in the Critical thinking section. Review your notes and add any new information.

2 Work in small groups with students who have the same opinion as you. Look at the main points you want to make in the discussion and plan what language you will use to make these points. Make notes. You can use language like this:

It seems to me …
What about … ?
Why not … ?
Personally, I …
I think that …
I've heard that …
It's a well-known fact that …

3 Make a list of arguments to support the opposite opinion. Then make notes about how you will respond to each argument. You can use language like this:

I see your point, but …
You may be right, but …

4 Refer to the Task checklist below as you prepare for your discussion.

TASK CHECKLIST	✔
Use adverbs for emphasis.	
Use phrases with *that* appropriately.	
Use the present perfect where appropriate.	
Interrupt, agree and disagree appropriately and politely.	
Show respect for other people's opinions.	

PRACTISE

5 Work in a group of four. Two people should agree with one side of the argument and two with the opposite side. Practise having your discussion. Take notes on the other students' performance during the practice and feed back to them on how they could improve their points.

DISCUSS

6 Work with a different group. Discuss the topic with students who agree with you and who disagree with you.

OBJECTIVES REVIEW

1 Check your learning objectives for this unit. Write *3*, *2* or *1* for each objective.

3 = very well 2 = well 1 = not so well

I can …

watch and understand a video about the Chinese tradition of moon cakes.	_____
identify cause and effect.	_____
listen for opinion.	_____
create a convincing argument.	_____
use the present perfect.	_____
be polite in a discussion.	_____
use adverbs for emphasis.	_____
use phrases with *that*.	_____
take part in a discussion about whether special occasions have become too commercial.	_____

2 Use the *Unlock* Digital Workbook for more practice with this unit's learning objectives.

UNLOCK DIGITAL WORKBOOK

WORDLIST

acceptable (adj) ⊙	generation (n) ⊙	political (adj) ⊙
agreement (n) ⊙	graduate (v) ⊙	prevention (n) ⊙
anniversary (n)	helpful (adj) ⊙	social (adj) ⊙
behaviour (n) ⊙	interact (v)	specialize (v)
celebration (n)	modernize (v)	strengthen (v) ⊙
commercial (adj) ⊙	multicultural (adj)	thoughtful (adj)
die out (phr v)	obligation (n) ⊙	traditional (adj) ⊙
endless (adj)	occasion (n) ⊙	
event (n) ⊙	personal (adj) ⊙	

⊙ = high-frequency words in the Cambridge Academic Corpus

UNIT 5

HEALTH AND FITNESS

LEARNING OBJECTIVES

Watch and listen
Watch and understand a video about brain health.

Listening skills
Listen for attitude; identify references to common knowledge.

Critical thinking
Brainstorm and evaluate ideas using an ideas map.

Grammar
Understand and use phrasal verbs.

Speaking skills
Use problem–solution organization; present persuasively.

Speaking task
Give a presentation to a group of students about an idea for a health product or programme.

UNIT 5 HEALTH AND FITNESS

UNLOCK YOUR KNOWLEDGE

Work with a partner. Look at the photo and answer the questions.

1 What are the people doing? Why do you think they're doing it?

2 What advice would you give to somebody who wants to live to be 100 years old? What should the person do or not do?

3 Do you think it is easier or harder to stay healthy now than it was 100 years ago? Why?

WATCH AND LISTEN

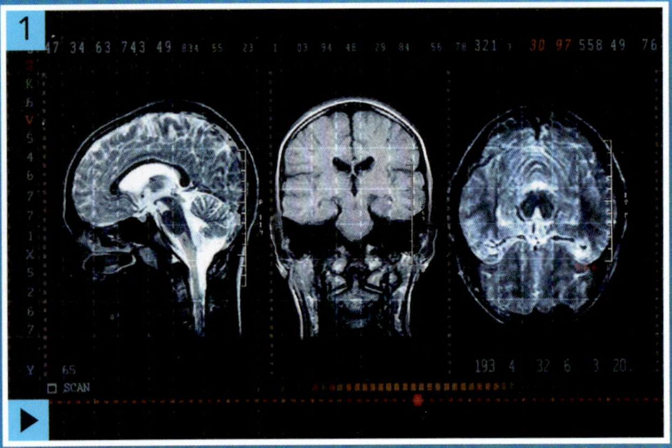

PREPARING TO WATCH

ACTIVATING YOUR KNOWLEDGE

1 Work with a partner and answer the questions.

1 What activities do you do to stay healthy? Do you have any unhealthy habits that you would like to stop?
2 In what ways can technology help us to stay healthy?

PREDICTING CONTENT USING VISUALS

2 You are going to watch a video about brain health. Before you watch, look at the photos from the video. Discuss the questions with your partner.

1 What are the people doing in photos 2 and 4? Why are they doing this?
2 How might photos 1 and 3 be connected in terms of people's health?
3 What do you think this video will tell you about health?

GLOSSARY

signal (n) an action that is intended to give a particular message

protein (n) something found in foods like meat and eggs which is necessary for the body to grow and be strong

focused (adj) giving a lot of attention to one particular thing

effectively (adv) in a way that is successful and achieves what you want

interpret (v) to decide what the intended meaning of something is

neuron (n) a tiny unit of the brain that carries information to and from other parts of the body

WHILE WATCHING

3 Watch the video. Number the ideas in the order you hear them.

UNDERSTANDING MAIN IDEAS

_____ How technology can help to maintain a training plan.
_____ The importance of sleep in keeping your brain healthy.
_____ The benefits that certain types of foods produce in our minds.
_____ What happens in the brain when we learn or exercise.
_____ The effects that different types of exercise have on the brain.
_____ Where technology can help to improve sleep and learning.

4 Watch again. Correct the mistakes in the sentences.

UNDERSTANDING DETAIL

1 Doing physical exercise encourages the proteins in the brain to grow.
2 Aerobic exercise, like running, is best for helping the brain to stay focused.
3 Foods with lots of fat and sugar tend to encourage neuron growth.
4 Nuts contain fatty acids which are particularly good for old people's brains.
5 People tend to work less effectively when they are feeling confused.
6 Research shows that getting a good night's sleep makes it easier to use smart devices successfully.

DISCUSSION

5 Discuss the questions below in a small group.

1 Of the activities shown in the video, which do you think are the most and the least effective in helping to stay healthy?
2 What other activities can somebody do to improve the health of their brain?
3 How is the way we use our brains today different from in the past?

LISTENING

LISTENING 1

PREPARING TO LISTEN

UNDERSTANDING KEY VOCABULARY

1 You are going to listen to a podcast about why some people live a long life. Before you listen, work with a partner to discuss the meaning and part of speech of the words and phrases in the box. Use a dictionary to help you.

habit	**illness**	**in shape**	**overweight**
prove	**ridiculous**	**unhealthy**	**work out**

2 Complete the sentences (1–8) with the correct form of the words and phrases from Exercise 1.

1 My grandmother is very healthy. She's never had a serious __________ .
2 Research __________ that exercising can improve your health.
3 I have a __________ of eating chocolate. I eat it almost every night after dinner!
4 He has an __________ lifestyle. He never exercises and hardly ever eats fruit and vegetables.
5 It's __________ that the government allows companies to advertise fast food.
6 Exercise is important to me, so I __________ at the gym three mornings a week.
7 I'm a few kilos __________ . I should probably eat less fast food.
8 The best way to stay __________ is to eat a good diet and do exercise.

USING YOUR KNOWLEDGE

3 Work in a group and discuss the photos below.

1 What are the differences between the health and the lifestyles of the people in the photos?
2 In what ways can lifestyles like the ones shown in the photos affect people's health?
3 Do you think that the genes we receive from our parents can affect our health? How?

a

b

WHILE LISTENING

LISTENING FOR MAIN IDEAS

4 5.1 Listen to the introduction to the podcast and answer the questions.

1 Do people who live to be 100 years old always have a healthy lifestyle?

___

2 What does the speaker say is more important than lifestyle for having a long and healthy life?

___

TAKING NOTES ON DETAIL

5 5.2 Listen to the podcast and complete the notes.

Speaker A

Many people believe eating only healthy food / exercising = a long life.

BUT: having the (1)________ *can make life shorter.*

Happiness better than always being in (2)________ .

Speaker B

Don't focus on healthy eating/exercise.

- *Example: grandfather died at* (3)________ *and never ate vegetables/exercised.*
- *Genes are more important for a long life than* (4)________ .

Exercise is good, but (5)________ *shouldn't be main focus in life.*

Speaker C

Prefers good diet and exercise.

People only know if they have good genes when they (6)________ .

- *Therefore, don't take risks.*
- *Unhealthy people get the* (7)________ *or* (8)________ *more easily.*

Unhealthy habits increase possibility of a (9)________ .

Speaker D

Children often overweight – eating too much junk food.

Some people can live (10)________ *despite their unhealthy habits.*

Prefers to = (11)________ *and take care of themself.*

c

d

PRONUNCIATION FOR LISTENING

SKILLS

Attitude and emotion

To understand a speaker's message, it is necessary to understand their attitude – what they are thinking or feeling. This is especially important in discussions, in which speakers might have different attitudes about a topic.

You can often learn about a speaker's attitude from the sound of their voice. When a speaker is expressing strong feelings, their voice often goes up and down more than usual. Listen to the difference in the way the speaker says this sentence:

5.3

I'm really surprised about that.

↘
I'm really surprised about that.

↗
I'm really surprised about that!

In the first sentence, the speaker's voice does not go up or down very much. He does not have strong feelings.
In the second sentence, the speaker's voice goes down. He feels upset.
In the third sentence, the speaker's voice goes up. He feels excited.

6 5.4 **Listen to the extracts. How do you think each speaker feels about what they are saying? Circle the correct answer. How do you know?**

1 I'm really happy about this new research!
The speaker feels *excited / upset / no strong feelings*. I know this because ______________________ .

2 There's no question that happy people live longer.
The speaker feels *excited / upset / no strong feelings*. I know this because ______________________ .

3 It's ridiculous to get too worried about healthy eating and exercise!
The speaker feels *excited / upset / no strong feelings*. I know this because ______________________ .

4 He certainly never went to a gym.
The speaker feels *excited / upset / no strong feelings*. I know this because ______________________ .

5 There's no doubt that bad health habits increase the chances of getting a serious illness.
The speaker feels *excited / upset / no strong feelings*. I know this because ______________________ .

Listening for attitude

SKILLS

You can also identify a speaker's attitude by listening for their use of:

Adjectives

A positive adjective can express a negative attitude depending on the speaker's intonation. A *sarcastic* intonation usually shows they mean the opposite of what they say.

I'm afraid I lost your gym membership card.

Well, that's just great! (*Great* is usually a positive adjective, but here the speaker is not happy.)

Rhetorical questions

A rhetorical question (a question you are not expected to answer) is sometimes used to express a negative attitude.

So, you didn't enjoy the yoga class?

What do you think? (The rhetorical question makes it clear the speaker did not enjoy the class.)

But be careful! Rhetorical questions do not always express a negative attitude. Listen to the intonation to decide if the speaker has a negative attitude.

LISTENING FOR ATTITUDE

7 Work with a partner. Read the sentences below and discuss whether you expect each speaker to sound positive or negative.

Speaker 1 I think it's great news!
Speaker 2 Oh, that's great.
Speaker 3 What's wrong with being healthy?
Speaker 4 So now we should all eat fast food and stop exercising?
Speaker 5 I'd say that it's always better to have a healthy lifestyle.

8 5.5 Listen to the extracts. Then discuss the questions with your partner.

1 Is the attitude of each speaker positive or negative?
2 What tells you their attitude – adjectives, rhetorical questions, intonation or a combination of these?

POST-LISTENING

Identifying references to common knowledge

SKILLS

Common knowledge means ideas which most people know about. Speakers often refer to common knowledge to make their arguments stronger and persuade other people that they are right. To express common knowledge, use phrases such as:

It's common knowledge that …
Everybody knows that …
There is no question that …
There is no doubt that …
Most people think that …

Sometimes speakers use these phrases with ideas which may not be completely true or which may not be shared by everybody, to persuade the listener that they are right.

9 Work with a partner. Read the statements. Do you agree with each statement? Why / Why not? Discuss your opinions.

1 **Most people think that** if they eat healthy food, they'll have a long, healthy life.
2 **There is no question that** happy people live longer.
3 **There is no doubt that** bad health habits increase the chances of getting a serious illness.
4 **Everybody knows that** exercise makes us happier.

10 Complete the sentences with your own ideas. Then discuss your ideas with a partner.

1 Most people think ____ .
2 There is no question ____ .
3 Everybody ____ .

DISCUSSION

11 Discuss the questions below with a partner.

1 Do you feel that you have a healthy lifestyle? What could you do to make your lifestyle healthier?
2 Do you know any very old, healthy people? What kind of lifestyle do they have?
3 What are the most important things to do to have a healthy lifestyle?

I think that my lifestyle is … but I should …
I know somebody who is … years old and who is still very healthy. Their lifestyle is …
For me, the most important things for a healthy lifestyle are …

12 You read the following on a health and fitness blog. Write a response.

> We are inviting readers to send in their response to this statement:
>
> **'There are more important things than a healthy lifestyle if you want to live a long life. Do you agree or disagree?'**
>
> The reader who sends in the best response (100–150 words) will win their choice from a range of sports clothing.

Before you write:

- Make notes on the reasons why you agree or disagree with the statement.
- Plan your response and then write at least 100 words.
- Use at least two phrases from the Skills box on page 109 that refer to common knowledge in your response.

It's common knowledge that staying in shape is …

LANGUAGE DEVELOPMENT

PHRASAL VERBS

GRAMMAR

Phrasal verbs are two- or three-word verbs. They consist of a verb and one or two particles (small words like *up*, *out*, *in*). It is not always easy to understand the meaning of a phrasal verb by focusing only on the meaning of the verb and the particle(s). The parts together often have a completely different meaning than the individual parts.

When you see a phrasal verb that you do not know, try to work out its meaning from the context.

*I **ran into** my old friend Henry at the gym. I was surprised to see him after so many years.*

The words *surprised* and *see him* can help you figure out that the phrasal verb *run into* means *to meet somebody you know when you are not expecting to.*

With some phrasal verbs, the object can come between the verb and the particle.

*Can you **write** the recipe **down** for that amazing healthy soup you make?*

However, the object must always come after a three-word phrasal verb.

*I'm really **looking forward to** our training session later on.*

Phrasal verbs are very common in informal, spoken English. When you see or hear a new phrasal verb, check you understand the meaning and try to memorize whether the object can come between the verb and the particle. Use a dictionary to help you do this.

1 Read the sentences. Underline the phrasal verb in each sentence.

1 If you want to lose weight, you should <u>cut down on</u> fatty foods.
2 Last winter, I came down with four colds. I hope I'm healthier this year!
3 I want to try something new. Maybe I'll take up tennis.
4 Tim is going to try out for the football team. I don't think he'll make it, though – he's not a great player.
5 No matter how good their genes are, these children will not be able to enjoy a long and happy life unless they give up crisps, chocolate bars and sugary drinks.
6 Why don't you sign up for a yoga class? Yoga is good exercise and it helps you relax.
7 Would you like to join in the game? You can be on our team.
8 It took me a long time to get over the flu. I was ill for two weeks.

2 Write the phrasal verbs from Exercise 1 next to the correct definitions. What words in the context helped you work out the correct definition?

1 ______________ to get an illness, especially one which is not serious
2 ______________ to stop a habit, often because it is unhealthy
3 ______________ to agree to become involved in an organized activity
4 ______________ to become involved in an activity with other people
5 ______________ to compete for a position on a sports team or a part in a play
6 ______________ to become healthy again after having an illness
7 ______________ to start doing a particular job or activity
8 ______________ to eat or drink less of something

3 Complete the questions with phrasal verbs in the correct form.

1 Have you ever ____*signed up*____ for exercise classes or for a gym membership?
2 Have you ever had a cold or the flu? How long did it take you to ______________ it?
3 Have you ever ______________ a bad habit, ______________ like buying things you don't need?
4 Have you ever ______________ for a team?
5 Have you ______________ any new activities ______________ in the past few years?
6 Are there any foods which you want to ______________ ?

4 Write a follow-up question for each of the questions in Exercise 3.

1 *What did you sign up for?*
2 ______________
3 ______________
4 ______________
5 ______________
6 ______________

5 Work with a partner. Answer the questions in Exercise 3. Ask your follow-up questions to find out more information.

Have you ever signed up for exercise classes or for a gym membership?

Yes, I have.

What did you sign up for?

I actually signed up for exercise classes at a gym, so both!

ADJECTIVES TO DESCRIBE WELL-BEING

cultural (adj) relating to the habits, traditions and beliefs of a society
educational (adj) relating to learning
emotional (adj) relating to feelings
intellectual (adj) relating to your ability to think and understand things, especially complicated ideas
personal (adj) relating to a single person rather than to a group
physical (adj) relating to the body
social (adj) relating to activities in which you meet and spend time with other people

6 Read the definitions in the box. Complete the questions with the words in bold. Then discuss your answers to the questions with a partner.

1 Does exercising have ________ benefits? For example, can it make you happier and calmer?
2 What's the best way to find new people to go out with and improve your ________ life?
3 Would you describe somebody as '________' if they enjoyed talking about literature and philosophy? Why / Why not?
4 Which is better for learning a language quickly: hiring a ________ tutor or studying in a class? Why?
5 Which ________ activity is best for helping your body stay strong and healthy?
6 When somebody moves to a new country, how long should it take for them to get used to the ________ differences?
7 People often think that travelling has ________ benefits, but what do people learn?

LISTENING 2

PREPARING TO LISTEN

UNDERSTANDING KEY VOCABULARY

1 You are going to listen to four presentations about programmes which can improve your health. Before you listen, work with a partner. Discuss the best definition for each word in bold.

1 I don't feel like going to the gym this afternoon. I just want to stay at home, **relax** and watch a film.
   a to sleep until later than usual
   b to enjoy your favourite hobby
   c to become less tense or worried

2 Marcus is feeling a lot of **stress** at work. It's giving him headaches.
   a worry caused by a difficult situation
   b an illness caused by not getting enough sleep
   c pains that come when something unexpected happens

3 Drinking a lot of water can be a good **treatment** for a stomachache.
   a a solution to a problem
   b a way to cure an illness or injury
   c something you can drink

4 If you **reduce** the number of calories you eat, you will lose weight.
   a to count the amount of something
   b to make (something) less in size, amount, etc.
   c to make (something) larger in size, amount, etc.

5 Exercise has a number of **mental** benefits, like improving memory.
   a relating to the mind
   b relating to movement
   c relating to happiness

6 Eating healthy food can improve your athletic **performance**. It makes your muscles and bones stronger and helps you stay healthy.
   a how often a person does an activity
   b how well a person does an activity
   c how easily a person can do an activity

7 Writing requires a lot of **concentration**. It's a good idea to be alone in a quiet room when you're writing.
   a the energy required to do something on your own
   b the ability to stay calm for long periods of time
   c the ability to give your whole attention to one thing

8 Anybody can **participate** in the game. You don't need to be an experienced player to join.
   a to be involved in an activity
   b to do something well
   c to improve quickly at something

USING YOUR KNOWLEDGE

2 Work with a partner. Look at the photos. What do you think are the benefits – if any – of each activity? Discuss your ideas.

taekwondo

team sports

cycling

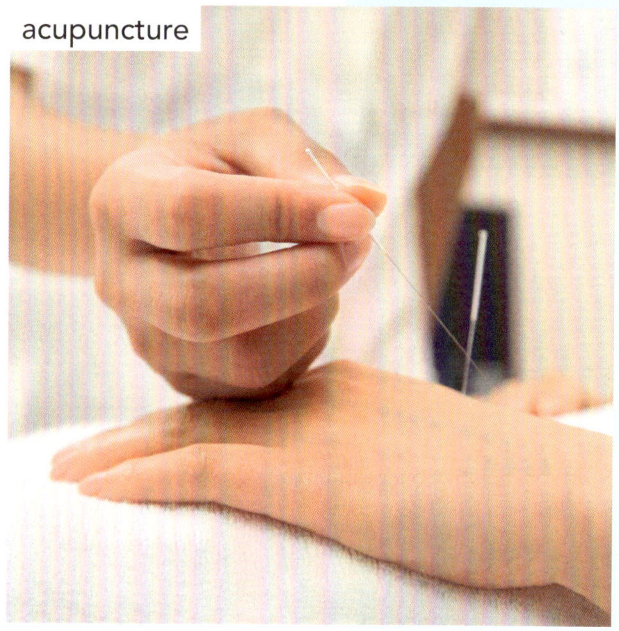
acupuncture

WHILE LISTENING

LISTENING FOR MAIN IDEAS

3 5.6 Listen to the four presentations. What is each one describing?

a cycling tour	acupuncture	a football club	taekwondo

Presentation 1: ____________________

Presentation 2: ____________________

Presentation 3: ____________________

Presentation 4: ____________________

TAKING NOTES ON DETAIL

4 5.6 Listen again. What are the benefits of each programme? Take notes.

Benefits of the health programmes

Programme 1:

Programme 2:

Programme 3:

Programme 4:

DISCUSSION

SYNTHESIZING

5 Work in small groups. Use ideas from Listening 1 and Listening 2 to answer the following questions.

1 What do you think each speaker in Listening 1 would think about the programmes in Listening 2? Why?
I think Speaker A would prefer to go on a CultureCycle tour because …

2 Do you still agree with your answer to this question from the start of the unit? Why / Why not?

> What advice would you give to somebody who wants to live to be 100 years old? What should the person do or not do?

I agree with my earlier advice, although …

3 Do you want to try any of the activities in the presentations in Listening 2? Which ones? Why / Why not?
I would like to try taekwondo because …
I wouldn't like to try the CultureCycle tour because …

SPEAKING

CRITICAL THINKING

At the end of this unit, you will do the speaking task below.

Give a presentation to a group of students about an idea for a health product or programme.

SKILLS

Brainstorming and evaluating ideas using an ideas map

Ideas maps are a good way to organize your notes as you listen. They help you see connections between the topic, the main ideas and the details.

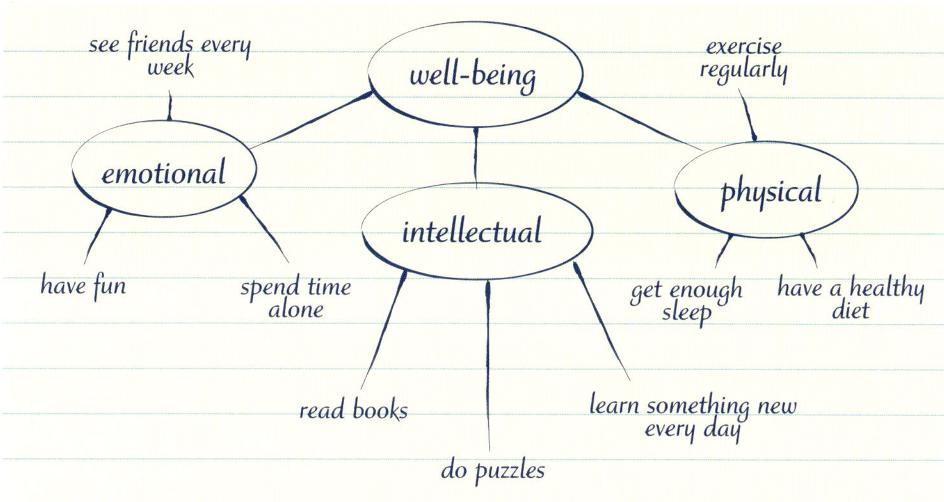

1 Choose one of the programmes from Listening 2 and complete the ideas map.

UNDERSTAND

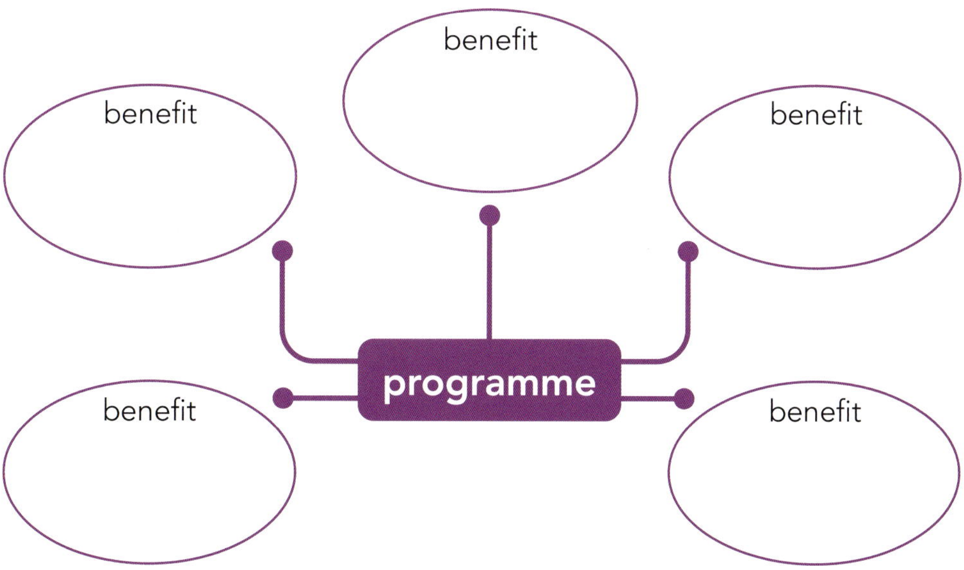

2 Work in groups. Brainstorm ideas for different health-related programmes which you might like to talk about. Write your ideas in the ideas map.

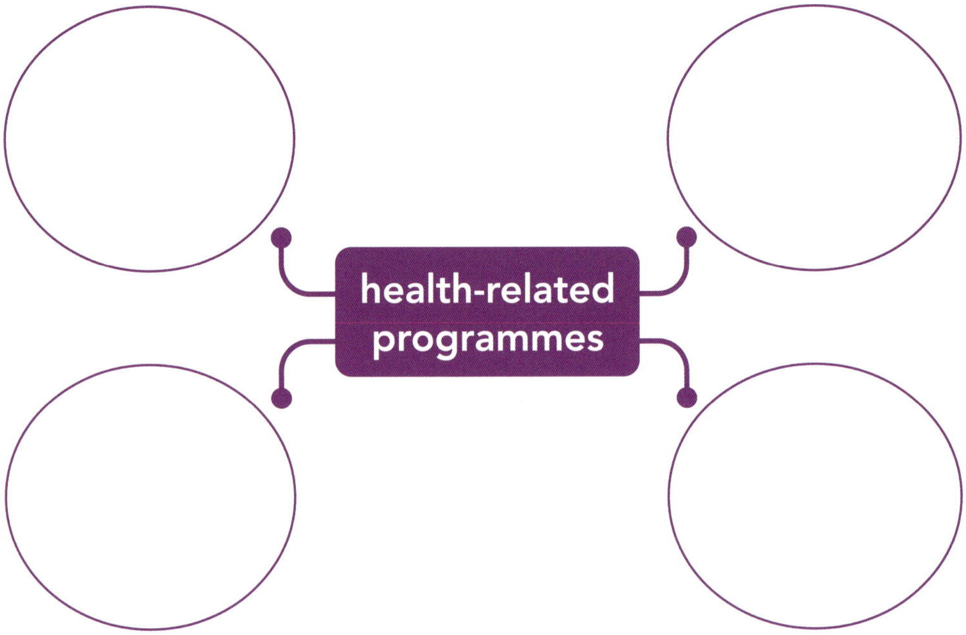

EVALUATE

3 Look at the health programmes you brainstormed in Exercise 2. Which has the most health benefits? Which has the fewest? Why? Choose one programme and write it in the centre of the ideas map below.

APPLY

4 Think of some benefits of the programme you are going to talk about and write them in the outside circles of the ideas map.

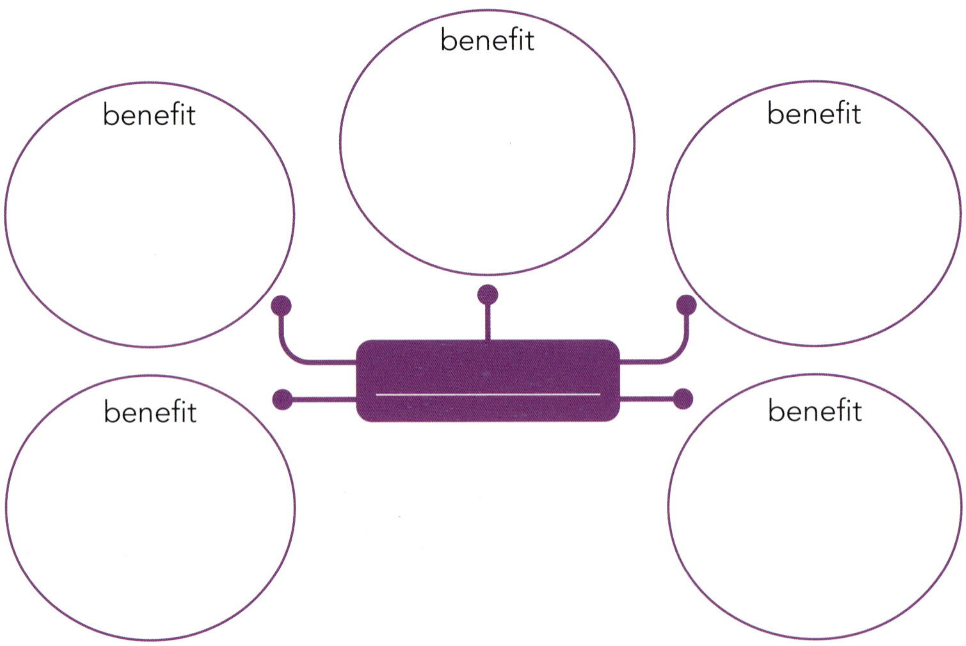

PREPARATION FOR SPEAKING

PROBLEM–SOLUTION ORGANIZATION

1 Work with a partner. Read the script below for a presentation about a programme and answer the questions.

1 Why does the script begin with rhetorical questions?

____

2 Why are all the rhetorical questions *yes/no* questions about *you*?

____

3 What three problems do the questions introduce?

____

____

____

4 What is the solution to the problems?

____

5 What is the purpose of the part of the script that begins 'And as we all know'?

____

6 What does the script say the programme is good for?

____

7 What information does the last part of the script provide?

____

2 What is the organization of the presentation? Number the information.

- specific information about the place, time, etc. ____
- background information about the programme ____
- rhetorical questions about the problems, to attract the listeners' attention *1*
- introduction of the solution ____

Script for presentation

Do you have problems focusing on your work? Are you under a lot of stress? Do you want to get more exercise while trying something new and exciting? If so, it's time to take up taekwondo! Taekwondo is great exercise. And as we all know, exercise improves your health. Taekwondo also has mental benefits – it has been shown to improve your concentration. In addition, it makes you feel good about yourself. This martial art was developed in Korea, and is now popular around the world. Whether you are looking for physical well-being, increased confidence or a life with less stress, Black Belt taekwondo club has it all. Sign up now for a free introductory class, starting on January 15th.

PRESENTING PERSUASIVELY

SKILLS

Speakers often try to persuade listeners to agree with them or to take action. Using rhetorical questions and identifying common knowledge are common persuasive techniques. Other persuasive techniques include:

1 **Using the imperative form.** The imperative form of a verb is strong and direct, so it is effective for persuasion. It is often used in advertisements.

Join us and take advantage of the many benefits of team sports.

2 **Using adjectives.** Adjectives help to persuade people by making them feel emotions.

So be kind to your body and your mind and come with us on an amazing adventure you'll never forget!

3 Read the extracts from the presentations. Underline the imperative verb forms.

1 Sign up now for a free introductory class, starting on January 15th.
2 If you're interested in learning more about our group, check out our website at www.footballsundays.cup.com.
3 This spring, join our six-month course in acupuncture.
4 Learn more about the course and visit us on our open days on the first Saturday of every month.

4 Work with a partner and answer the questions.

1 What effect do the imperatives have on the listener?

____

2 Why are imperatives used in the presentations?

____

____

5 Work with a partner. Take turns reading the sentences (1–6). Your partner listens and rephrases it more persuasively.

A: If you want, you can come along to our shop and buy our new product.
B: Come along and buy our new product!

1 It is possible to buy one and get one free.
2 You should hurry and purchase a ticket now.
3 People must not forget that our shops are open on Sundays.
4 If you would like to register for our course, you should do this before it's too late!
5 Our running club is a great club for you to come along and join. It's fun, friendly and free.
6 We predict you will become happier and healthier by cooking with our recipes.

6 **Read the extracts. Underline the adjectives.**

1 Do you want to get more exercise while trying something new and exciting?
2 Would you like to improve your social life, your intellectual performance, your physical fitness and your team-building skills?
3 Not only does this trip provide terrific exercise and a fascinating cultural experience, it's the best way to learn.
4 Are you interested in alternative treatments?
5 Have you ever wanted to explore the secrets of traditional Chinese medicine?

7 **Work with a partner and answer the questions.**

1 Do the adjectives in Exercise 6 have a positive or a negative meaning?

____

2 What images come to mind when you hear these adjectives?

____

____

3 Think of other adjectives you often hear in advertisements and persuasive presentations. Look at Exercise 5 again. Where you can, write a second sentence using a positive adjective.

Come along and buy our new product! It's amazing.

SPEAKING TASK

Give a presentation to a group of students about an idea for a health product or programme.

PREPARE

1 **Look at the ideas map you created in Exercise 4 in the Critical thinking section. Review your notes and add any new information.**

2 **Make notes about what you will say. Use this organization:**

1 rhetorical questions to introduce the problem and attract the listener's attention
2 introduction of the product or programme and explanation of how it solves the problem
3 background information about the product or programme
4 specific details about the place, time and/or costs

3 **Plan which phrasal verbs and adjectives you will use to talk about your product or programme.**

It's time to ***take up*** *taekwondo!*
This trip provides ***terrific*** *exercise and a* ***fascinating*** *cultural experience.*

4 Make notes about common knowledge which you can use to help persuade your audience. You can use language like this:

It's common knowledge that …
There is no question that …
Everybody knows that …
Most people think that …
There is no doubt that …

5 Refer to the Task checklist below as you prepare your presentation.

TASK CHECKLIST	✔
Use phrasal verbs correctly.	
Use adjectives to describe well-being correctly.	
Use problem–solution organization correctly.	
Use imperatives to persuade the listener.	
Use adjectives to persuade the listener.	

PRACTISE

6 Work in small groups. Take turns practising your presentations. Take notes on your classmates' presentations and feed back to them on how persuasive it was.

PRESENT

7 Take turns giving your presentations to the class.

OBJECTIVES REVIEW

1 Check your learning objectives for this unit. Write *3*, *2* or *1* for each objective.

3 = very well 2 = well 1 = not so well

I can …

watch and understand a video about brain health	____
listen for attitude.	____
identify references to common knowledge.	____
brainstorm and evaluate ideas using an ideas map.	____
understand and use phrasal verbs.	____
use problem–solution organization.	____
present persuasively.	____
give a presentation to a group of students about an idea for a health product or programme.	____

2 Use the *Unlock* Digital Workbook for more practice with this unit's learning objectives.

UNLOCK DIGITAL WORKBOOK

WORDLIST

come down with (phr v)
concentration (n) ⊙
cultural (adj) ⊙
cut down on (phr v)
educational (adj) ⊙
emotional (adj) ⊙
get over (phr v)
give up (phr v)
habit (n) ⊙
illness (n) ⊙
in shape (adj)
intellectual (adj) ⊙
join in (phr v)
mental (adj) ⊙
overweight (adj)
participate (v) ⊙
performance (n) ⊙
personal (adj) ⊙
physical (adj) ⊙
prove (v) ⊙
reduce (v) ⊙
relax (v)
ridiculous (adj)
sign up for (phr v)
social (adj) ⊙
stress (n)
take up (phr v)
treatment (n) ⊙
try out for (phr v)
unhealthy (adj)
work out (phr v)

⊙ = high-frequency words in the Cambridge Academic Corpus

UNIT 6

DISCOVERY AND INVENTION

LEARNING OBJECTIVES

Watch and listen
Watch and understand a video about research scientists.

Listening skills
Understand references to earlier ideas; understand lecture organization.

Critical thinking
Summarize information using *Wh-* questions.

Grammar
Use passive verb forms.

Speaking skills
Preview a topic; organize ideas; explain how something is used.

Speaking task
Give a presentation about an invention or a discovery which has changed our lives.

UNIT 6 DISCOVERY AND INVENTION

UNLOCK YOUR KNOWLEDGE

Work with a partner. Look at the photo and answer the questions.

1 The photo shows an early computer. When do you think this photo was taken?
2 How does this computer compare to modern ones?
3 What do you think is the most important invention or discovery in the last 50 years? Why is it important?

WATCH AND LISTEN

1

2

PREPARING TO WATCH

ACTIVATING YOUR KNOWLEDGE

1 Work with a partner and answer the questions.

1 What are the four 'STEM' subjects?
   a Science, Technology, Engineering, Mechanics
   b Science, Technology, Engineering, Maths
   c Science, Technology, Economics, Maths
2 Can you think of any famous people who work in a STEM industry? How did they become famous?
3 What do you think makes somebody a good research scientist? What interests and abilities do they have?

PREDICTING CONTENT USING VISUALS

2 You are going to watch a video about research scientists. Before you watch, look at the photos from the video. Discuss the questions with your partner.

1 What is happening in each photo? Which job do you find most interesting? Why?
2 What do you think the main topic(s) of the video will be?
3 In the video you will hear about three inventions. What do you think these might be?

GLOSSARY

fundamental (adj) more important than anything else
treatment (n) the use of medicine to make a sick or injured person healthy
immune system (n) the system in the body that protects it against infection
vaccine (n) a special substance that you take into your body to prevent a disease
cataract (n) a disease which affects somebody's eye so that they can not see clearly
pandemic (n) a dangerous disease that infects many people at the same time

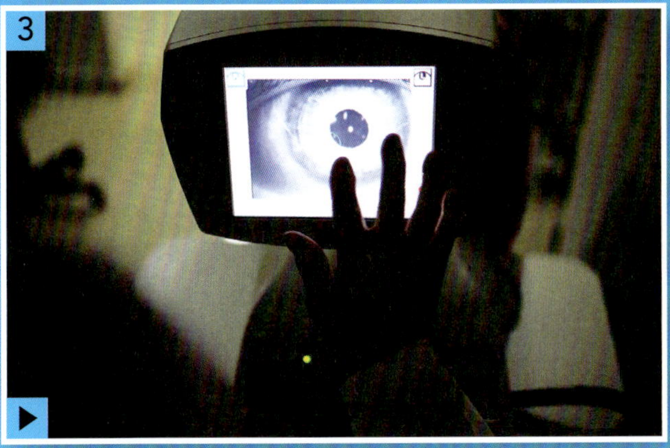

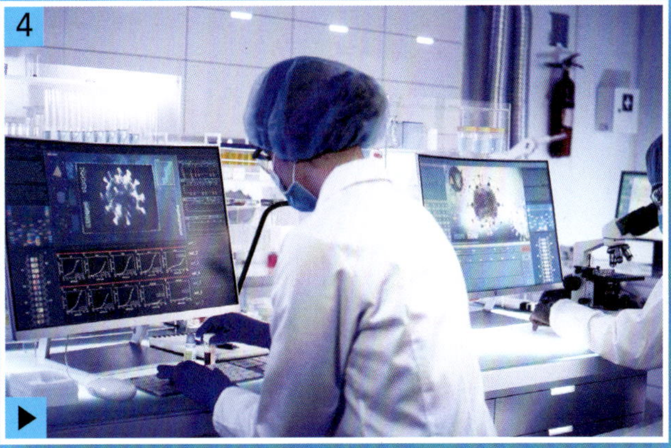

WHILE WATCHING

SUMMARIZING

3 Read the paragraph and try to predict the words you will hear. Then watch the video and complete the paragraph.

Research scientists have a range of skills. They enjoy testing their ideas and assessing (1)__________ – a fundamental part of science. They also possess (2)__________ flexibility and know that there is rarely a single (3)__________ . They should be able to accept changes in their working life, because their job can take them to a range of (4)__________ . A research scientist often works in this industry because they want to make a difference to the (5)__________ of others.

UNDERSTANDING DETAIL

4 Watch again. Circle the correct answer. In some items, more than one answer is possible.

1 Which type of thinking does the speaker say is 'fundamental to science'?
   a critical   b logical   c practical
2 What did James Dyson use during his first attempt at creating a vacuum cleaner?
   a cardboard   b plastic wire   c sticky tape
3 In which location(s) might a research scientist work?
   a underwater   b in space   c in a lecture hall
4 Which area did the creators of BioNTech first want to research?
   a Covid-19   b cancer   c the immune system

DISCUSSION

5 Discuss the questions below in a small group.

1 Which of the people mentioned in the video has had the most positive effect on the world? Why?
2 Based on the video, what effects has the work of research scientists had on your life?

LISTENING

LISTENING 1

PREPARING TO LISTEN

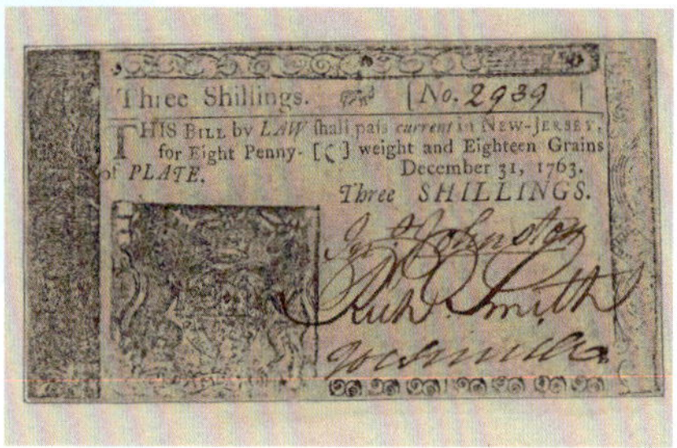

1 Work in groups. Look at the photos and discuss the questions.

1 Which of these inventions do you think is the oldest?
2 Which do you think is the newest?
3 Which do you think has been the most useful?
4 Where in the world do you think they were invented? Why do you think this?

UNDERSTANDING KEY VOCABULARY

2 You are going to listen to a museum tour about inventions from the Middle Ages. Before you listen, work with a partner and complete each sentence with the correct form of a noun from the box. Use a dictionary to help you.

contribution	**device**	**diagram**	**discovery**
outcome	**scholar**	**technology**	**weapon**

1 In the twelfth century, al-Jazari drew ________ and gave detailed descriptions of machines for farming.
2 Certain people who have made a huge ________ to science and the arts receive an award called the Nobel Prize.
3 Iron is a material that people first used to make ________ in the twelfth century BCE.
4 The ________ of electricity in the eighteenth century changed the organization of human society.
5 A baby monitor is a ________ which lets parents watch their child when they're in a different room.
6 Although we believe our company's new invention will be very popular with customers, it is too early to predict the ________ .
7 There are many important ________ at universities today whose work will have a huge effect on the world as we know it.
8 Modern ________ , such as computers and mobile phones, has completely changed our lives over the past 50 years.

USING YOUR KNOWLEDGE

3 Work with a partner. Match the inventions (1–4) to the photos (a–d). Tell your partner when you think they were invented.

1 the fountain pen ______
2 glasses ______
3 gunpowder ______
4 the crankshaft ______

a

b
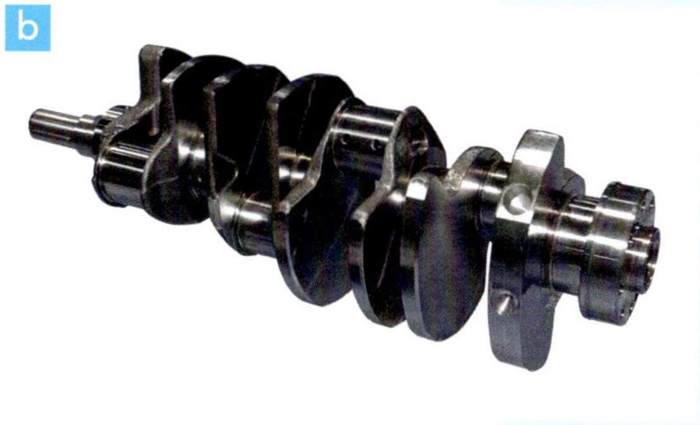
c

d

WHILE LISTENING

LISTENING FOR MAIN IDEAS

4 6.1 Listen to the museum tour. Number the topics (a–f) in the order they are mentioned.

a ______ A problem that fountain pens solved.
b ______ How and when glasses were invented.
c ______ The inventions of a great engineer.
d ______ Where these inventions were brought from and to.
e ______ How gunpowder changed the world.
f ______ Why the Middle Ages were important in the development of science.

5 6.1 Work with a partner. Complete the notes with the information you can remember. Then listen to the tour again to check and finish completing the notes.

Fountain pen
invented in the year (1) ____________ *in* (2) ____________
people previously wrote with (3) ____________ *and they used to get* (4) ____________ *on their fingers / clothes*
first fountain pen used a small container to avoid this problem

Glasses
invented in (5) ___________ *in the* (6) ___________ *century*
people held them in front of their eyes or rested them on their noses
al-Jazari
a famous (7) ___________ *from the Middle Ages, lived in* (8) ___________ *in the* (9) ___________ *century*
examples of inventions:
- *a mechanical clock that needed* (10) ___________ *and* (11) ___________ *to work*
- *the crankshaft – a device that keeps machines going in a* (12) ___________ *(used today in* (13) ___________*)*

Gunpowder
invented in (14) ___________ *in the* (15) ___________ *century*
the inventors were searching for a way that would allow people to (16) ___________
first instructions for making gunpowder came in the (17) ___________ *century*
gunpowder had a big effect on the methods and outcomes of (18) ___________

POST-LISTENING

SKILLS

Understanding references to earlier ideas

To refer to things they talked about earlier, speakers often use words such as *it, he, she, they, then* and *there*. This sounds more natural than repeating the same words. In this sentence, the word *it* refers back to the invention of the telephone:

In 1876, Alexander Graham Bell invented the telephone. ← It changed the way we communicate.

6 Read the sentences. Underline the words which the words in bold refer to.

1. The first fountain pen was made in 953 in Africa. Before **then**, people used bird feathers and ink to write with.
2. As some of you may know, the Middle Ages have often been called the 'Dark Ages'. During this tour, you will find out that **they** were not.
3. Glasses were invented in Italy in the thirteenth century. Nobody knows who invented **them**.
4. The invention of gunpowder has changed the way we fight wars. **It** changed the outcome of many medieval battles and affected the history of the world.

PRONUNCIATION FOR LISTENING

SKILLS

Weak and strong forms

In spoken English, people don't usually stress words which do not carry the main meaning in a sentence, such as *a*, *an*, *in*, *the*, *do*, *does*, *to*, *from*, *and* or *of*. When these words are unstressed, they are called *weak forms*.
The unstressed vowel in these weak forms is pronounced /ə/ (*to* = /tə/, *the* = /ðə/, etc.). However, speakers sometimes stress these types of words to make them the main part of their message. When these words are stressed, they are called *strong forms*.

Andrea is funny and intelligent. (The speaker is stressing that Andrea has both of these qualities.)

7 6.2 **Listen for the weak forms and complete the sentences.**

1 Inventions ________ technology from India, China, North Africa, ________ ________ Middle East were brought ________ Europe.
2 ________ first glasses were held in front ________ the eyes or balanced on ________ nose.
3 ________ crankshaft is ________ long arm which allows machines ________ move ________ ________ straight line.
4 As we move along, you'll find one ________ ________ most important inventions ________ medieval times.

8 6.3 **Listen to the extracts. Match the extracts (1–3) to the reasons for using strong forms (a–c).**

1 The Middle Ages **were** an interesting time and they were full of scientific discoveries. ____
2 Inventions and machines designed by medieval scholars made a great contribution to society and many are still in use today. **And** some of these inventions are very common. ____
3 Many people think gunpowder is **the** most important invention in history. ____

Strong forms are used …

a to emphasize that there is nothing better or more than this.
b to contrast with an earlier idea that the Middle Ages were **not** an interesting time.
c to emphasize that there is more information.

DISCUSSION

9 Look at the photos of some Chinese inventions. Think about the questions and make notes.

1 How did the inventions make people's lives better?
The compass made people's lives better by … After somebody invented paper, people …

2 Which inventions were very important in the past but are less important now?
All of the inventions were important because …

3 Which invention was the most important in the past? Is it the same now?
In the past, I think paper was the most important invention because …

10 Work in a group. Take turns explaining why the invention you chose is the most important.

the compass

making paper

printing

LANGUAGE DEVELOPMENT

USES OF THE VERB *MAKE*

VOCABULARY

The verb *make* has three main meanings: *force*, *cause* or *produce*.
Force: *My boss* ***made*** *me work late last night.*
Cause: *Water and weights* ***make*** *the mechanical clocks work.*
Produce: *The first fountain pen was* ***made*** *in 953.*

1 Work with a partner. Discuss the meaning of *make* in each sentence. Write *C* (cause), *F* (force) or *P* (produce).

1 Gunpowder was first **made** in China. _P_
2 My professor **made** me rewrite my assignment because there were too many mistakes. ____
3 Social media **makes** it easy for people to stay in touch. ____
4 The new discovery **made** a lot of people very happy. ____
5 I **made** myself stay up late to finish the work. ____

2 Work with a partner. Which of the nouns in the box below are used with *make*? Which nouns are not used with *make*? What verb do you use instead?

attempt	comparison	contribution	decision	difference
experiment	improvement	investment	public	research

3 Complete the sentences with the correct form of *make* and a noun from Exercise 2. Then compare your answers with a partner.

1 If you ________ between these two TVs, you'll see that this one has a much clearer picture.
2 I like both of these bikes a lot. I'm finding it hard to ________ about which one to buy.
3 Medieval scholars ________ to the world by inventing things that allowed societies to grow and become wealthier.
4 Inventors ________ on many occasions to build flying cars, and they are getting closer to something drivers can buy.
5 Ten years ago, Andrew ________ in a new technology company. He's now a millionaire.
6 The invention of the light bulb ________ to people's lifestyles. After it was invented, people could work indoors for longer, even when it was dark.
7 This is a good smartphone, but they could still ________ to it, like longer battery life.
8 The government won't ________ who the people are until the police confirm the details.

4 Work with a partner. Match the sentences (1–8) in Exercise 3 to the definitions (a–h) of *make* + noun.

a to try ________
b to choose ________
c to make a situation better for people ________
d to consider the similarities between two things ________
e to change or add to something to make it better ________
f to put money into something to make more money ________
g to share information about something to a wider group of people ________
h to create, give or do something to create more success for something else ________

5 Write two questions using the correct form of *make* + a noun from Exercise 2. Then ask your partner.

Do you think planting trees will make a difference to climate change?

PASSIVE VERB FORMS

GRAMMAR

In an *active sentence* we focus on the person or thing that *causes* an effect or a result.

In a *passive sentence* the focus is on the person or thing that *experiences* the effect of an action, or what comes *as a result of* an action.

Active: *Alan Turing invented the digital computer.* (focus on the inventor)

Passive: *The digital computer was invented in 1936.* (focus on the invention)

You can use the passive when you don't know who does an action, when it is not important to give that information, or when it is obvious.

*The wooden cannon **was invented** in the thirteenth century. (It's not known or not important who invented the cannon.)*

*Maria Ressa and Dmitry Muratov **were awarded** the Nobel Peace Prize in 2021. (It's obvious that the Nobel Prize organization gave them the award.)*

If you want to make it clear who did something, use *by* at the end of a passive sentence.

The digital computer was invented in 1936 by Alan Turing.

To form the passive, use *be* + *past participle*. (Remember: the passive can be used in all tenses, and with regular and irregular past participles).

*All students **are invited** to attend a talk by one of the country's most successful inventors.*

*Many museum members complained they **were not told** about the new science exhibition.*

6 **Work in a group. Time yourselves to see who is quickest to find the correct number of passive verb forms in these extracts from Listening 1.**

1 The Middle Ages were an interesting time, and they were full of scientific discoveries. During this time, inventions and technology from India, China, North Africa and the Middle East were brought to Europe.

2 And some of these inventions are very common. For example, the first fountain pen was made in 953 in Africa.

3 Glasses were invented in Italy in the thirteenth century. No one knows who invented them. The first glasses were held in front of the eyes or balanced on the nose. They were developed to help people with bad vision to read.

4 His most important invention was the crankshaft. The crankshaft is a long arm which allows machines to move in a straight line. It was first used for watering gardens.

7 **Compare your answers with a partner and check that you have both underlined the correct verbs.**

8 Find and correct the verb errors in the sentences (one sentence does not have an error). Then compare your answers with a partner.

1 The first smartphone, named Simon, were created by IBM.

____

2 The first newspaper was print in 1605 in Germany.

____

3 The first computer program was wrote by Ada Lovelace.

____

4 Hearing aids were developed to help people hear better.

____

9 Work with a partner. Write each sentence in the passive form.

1 Apple's first tablet computer – develop – the 1990s
Apple's first tablet computer was developed in the 1990s.

2 the law of gravity – discover – Isaac Newton – the seventeenth century

____

3 the first computer chip – invent – the 1950s

____

4 the first smartphone – create – after 1997

____

5 penicillin – first discover – 1928 – Alexander Fleming

____

10 Work with a partner. Take turns reading the sets of words (1–8). Your partner says a complete sentence with the verb in the correct active or passive form.

Student A: *paper discover ancient China*
Student B: *Paper was discovered in ancient China.*

1 first email **send** 1971
2 telephone **invent** 1876
3 Edison **develop** first light bulb 1879
4 720,000 hours video **share** social media every day
5 Egyptian architect called Imhotep **design** pyramid of Djoser
6 very early calculator **create** Blaise Pascal
7 millions people **download** smartphone apps every hour
8 letters **write** fountain pens many years now.

11 Work with a partner. What do you know about the inventions mentioned in Exercises 8, 9 and 10?

LISTENING 2

PREPARING TO LISTEN

PREDICTING CONTENT USING CONTEXT

1 Read the introduction to a lecture about an invention. Answer the questions.

1 Can you guess the name of the invention? ______________

2 What two words are used to refer to it? __________ and __________

In today's lecture, I want to discuss an invention which has changed our lives. This product has made a huge difference in the way we work, travel, communicate and socialize with friends. Can you guess what it is? I'm talking here about mobile phone [redacted]. The word [redacted] comes from [redacted]. Traditionally, [redacted] were used in computers to help them perform better. However, with the invention of smartphones, the word [redacted] is used to refer to phone [redacted]. In this lecture, we'll start by discussing the very first [redacted] and their development. We will then discuss how [redacted] have changed our lives. Finally, we'll focus on some of the most popular [redacted] used by people today.

2 6.4 Listen to the introduction. Check your answers to Exercise 1.

UNDERSTANDING KEY VOCABULARY

3 Work with a partner. Circle the best word to complete each sentence. Then write the words next to the correct definitions (a–g) on page 137.

1 I need a password to __________ the Wi-Fi connection in this café.
 a access b connect c enter

2 After you download the app, __________ it on your smartphone.
 a produce b install c add

3 This software lets you __________ your own apps. I have some great ideas I'd like to try to design.
 a create b start c form

4 In a recent study, 45% of American smartphone __________ said they would rather give up their holidays than their phones.
 a keepers b holders c users

5 I always read __________ reviews before I buy an expensive item.
 a goods b equipment c product

6 IT (information technology) is an extremely fast-growing __________ .
 a industry b custom c trade

7 Smartphones __________ us to stay in touch with each other.
 a mean b allow c let

a the people and activities involved in one type of business ___________
b somebody who uses a product, machine or service ___________
c the right or opportunity to use something ___________
d something that is made to be sold ___________
e to make something new, or invent something ___________
f to make it possible for something to happen ___________
g to put a program onto a computer so you can use it ___________

WHILE LISTENING

4 Discuss the questions below in a small group.

1 How have smartphones and tablets changed our lives?
2 What would your everyday life be like without your smartphone?

USING YOUR KNOWLEDGE

5 Work with a partner. Read the text and answer the questions.

> It's hard to imagine life before smartphone apps! But let's try anyway. Imagine for a moment that you're taking a road trip in the days before smartphones were invented.

1 How can you find information about the place that you want to visit?
2 Which forms of entertainment could you use in the car while you drive?
3 How will you find your way to your destination? What will you do if you get lost?
4 Where are the address and phone numbers of the hotels where you want to stay?

LISTENING FOR MAIN IDEAS

6 6.5 Listen to the lecture. Are your answers to the questions in Exercise 5 similar to the speaker's? Check your notes and add ideas.

TAKING NOTES: JIGSAW READING

7 Work in groups of three students, A, B and C. Your teacher is going to give a text to each student in the group. Read your text and underline the key information in it. Then make notes about it.

8 Work in your group from Exercise 7. Use your notes to tell each other about the key information in your text.

9 Work in your groups again. Use your notes to underline eight mistakes in the notes. Write the correct words or numbers in gaps 1–8 on page 138.

first apps used for:	*second generation apps:*	*another effect of apps:*	*negative effects of apps:*
- accessing the internet *- check voicemail* *- send photos*	*- first app store opened in 2009* *- by 2011, 20 billion downloads – people used apps more than internet browsers* *- by 2018, 180 billion downloads*	*- there is a need for skilled IT specialists*	*- people are more stressed* *- people are less tolerant*

1 ______________	5 ______________
2 ______________	6 ______________
3 ______________	7 ______________
4 ______________	8 ______________

LISTENING FOR DETAIL

10 6.5 Listen to the lecture again. Check your answers to Exercise 9.

POST-LISTENING

SKILLS

Understanding lecture organization

Lecturers often use special phrases to help the audience follow the lecture. In the introduction, they explain what they'll talk about and in what order.

First, we'll discuss … I'd like to start by talking about …

They also use special expressions to show transitions from one topic to another.

Next, I will discuss … Now I'd like to talk about …

Transition phrases like these are very common in academic contexts. Lecturers use them to help you understand the material and to take better notes while you are listening. They are also useful for organizing presentations.

11 Read the extracts from the lecture. Underline the expressions the lecturer uses to say what will happen next.

1 We'll start by discussing the very first apps and their development.
2 We will then discuss how apps have changed our lives.
3 I'd like to start by talking a little bit about the first apps.
4 I'm going to briefly talk about how these apps have changed our lives.
5 Now I'd like to mention another important effect of the invention of apps.
6 In the next part of the lecture, I'll discuss some of the most common apps in more detail.

DISCUSSION

SYNTHESIZING

12 Think of an app that you use very often. Then work with a partner to answer the questions below.

1 What is the app designed to do?
2 What do you use it for?
3 What are the advantages and disadvantages of the app?
4 Who would you recommend it to?

13 Write a review of the app you discussed in Exercise 12. Use the language from Exercise 11 and the Skills box. Start by saying what the app is called. Write between 150–180 words.

An app which I use a lot is called … *This app is designed for …*

SPEAKING

CRITICAL THINKING

At the end of this unit, you will do the speaking task below.

Give a presentation about an invention or a discovery which has changed our lives.

Summarizing information using *Wh-* questions

SKILLS

When you do research on a topic, try asking yourself the following questions: *Who? What? When? Where? Why?* Many researchers add *How?* to this list. Then search for the answers to these questions. To organize your research, it is helpful to make an ideas map like the one in Exercise 1. This is a quick and easy way to focus on the key details of a topic.

UNDERSTAND

1 Choose one of the inventions from Listening 1 or one of the apps from Listening 2. Write this in the Topic box below. Complete the ideas map for the invention or app. Use information from your notes on page 130 or 137. Try answering some of these questions:

1 When was the last time you used this thing?
2 What are its uses?
3 What would life be like without it?
4 How has it affected our lives?

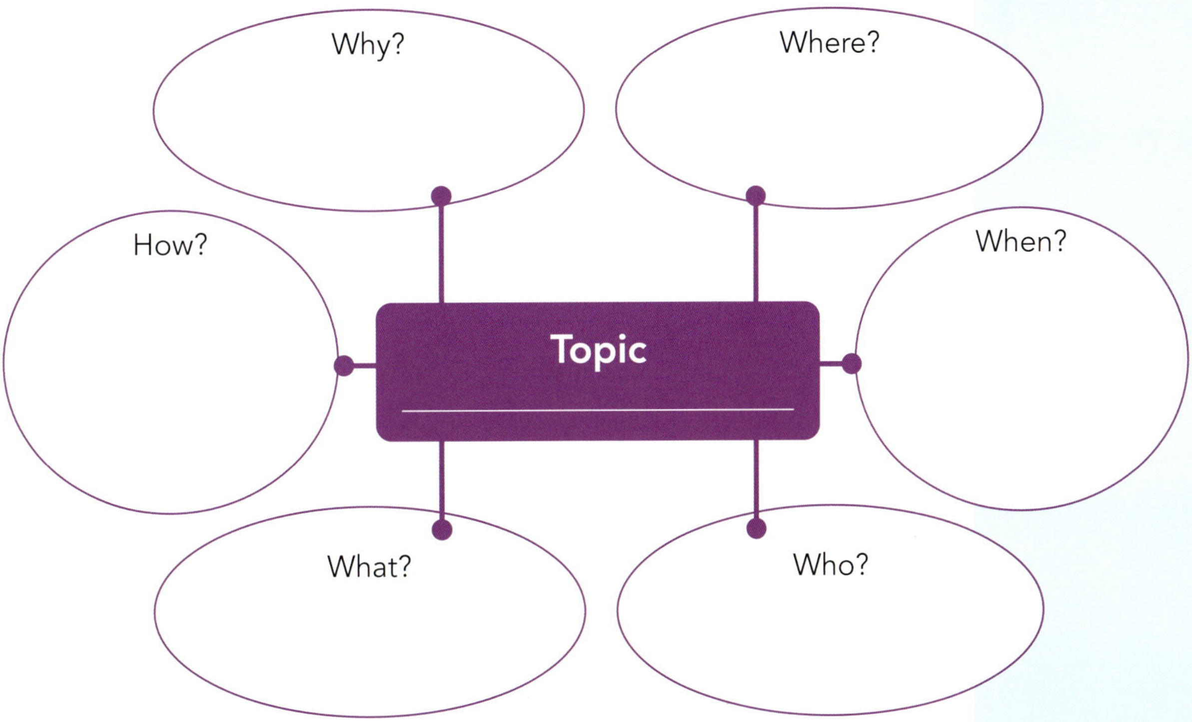

2 Work with a partner. Share your ideas map. Make suggestions about information which your partner could add.

APPLY

3 Choose an invention to talk about in the speaking task. You can talk about one of the inventions in the photos below or use your own idea.

contactless payment

the microwave

the refrigerator

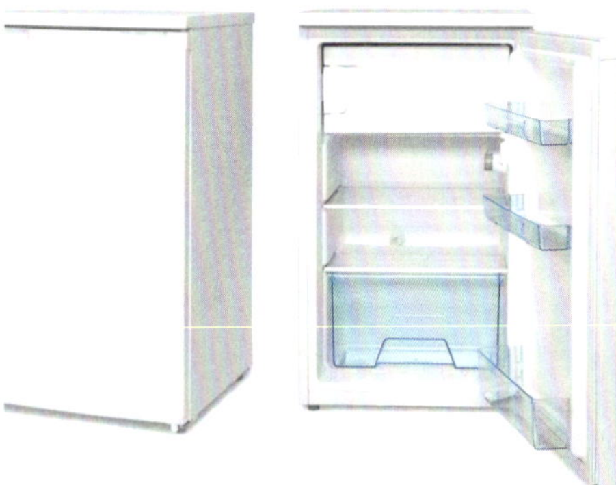

the electric car

4 Complete an ideas map about the invention you chose.

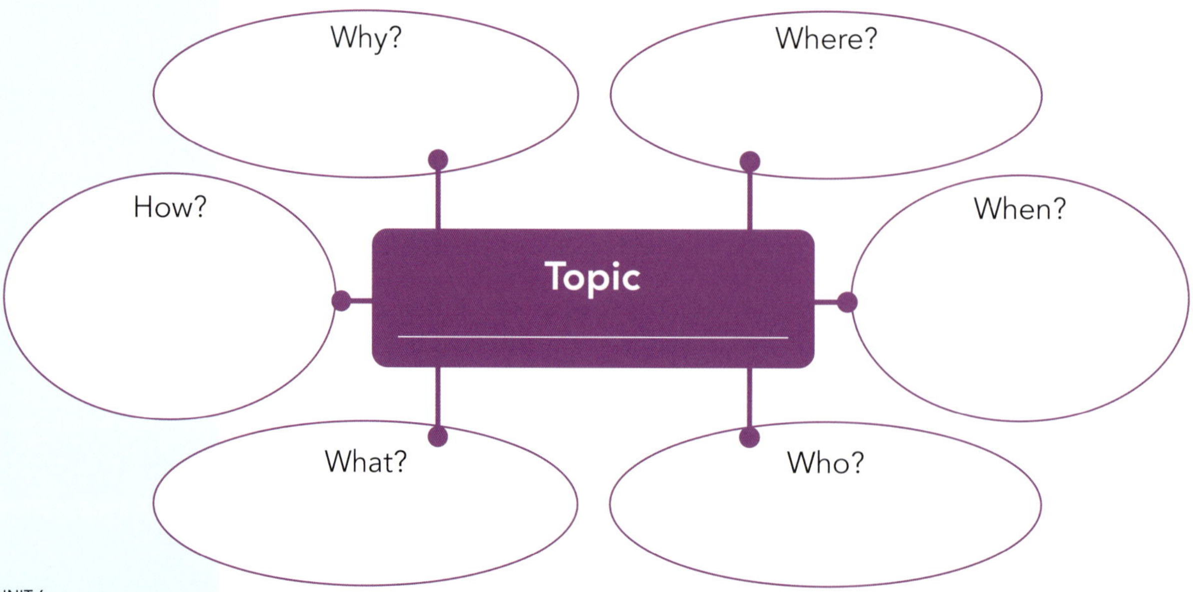

5 Work with a partner. Share your ideas map. Make suggestions about information which your partner could add.

PREPARATION FOR SPEAKING

PREVIEWING A TOPIC

SKILLS

In the introduction to a presentation, give a preview of what you will talk about. This helps your audience follow your talk. Here are some examples of language you can use to preview a topic:

I'd like to begin my talk by looking at …
After that, I'm going to explain …
Then, I'll discuss …
Finally, I'll explore …

1 6.6 Listen to an introduction to a presentation which previews what the speaker will talk about. Circle the things that the speaker does.

1 mentions the invention's name in the first sentence
2 gives a description of the invention
3 says how you can use it
4 gives specific details of how it was invented
5 explains what will happen next in the presentation

2 Work with a partner. Practise giving an introduction about a simple invention. Use the preview below to organize your ideas.

Student A: give an introduction to a presentation about the **paperclip**.
Student B: give an introduction to a presentation about the **ballpoint pen**.

I would like to present an invention which has changed the way we ____________ . It's a simple invention and we have all used it.
It's the ____________ .
A ____________ is ____________ .
(explain the invention here)
You can ____________ .
(explain how it is used in general)
First, I am going to talk about ____________ . Then, I will explain how it has improved our lives.

ORGANIZING IDEAS

SKILLS

Before you write a presentation outline, decide in what order you will present your ideas. First, brainstorm some ideas and write them down. Then put them in order to create the framework for your outline. This will help you make sure that your ideas are in a logical order when you start writing. For example, it is logical to tell your listeners background information before you tell them why something is useful. You can use *Wh-* questions to organize your presentation.

3 **Read the next part of the presentation. Number the questions (a–g) in the order they are answered in the presentation. Then compare your answers with a partner.**

a Why do people use them? _____
b Who invented them? _____
c Where can people use them? _____
d Why were they invented? _____
e When were they invented? __1__
f What is the best thing about the invention? _____
g When were they first sold? _____

To start with, Post-it® notes were invented in 1974 by Art Fry. Fry needed a bookmark which would stay inside the book and didn't fall out. He used a special type of glue invented by his colleague Spencer Silver. The glue was not very strong and made it easy to remove the notes.

In 1977, the first Post-it® notes were sold in shops. Since then, they have become a global phenomenon. People all over the word recognize the small, yellow sticky notes. We use them at work, at school and at home.

Because the glue does not leave any stains, people can stick Post-it® notes to anything. They allow us to remember important information and take notes. The best thing is that you can stick a Post-it® note anywhere to help you remember something.

SKILLS

EXPLAINING HOW SOMETHING IS USED

We can use the words and expressions in bold to talk about how something is used.

Without *the crankshaft, car engines wouldn't work.*	*(without + noun)*
Post-it® notes ***help people to*** *remember things.*	*(help + noun/pronoun + to + infinitive)*
The light bulb ***allows us to*** *see at night.*	*(allow + noun/pronoun + to + infinitive)*
The microwave ***makes it*** *possible to cook food quickly.*	*(make + it + adjective)*
Social media ***is useful for*** *communicating with friends.*	*(useful + for + gerund)*

4 Complete the sentences with phrases from the box.

allows us	are useful for	helps people to	makes it	without

1 GPS ________________ to find our way around unknown places.
2 The mobile phone ________________ stay in touch.
3 Translation apps ________________ learning another language.
4 Television ________________ easy to learn about the world.
5 ________________ the computer chip, we wouldn't be able to use laptops.

5 Write between two and four sentences about an invention of your choice. Use phrases from Exercise 4. Do not use the same invention that you chose in the Critical Thinking section.

____
____
____
____

6 Work with a partner. Take turns saying your sentences. Do not say the name of your invention – instead, say 'this invention'. Your partner should try to guess what is being described.

This invention allows us to work or study at home more easily.

Is it a smartphone?

No. I'll give you another clue.Without this invention, we would have to sit in one place to work or study …

SPEAKING TASK

Give a presentation about an invention or a discovery which has changed our lives.

PREPARE

1 Look at the ideas map you created in Exercise 4 in the Critical thinking section. Add any new information. Decide in what order you will answer the *Wh-* questions and write them below.

1 ______
2 ______
3 ______
4 ______
5 ______
6 ______

2 Make notes about the language you will use. Use language like this:

To preview your topic

I'd like to start by talking about …
Then, I'll discuss …
Finally, I'll explore …

To explain how something is used

______ *helps people to …*
Without ______, …
______ *makes it* ______ *to …*

Passive verbs

The Post-it® note ***was invented*** *in …*

References to earlier ideas

After ***it*** *was invented …*

3 Refer to the Task checklist below as you prepare your presentation.

TASK CHECKLIST	✔
Use phrases with *make* correctly.	
Clearly preview a topic and explain how something is used.	
Logically organize your ideas and make references to earlier ideas with words such as *this*, *it*, etc.	
Use passive verbs correctly and appropriately.	

PRACTISE

4 Work with a partner. Take turns practising your presentation.

PRESENT

5 Work in small groups. Take turns giving your presentations. Discuss which one of your inventions or discoveries has had the biggest influence.

The laptop computer has had a huge effect on our lives, because is has allowed us to …

OBJECTIVES REVIEW

1 Check your learning objectives for this unit. Write *3*, *2* or *1* for each objective.

3 = very well 2 = well 1 = not so well

I can …

watch and understand a video about research scientists.	_____
understand references to earlier ideas.	_____
understand lecture organization.	_____
summarize information using *Wh-* questions.	_____
use passive verb forms.	_____
preview a topic.	_____
organize ideas.	_____
explain how something is used.	_____
give a presentation about an invention or a discovery which has changed our lives.	_____

2 Use the *Unlock* Digital Workbook for more practice with this unit's learning objectives.

WORDLIST

access (v) ⊙
allow (v) ⊙
app (n)
contribution (n) ⊙
create (v) ⊙
device (n) ⊙
diagram (n) ⊙
discovery (n) ⊙
industry (n) ⊙
install (v)
make a comparison (v phr)
make a contribution (v phr)
make a decision (v phr)
make a difference (v phr)
make an investment (v phr)
make attempts (v phr)
make improvements (v phr)
make public (v phr)
outcome (n) ⊙
product (n) ⊙
scholar (n) ⊙
technology (n) ⊙
user (n) ⊙
weapon (n) ⊙

⊙ = high-frequency words in the Cambridge Academic Corpus

UNIT 7

FASHION

LEARNING OBJECTIVES

Watch and listen
Watch and understand a video about a College of Art graduate.

Listening skills
Take notes on main ideas and detail; identify auxiliary verbs for emphasis.

Critical thinking
Create a purpose statement; evaluate interview questions.

Grammar
Talk about recent events and actions using adverbs; make predictions and talk about expectations for the future.

Speaking skills
Ask for opinions and check information; ask follow-up questions.

Speaking task
Take part in an interview about attitudes on uniforms.

UNIT 7 FASHION

UNLOCK YOUR KNOWLEDGE

Work with a partner. Look at the photo and answer the questions.

1 What is the person doing?
2 What do young people like to wear in your country at the moment?
3 Has fashion changed a lot in your country in the last 50 years? How has it changed?
4 What do you think are some reasons why fashions change?

WATCH AND LISTEN

1

2

PREPARING TO WATCH

ACTIVATING YOUR KNOWLEDGE

1 Work with a partner. Read the definitions. Discuss the questions.

> **ethical brand** (n phr) a product which is produced in a way that does not hurt anybody or anything, for example, animals
> **sustainable brand** (n phr) a product which is produced in a way that does not damage the environment

1 What ethical and sustainable brands of clothing do you know of?
2 What are the advantages of buying these brands?
3 Are there any disadvantages of buying these brands?

PREDICTING CONTENT USING VISUALS

2 You are going to watch a video about a fashion brand. Before you watch, look at the photos from the video. Circle the ideas you think you will hear.

1 The brand is from *England / the US / China*.
2 They make their clothes in *England / the US / China*.
3 They make the clothes with *new / special / recycled* materials.

GLOSSARY

military (adj) relating to the army
parachute (n) a large piece of material that helps you to drop safely from an aircraft
production (n) all the things that you do in order to make a product which you then sell
fabric (n) cloth, material
garment (n) a piece of clothing

WHILE WATCHING

UNDERSTANDING MAIN IDEAS

3 Watch the video and check your ideas in Exercise 2. Then complete the sentence.

Christopher Raeburn's fashions are sustainable and ethical because
____.

3

4

UNDERSTANDING DETAIL

4 Watch again. Write *T* (true) or *F* (false) next to the statements below. Then correct the false statements.

_____ 1 Christopher Raeburn started recycling military uniforms at university.
_____ 2 He only uses old military uniforms to make his clothes.
_____ 3 He employs people all over the world to make his clothes.
_____ 4 Some of Christopher's clothes are made from British wool.
_____ 5 At London Fashion Week, Christopher is showing his fashions in an old underground station.

WORKING OUT MEANING FROM CONTEXT

5 Match the words in bold to their meaning. Circle *a* or *b*. Watch again and check your answers.

1 I'm **based** here in London in the East End, Hackney Wick …
 a from b living and working
2 I never really **set out** to create an ethical or sustainable brand.
 a planned b wanted
3 This season we're actually **splitting** the collection into three sections.
 a dividing b choosing
4 That's very much focused on **incredibly** good quality … wools.
 a definitely b extremely
5 … we'll be getting in and doing a very different event, it'll be **multimedia**.
 a many journalists will come there b using film, pictures, music, words, etc. together.

DISCUSSION

6 Discuss the questions below in a small group.

1 Why do you think Christopher Raeburn has been so successful?
2 What do you think of the designs you saw in the video?
3 Do you care about where the clothes you wear are made? Why / Why not?

LISTENING

LISTENING 1

PREPARING TO LISTEN

UNDERSTANDING KEY VOCABULARY

1 You are going to listen to a discussion about fast fashion. Before you listen, read the article below to get a general understanding of fast fashion. Then read the definitions and complete the article with the correct form of the words in bold.

convert (v) to change something into something else
collaborate (v) to work with somebody for a special purpose
criticize (v) to express that you believe something or somebody is bad
copyright (n) the legal right to control the use of a design, an artwork, a piece of music, etc.
ethical (adj) something that meets society's standards of acceptable and honest behaviour
focus on (phr v) to give a lot of attention to one subject or thing
image (n) a picture or photograph
practical (adj) able to be done or put into action

'Fast Fashion'

'Fast fashion' is the term used to describe clothing designs that move quickly from fashion shows to clothing stores. Customers can buy the 'new look' at an affordable price from a local store, rather than from an expensive designer shop in a big city.

However, the clothing companies are often (1) __________ because they produce low-quality items that consumers wear only a few times before throwing away. So there are a number of environmental problems with fast fashion. For example, it isn't (2) __________ to recycle all the clothes, which creates a lot of waste.

Additionally, these companies don't only (3) __________ copying designs from fashion shows. Some companies take (4) __________ they find on the internet and (5) __________ them into designs, which they sell for a large profit.

There are both legal and (6) __________ issues when fashion companies do this. Firstly, they often pay no attention to (7) __________ laws that protect an artist's work. Secondly, it is very rare for an artist either to (8) __________ with a fast fashion company or to give permission for their designs to be used. As a result, they hardly ever receive any payment for the use of their work.

WHILE LISTENING

GLOSSARY

intellectual property (n) – somebody's work that is protected by law from being copied
copyright infringement (n) – using all or a part of somebody else's work without their permission
lift (v) (informal) – to use somebody's work, without their permission; steal
plagiarize (v) – to use another person's ideas or work and pretend that it is your own
go viral (idiom) – quickly become very popular or well known by being published on the internet
resources (n) – something that a country, person or organization has that they can use

LISTENING FOR MAIN IDEAS

2 7.1 Listen to the discussion and take notes to answer the questions. Then compare your answers with a partner.

1 Which aspect of fast fashion will Hamed and Yoriko be doing their presentation on?
2 How many different artists are Hamed and Yoriko going to use as examples?
3 Which of the artists argued with a fast fashion company after it used her images?
4 In general, do Hamed and Yoriko feel positive about fast fashion companies?

SKILLS

Taking notes on main ideas and details

Using an outline is an effective way to take notes while you listen. An outline helps you organize main areas of focus and details in a way that is easy to review later. An outline can be organized like this:

I Topic

A Main focus 1	*B Main focus 2*
1 Detail 1	*1 Detail 1*
2 Detail 2	*2 Detail 2*

TAKING NOTES ON MAIN IDEAS AND DETAILS

3 7.1 Listen to the discussion again and complete the outline.

Fast fashion
A Vanessa Bowman
Artist who lives in southern (1) ____________ .
Paints what she sees in her (2) ____________ */ natural scenes.*
A fast fashion company took images from her (3) ____________ *to use on* (4) ____________ .
B Kirstie Moran
Artist who creates interesting images of (5) ____________ .
An example of a company using somebody else's designs for (6) ____________ .
Some large fashion companies have taken (7) ____________ *when their designs are lifted, but this is far more difficult for an* (8) ____________ *(like Kirstie Moran) to do.*

C Elora Pautrat

Her designs were lifted and used on clothes and (9) ___________ .

She used (10) ___________ *to complain about the situation. As a result, she received an* (11) ___________ .

She has had only one (12) ___________ *for frequent use of her artwork by the same company.*

D Overall:

Fast fashion companies have the ability and (13) ___________ *to work together with the artists but decide not to.*

They are unlikely to follow copyright (14) ___________ *in the future.*

POST-LISTENING

SKILLS

Auxiliary verbs for emphasis

7.2 In fluent speech, speakers usually contract auxiliary verbs (*am* → *'m*, *have* → *'ve*, etc.). However, to emphasize a point or show contrast, they sometimes use the full form and stress the auxiliary verb.

I've seen some examples of artists defending their intellectual property, but not many.

I have seen some examples of artists defending their intellectual property, but not many.

(= speaker is emphasizing that there are examples, or is contrasting the idea that there are no examples)

Can you see the situation changing any time soon?

No, I don't think it will change. (= emphasizes that the situation won't change)

Speakers sometimes add *do*, *does* or *did* to an affirmative sentence to emphasize a point.

I agree. (= affirmative sentence)

I do agree. (= emphasizes the agreement, or shows contrast with somebody's disagreement)

She did something about it. (= affirmative sentence)

She did do something about it. (= emphasizes the action, or contrasts the idea that she didn't do anything)

These companies have the ability and the resources to collaborate with artists. (= affirmative sentence)

These companies do have the ability and the resources to collaborate with artists. (= emphasizes what the companies have, or contrasts the idea that companies don't have resources for this)

4 Work with a partner. Change each sentence to give it more emphasis. In some items, more than one answer is possible.

1 a That's amazing.
  b ___________________________

2 a You've asked me that before, you know.
  b ___________________________

3 a I agree that it's not very practical.
b ______________________________
4 a I think it'll be interesting.
b ______________________________
5 a I know I look tired, but I've been working very hard.
b ______________________________

5 7.3 Listen and check your answers.

6 Work with a partner. Read the sentences from Exercise 4 to each other with the correct emphasis.

PRONUNCIATION FOR LISTENING

Vowel omission

Speakers don't always pronounce every letter in a word. Unstressed vowels are sometimes not pronounced when they appear between a consonant and /l/ or /r/.

Every is usually pronounced /'ev·ri/. **Family** is often pronounced /'fæm·li/.

Common words in which a vowel is often omitted

typically	favourite	camera
jewellery	average	temperature
finally	separate (adj)	natural
chocolate	several	general

SKILLS

7 7.4 Listen to the extracts. For the words in bold, circle the vowels which are not pronounced.

1 She creates **interesting**, unusual designs of animals.
2 It's plagiarism, **basically**.
3 The company's lifted her work **several** times since then.
4 She tried a **different** approach.
5 **Finally**, the company wrote to her offering an apology.

8 Write five sentences using words from the Skills box. Then work with a partner. Take turns reading your sentences to each other. Correct your partner's pronunciation if necessary.

DISCUSSION

9 Discuss the questions below with a partner.

1 Is fashion important to you? Why / Why not?
2 Do you often buy fast fashion clothing? Do you think it is ethical? Why / Why not?
3 Have you ever seen examples of plagiarism at school, work or university? How is it dealt with?

10 Imagine you are an artist. A fast-fashion company has copied your designs and printed them onto a new clothing range. Write a short social media statement (around 150 words) to explain to your followers what has happened and how you feel about it.

I have just found out that ...　　*As an artist it is important to me that ...*

LANGUAGE DEVELOPMENT

TALKING ABOUT RECENT EVENTS AND ACTIONS

GRAMMAR

Already, just, yet and *still* are used with present perfect verbs to give more information about when a recent event or action happened (or didn't happen).

Already means 'before now' and refers to events or actions which are complete. You use *already* with positive present perfect verbs and questions.

Danial and Samia have ***already*** *finished writing their part of the presentation.*

Have you ***already*** *finished your essay?*

Already can come between the auxiliary and the main verb, or at the end of the clause.

Danial and Samia have finished writing their part of the presentation ***already****.*

Just means 'a short time before the present' and also refers to events or actions which are complete. You use *just* with positive present perfect verbs.

We've ***just*** *started on our presentation.*

Just comes between the auxiliary verb (*have/has*) and the past participle.

My sister has ***just*** *sent me a message.*

Yet means 'at any time up to now' and refers to things which were expected or possible, but did not happen. You use *yet* with negative present perfect verbs and questions. *Yet* comes at the end of a sentence or question.

I haven't read the article about her ***yet****.*

Still means 'continuing (not) to happen, or (not) to be done' and emphasizes that we expected the event or action to be complete by now. You use *still* with negative present perfect verbs. *Still* comes between the subject and auxiliary verb.

She ***still*** *hasn't received any sort of payment.*

1 Circle the correct answer.

1 Have you decided what to write about in your essay ________ ?
a yet　b still　c already

2 That jacket I ordered online ________ hasn't arrived.
a just　b already　c still

3 Has Mila ________ come home? She wasn't out long.
a still　b already　c yet

4 Are you trying to find Professor Haidar? I've ________ seen her going into her office.
a just　b already　c still

2 Work with a partner. Add *already*, *just*, *yet* or *still* to the present perfect verbs in sentences 1–5. In some items, more than one answer is possible.

1 It's my brother's birthday tomorrow and I haven't bought him a present.
2 Have you finished your English homework? That was quick!
3 You've been in this store for nearly an hour and you haven't decided what to buy. Hurry up!
4 Go and get something to eat if you're hungry. I've eaten, so I don't need anything.
5 I've found out a fast fashion company has lifted my designs and put them on a clothing range!

PREDICTIONS AND EXPECTATIONS ABOUT THE FUTURE

GRAMMAR

There are several ways to make predictions or talk about your expectations for the future.

be going to

*She's **going to be** disappointed this time, I imagine.* (expectation)

will

*I think that very little **will happen** to stop this sort of thing.* (prediction)

Future continuous

The future continuous describes an action which will/won't be in progress at a specific time in the future. Form the future continuous with *will/won't* or *be going to* + *be* + verb + *-ing*.

*I expect that people **will be buying** clothes from fast fashion companies in 50 years' time.*

*A few years from now, these companies **are going to be ignoring** copyright law just like they do now, and artists still **won't be getting** recognized for their work.*

3 Complete the sentences with the future continuous form of the verbs from the box.

arrive	do	earn	live	print	throw away	use

1 In a few years, maybe people ________ most of their clothes instead of shopping for them. The 3D technology is already available.
2 I hope that in 25 years, people ________ their clothes after wearing them only a few times.

3 I don't think anybody ________ laptops, tablets or phones ten years from now. I think we ________ all our computing with technology that you can wear.
4 Emi just called – her flight has been delayed. She ________ until after midnight now.
5 My friend Adam is the CEO of a successful eco-clothing company. In a few years, it's likely that he ________ millions of dollars. I expect he ________ in a mansion.

USING YOUR KNOWLEDGE

4 Complete the sentences to make predictions about the future. Use each future form (*will*, *be going to*, future continuous) at least once. You can write about topics from the box, or other topics.

cars	communication	fashion	homes	science
space travel	technology	the environment	your life	

1 Ten years from now, ____
____
2 By the time I'm ____
____
3 In the near future, ____
____
4 This time next year, ____
____

5 Work with a partner. Share your answers to Exercise 4 and ask follow-up questions.

Ten years from now, I'll be living in Japan!
Really? What will you be doing there?

LISTENING 2

PREPARING TO LISTEN

UNDERSTANDING KEY VOCABULARY

1 You are going to listen to a radio interview. Before you listen, read the sentences (1–5) below. Then work with a partner and discuss the meaning of the words in bold. Use a dictionary to help you.

1 Aysha's **collection** was presented during the last Fashion Week in Doha.
2 I have always tried to **combine** my culture with fashion.
3 As a teenager, I would make my own skirts and scarves. I wanted my designs to be **individual**. They were **unique** and, eventually, people **admired** my clothes rather than laughed at me.
4 Many traditional clothing **styles** are being reused by young designers.
5 My philosophy is to create clothes which are **modest** but, at the same time, give women **confidence**.

2 Complete the sentences with a different form of the words in bold from Exercise 1. There are two words you do not need to change.

1 Aysha brings a *combination* of culture and fashion to her designs.
2 I have a great __________ for all that she has achieved in her career – it's extremely impressive.
3 If you __________ together all of her designs in one place, it would be an amazing exhibition.
4 In my opinion, Aysha is a __________ designer – there's nobody else doing what she does.
5 In the studio, each T-shirt is made __________ by hand.
6 She has created a range of __________ clothing for young people.
7 'I designed clothes for people who like colourful fashion but also want to dress in a __________ way,' she says.
8 We're completely __________ that our new designs are going to be popular with customers.

3 Discuss the questions below with a partner.

1 Do you have a friend that you admire the style or fashion choices of?
Yes, I do. My friend Ana has …
2 Does fashion allow people to show their personality or does it make people look and act the same?
Fashion does allow people to show their personality, I think …
3 Do you like the clothes in the photo? Why / Why not?
I think the woman in the photo looks great because …

WHILE LISTENING

4 7.5 Listen to the first part of the interview. Answer the questions.

LISTENING FOR MAIN IDEAS

1 Who is Aysha Al-Husaini? __________
2 Where was she born? __________
3 What is she famous for? __________

TAKING NOTES ON DETAIL

5 7.6 Listen to the second part of the interview and complete the outline. Listen for the interviewer's questions to help identify the main ideas.

Interview with Aysha Al-Husaini

A Feelings about (1) ____________________

(2) ____________________

(3) ____________________

made own clothes – colourful skirts, scarves, etc.

B Misunderstandings about (4) ____________________

(5) ____________________

(6) ____________________

(7) ____________________

C Aysha's fashion

modest clothes which give women confidence

(8) ____________________

(9) ____________________

people like to be individuals, show their cultural roots

(10) ____________________

6 7.7 Listen to the interview again. Circle the numbers of the statements that are true. Then compare your answers with a partner and correct the false statements.

1 Aysha grew up in Doha.

____

2 Aysha started making clothes when she was a teenager.

____

3 Aysha's teachers asked her why she didn't design Western styles of clothing.

____

4 Aysha's designs are for women who like to dress in a modest way.

____

5 Many Muslim women want to wear fashionable clothes.

____

6 Chinese and Indian designers don't use traditional designs.

____

7 You can buy Aysha's collection in Malaysia and Singapore.

____

POST-LISTENING

MAKING INFERENCES

7 Read your notes from the interview in Exercise 5 and answer the questions. Give reasons for your answers.

1 Is Aysha's work popular in the fashion world?

____

____

2 Did Aysha have problems growing up in New York?

____

____

3 Do some non-Muslim people understand what Muslim fashion is?

____

____

4 Was becoming a fashion designer easy for Aysha?

____

____

5 Is Aysha's fashion company successful?

____

____

DISCUSSION

SYNTHESIZING

8 Work in small groups. Use ideas from Listening 1 and Listening 2 to answer the following questions.

1 Why is it important for fashion designers to create original designs and not simply lift somebody else's artwork?
2 Do you think it's possible to combine fashion with tradition? Why / Why not?
3 Aysha says that her clothes 'give women confidence'. Do you agree that clothes can influence how people feel about themselves? Why / Why not?
4 Do you think it's better to dress in an individual way or to dress in a similar way to everybody else? Why?

If you use somebody's intellectual property and say it is your own …
I think that Aysha has shown that it definitely is possible to combine fashion with tradition …
Clothes can influence how people feel about themselves because …
I prefer to dress in an individual way …

SPEAKING

CRITICAL THINKING

At the end of this unit, you will do the speaking task below.

Take part in an interview to find out attitudes about uniforms and dress codes.

SKILLS

Creating a purpose statement

Before interviewing somebody, it is helpful to create a purpose statement – that is, a sentence about what you want to learn from the interview. A good purpose statement:

- is just one sentence.
- states the goal of the interview.
- uses qualitative words (*explore*, *understand*, *discover*, *learn about*).

The purpose of the interview is to learn how fashions have changed in the last five years and to explore fashion trends of the next decade.

ANALYZE

1 Look at your outline from Listening 2 on page 158. Then circle the number of the best purpose statement for the interview with Aysha Al-Husaini from the list below. Why do you think it is best? What is wrong with the other statements?

1 The purpose of the interview is to explore fashions from around the world.

____

2 The purpose of the interview is to find out about Aysha Al-Husaini's background and why she got into fashion design. In addition, I plan to learn about Muslim fashion and about Aysha's plans for her business.

____

3 The purpose of the interview is to learn about Aysha Al-Husaini's career as a fashion designer and her chic yet traditional Muslim fashions.

____

2 Discuss the questions below in a small group. Reflect on your own experiences.

1 What is a dress code?
2 Why do some schools, universities and companies have a dress code?
A dress code is a set of rules about …
In schools, dressing correctly shows … / A dress code makes sure that people …

APPLY

3 Read the speaking task. Write a purpose statement for your interview. Then work in a group to compare your purpose statements. Suggest ways to improve each other's ideas.

My purpose statement: ____

____

SKILLS

Evaluating interview questions

In order to get interesting and relevant information from an interview, you need to ask good questions.

Good interview questions have these characteristics:

1 **They are open.** *Open questions* allow many possible answers. *Closed questions* limit the possible answers.

Closed questions:

Do you prefer the fashions of a decade ago or of today?
(Answer choices: *a decade ago / today*)
Are you interested in fashion? (Answer choices: *yes / no*)

Open questions:

What decade do you think had the most interesting fashions?
How did you become interested in fashion?

2 **They are not biased**. Biased questions encourage the interviewee to answer in a certain way.

Biased question: *Don't you think fashions have become less attractive in the last five years?* (Encourages a *yes* answer)

Unbiased question: *What's your opinion of how fashion has changed in the last five years?* (Doesn't encourage a particular answer)

3 **They only have one part.** Two-part questions can confuse the interviewee. After they answer the first part, they might forget what the second part was.

Two-part question: *What is your opinion of how fashions have changed in the past five years and what do you think of today's fashions?*

One-part question: *What do you think of today's fashions?*

4 **They are focused**. Focused questions make it clear what type of answer you're looking for.

Unfocused question: *What do you think about the future?* (It's not clear what aspect of the future you want to know about.)

Focused question: *What do you think fashions will be like in the future?*

5 **They relate to your purpose**.

Purpose: *The purpose of the interview is to explore the future of fashion.*

Unrelated question: *Who is your favourite fashion designer?* (This doesn't relate to the future of fashion.)

Related question: *How do you think fashion will change in the next ten years?*

ANALYZE

4 Read the purpose statement and the interview questions. What is wrong with each question? Match the questions (1–5) to the problems (a–e).

Purpose statement: The purpose of the interview is to learn about the fashions of the 1950s.

1 How did you become interested in 1950s fashion and when did you start researching it? ______
2 Do you like 1950s fashions? ______
3 What do you think of the films from the 1950s? ______
4 What do you think of fashion? ______
5 Don't you think that the fashions of the 1950s were boring? ______

a closed
b biased
c two-part
d unfocused
e doesn't relate to the purpose

APPLY

5 Work in small groups. Try to make a list of ten questions for your interview.

1 *What reasons do you think there are for students wearing uniforms at school?*
2 ______
3 ______
4 ______
5 ______
6 ______
7 ______
8 ______
9 ______
10 ______

EVALUATE

6 Read your questions in Exercise 5. Which are the best? Are there any which could be combined? Are there any which are not very interesting? In the same group, identify the five specific questions you would like to ask in your interview.

1 ______
2 ______
3 ______
4 ______
5 ______

PREPARATION FOR SPEAKING

ASKING FOR OPINIONS AND CHECKING INFORMATION

SKILLS

To ask somebody for their opinion, you can use expressions like *Do you think that*, *Would you say that* and *Do you feel that* to introduce your questions.

Do most people know much about Muslim clothes? (= direct question)

Do you feel that / Would you say that / Do you think that most people know much about Muslim clothes? (= indirect question)

When you ask somebody for their opinion, you can add phrases like *Can you tell me* and *Could you tell me* before questions to make them more indirect and polite.

How do you feel about Muslim fashion? (= direct question)

Can you tell me how you feel about Muslim fashion? (= indirect question)

Notice that indirect questions use positive word order and do not use *do/does*:

*Could you tell me what **you think** Muslim men prefer to wear?*

To check that you understood something correctly, you can use the following phrases:

*So, **are you saying that** there is a need for fashionable clothes for Muslim women?*

***Do you mean that** Muslim women sometimes have a hard time finding fashionable clothes?*

1 Circle the phrase which correctly completes each question. Then compare your answers with a partner.

1 *Can you tell me / Are you saying that* it's important to educate people about Muslim fashion?
2 *Do you mean that / How do you feel about* the idea of opening shops in Singapore and Malaysia?
3 *Would you say that / Could you tell me* many women are looking for modest clothes?
4 *Are you saying that / Can you tell me* how you feel about Muslim fashion?
5 Could you tell me *what you enjoy / what do you enjoy* about designing clothes?

2 Work with a partner. Read the dialogue and consider the direct questions. Think of an indirect question to make it more polite or check information. Then write your indirect questions onto the lines.

A: *What is the best way to dress for a job interview?*
(1)____?

B: I think you should wear a suit and a tie.

A: *Should I wear a suit even if I don't usually wear one?*
(2)____?

B: Yes, absolutely. As I see it, you only have 30 minutes to impress your future boss at the interview. You should look your best.

A: I'm not sure I agree. *Are my skills less important than what I look like?*

(3) ____?

B: No, I'm just saying that you should dress appropriately. *Are you really going to wear jeans and a T-shirt to your job interview?*

(4) ____?

A: I think so. The company I want to work for isn't interested in appearances.

B: *Why do you think it's a good idea?*

(5) ____?

3 Compare your sentences with another pair.

ASKING FOLLOW-UP QUESTIONS

SKILLS

Asking follow-up questions is a useful interviewing strategy. If a person you are interviewing says something which you find interesting and you want to know more, you can ask follow-up questions to get more information about the topic.

To ask follow-up questions, use phrases like:

Can you explain why *you decided to design fashions for Muslim women?*

Why do you think that *there is so much misunderstanding about Muslim clothes?*

What do you mean by *'traditional chic'?*

You mentioned that *when you were a teenager, your friends thought you dressed strangely in the summer.* ***How did you feel about that?***

Could you expand on that point?

Can you tell me more about *your plans to open shops in other cities?*

4 For each statement, write a good follow-up question. Use phrases from the Skills box. Try not to use the same phrase more than once.

1 I'm planning to change my individual fashion style.
Follow-up question: ______________________________?

2 When I was in school, I used to hate my uniform.
Follow-up question: ______________________________?

3 My best friend Ellie has started to dress too young for her age.
Follow-up question: ______________________________?

4 A lot of people have strong feelings about dress codes at work.
Follow-up question: ______________________________?

5 Research has shown that students behave better in school when they wear uniforms.
Follow-up question: ______________________________?

5 Work in small groups. Share your questions in Exercise 4. For each statement, whose question do you think is the best? Why?

6 Read the topics below. What is your opinion about them? Make notes about each of the topics.

- People should dress smartly for work every day.

  ____

  ____

  ____

- Secondary school students should wear uniforms to school.

  ____

  ____

  ____

- It's important to have an individual style and not to dress like everybody else.

  ____

  ____

  ____

- You should always look your best, even when you're just going out for coffee or to the supermarket.

  ____

  ____

  ____

7 Work in small groups. Share your opinions on the topics in Exercise 6. Ask the others in the group follow-up questions.

Student A: *Dressing smartly makes you look and act …*
Student B: *Secondary students should focus on …*
Student C: *Having an individual style means that other people …*
Student D: *It is important to make an effort to look your best because …*

SPEAKING TASK

Take part in an interview to find out attitudes about uniforms and dress codes.

PREPARE

1 Read the purpose statement and questions you created in Exercises 3 and 6 in the Critical thinking section. Review your notes.

2 Make your questions more polite. You can use language like this:

Could you tell me …	*Would you say that …*
Do you think that …	*Do you feel that …*

3 Read your questions again from the Critical thinking section, page 162 Exercise 6. Are they in an order which makes sense? If not, change the order so it does make sense.

4 Refer to the Task checklist below as you prepare for your interview.

TASK CHECKLIST	✔
Ask questions in an order which makes sense.	
Ask for opinions politely and clearly.	
Check information where necessary.	
Ask follow-up questions.	

PRACTISE

5 Work with a partner. Practise your interview questions. Take notes on your partner's questions and interview technique.

6 Give each other feedback about your performance.

1 Were there enough questions? What other questions could you add?
2 Did the interviewer check information?
3 Did the student give clear opinions?

7 Make improvements to your questions based on your partner's feedback.

PRESENT

8 Work with a different partner. Interview your partner. Then change roles and let your partner interview you.

OBJECTIVES REVIEW

1 Check your learning objectives for this unit. Write *3*, *2* or *1* for each objective.

3 = very well 2 = well 1 = not so well

I can …

watch and understand a video about College of Art graduate Christopher Raeburn. _____

take notes on main ideas and detail. _____

identify auxiliary verbs for emphasis. _____

create a purpose statement. _____

evaluate interview questions. _____

make predictions and talk about expectations for the future. _____

talk about recent events and actions using *already*, *just*, *yet* and *still*. _____

ask for opinions and check information. _____

ask follow-up questions. _____

take part in an interview to find out attitudes about uniforms and dress codes. _____

2 Use the *Unlock* Digital Workbook for more practice with this unit's learning objectives.

UNLOCK DIGITAL WORKBOOK

WORDLIST

admire (v)	copyright (n)	individual (adj) ⊙
collaborate (v) ⊙	criticize (v) ⊙	modest (adj) ⊙
collection (n) ⊙	design (n) ⊙	practical (adj) ⊙
combine (v) ⊙	ethical (adj) ⊙	smart (adj)
confidence (n) ⊙	focus on (phr v)	style (n) ⊙
convert (v) ⊙	image (n)	unique (adj) ⊙

⊙ = high-frequency words in the Cambridge Academic Corpus

UNIT 8

ECONOMICS

LEARNING OBJECTIVES

Watch and listen
Watch and understand a video about money management.

Listening skills
Understand paraphrases.

Critical thinking
Evaluate arguments.

Grammar
Use conditional sentences.

Speaking skills
Use gerunds as subjects to talk about actions; present reasons and evidence to support an argument; use paraphrases.

Speaking task
Take part in a discussion about whether young people should be allowed to have credit cards.

UNIT 8 ECONOMICS

UNLOCK YOUR KNOWLEDGE

Work with a partner. Look at the photo and answer the questions.

1 What can young people do in your country to earn money?
2 How do you save money?
3 Why do some people spend a lot of money on things like designer clothes and expensive cars?

WATCH AND LISTEN

PREPARING TO WATCH

ACTIVATING YOUR KNOWLEDGE

1 Work with a partner and answer the questions.

1 At school, were you taught how to manage your money? Is it important to teach children about this? Why / Why not?
2 Are you confident that you have – or will develop – good financial habits? Why / Why not?

PREDICTING CONTENT USING VISUALS

2 You are going to watch a video about money management. Before you watch, look at the photos from the video. Discuss the questions with your partner.

1 What are each of the people doing in the photos? Have you ever done any of these things?
2 Which of the people in the photos do you think has developed good financial habits?
3 What knowledge or skills are needed for somebody to manage their personal finances?
4 Based on the photos, what do you think the video will be about?

GLOSSARY

satisfaction (n) a pleasant feeling you get when you receive something you want, or when you have done something you wanted to do

psychologist (n) / **psychology** (n) – somebody who studies / the study of the human mind and human emotions and behaviour

purchase (n) something you buy

budget (n) a plan of how much money you will spend and how you will spend it

deal (n) an agreement, especially in business, on exactly how to pay for or do something

savings account (n) an account in a bank or similar financial organization for keeping money not used for day-to-day spending

WHILE WATCHING

UNDERSTANDING MAIN IDEAS

3 Work with a partner. Think about the best word to complete each sentence.

1 The average person spends about one third of their life *earning* / *saving* money.
2 According to psychologists, *spending* / *saving* more money increases a person's life satisfaction.
3 Most people find it quite *difficult* / *easy* to manage their money.
4 The best way to learn how to manage money is through *education* / *experience*.

4 Watch the video and check your answers.

UNDERSTANDING DETAIL

5 Watch again. Complete the sentences with a word or short phrase.

1 Dopamine is released in the brain when you shop in stores or get an ________ .
2 We often find it enjoyable to buy gifts or to help ________ .
3 Many people would describe developing good financial habits as '________'.
4 Good financial habits, such as following a budget, are important ________ .
5 If an adult has an understanding of ________ , they will be less likely to find themselves in ________ .

DISCUSSION

6 Discuss the questions below in a small group.

1 Which is most important in learning good financial habits: psychology, education, or being confident with maths / figures?
2 How can we encourage people to become better at managing their finances?

LISTENING 1

PREPARING TO LISTEN

UNDERSTANDING KEY VOCABULARY

1 You are going to listen to a podcast about millionaire lifestyles. Before you listen, work with a partner. Circle the best word in bold to complete each sentence. Use a dictionary to help you.

1 If you want to **save** / **afford** money, you could stop eating out in expensive restaurants.
2 Sarah got a big **debt** / **loan** to help her buy her first house.
3 I borrowed money to buy my car. Every month I have to make a £300 **payment** / **saving**.
4 My cousin is a **million** / **millionaire**. He has three houses, four cars and he goes on exotic holidays every year.
5 Jacinta used her credit card to go on holiday. Now she has a huge **payment** / **debt**.
6 I've just paid my university tuition fees. That's why I can't **afford** / **save** to go out this weekend.
7 Marta puts 10% of every monthly salary into the bank. She already has £15,000 in **savings** / **payments**.

2 Work with a partner. Read the sentences (1–5) and decide which phrasal verb from the box should replace the verbs and phrases in bold. Use a dictionary to help you. Write the answers in the correct form at the end of each sentence.

come up with	get into	pay off	put aside	take out

1 I don't think I'm ever going to **have** debt in the future – I'm very careful with money. ________
2 The bank has given Naseem 30 days to **find and pay** £1,000. If not, they'll close his account. ________
3 It's important to start **saving** as much money as you can from a young age. ________
4 When Shireen started her own business, she **got** a loan to buy some office equipment. ________
5 The bank gave me a loan two years ago, but I haven't **given** it **back** yet! ________

3 Work with a partner and answer the questions.

1 How does somebody become a millionaire?
2 Do you think millionaires are more likely to spend or save money? Why?
3 What kinds of cars do you think they drive? What kinds of houses do they live in? What kinds of clothes do they wear? Do you think these things are important to them?

4 8.1 Look at the book cover and listen to the introduction to a podcast about millionaire lifestyles. Discuss the questions with your partner.

1 The speaker says that the results of the study were surprising. Can you guess why they were surprising?
2 What does *wealthy* mean?
3 What do you think the rest of the podcast will be about?

WHILE LISTENING

LISTENING FOR MAIN IDEAS

5 Circle the numbers (1–8) for the behaviours of millionaires which you think are true. Then compare and discuss your ideas in small groups.

Millionaires …
1 drive luxury cars and eat in expensive restaurants.
2 know how much money they spend on food, clothes, etc.
3 live in the same place for a long time.
4 don't spend a lot of money on cars.
5 have successful relationships.
6 borrow money from the bank.
7 are happy with what they have.
8 buy expensive things to feel better.

6 8.2 Listen to the podcast and underline the behaviours in Exercise 5 which it says are true of millionaires.

TAKING NOTES ON DETAIL

7 8.2 Listen to the podcast again. Complete the notes with numbers and percentages.

Around (1)__________ *% of millionaires know how much they spend every year.*
(2)__________ *% of millionaires have lived in the same house for* (3)__________ *years.*
About (4)__________ *% of millionaires live in homes which cost around the national* (5)__________ .
(6)__________ *% of luxury cars are owned by people who can't afford them.*

POST-LISTENING

SKILLS

Understanding paraphrases

To help listeners understand what they're saying, speakers sometimes paraphrase. That is, they explain an idea in different words, often in a simpler or shorter way. To recognize paraphrases, listen for the phrases in bold, which often introduce paraphrases.

Most people think that rich people live lavish lifestyles – ***that is****, they drive very expensive cars, eat in expensive restaurants, own a yacht or live in big houses.*

Millionaires are often financially savvy. ***To put it another way****, they're smart about how to save and spend money.*

Most millionaires actually seem to have ordinary lifestyles. ***In other words****, they have normal cars, average houses and so on.*

Sometimes speakers paraphrase without using an introductory phrase.

John Holm decided to study the behaviour of wealthy people. He paid close attention to what rich people do.

8 **Read the sentences. Underline the words or phrases in each sentence which mean the same thing.**

1 The important lesson here is to live within your means – that is, don't spend more money than you have.
2 Instead, they have spent all their money trying to show off – showing other people that they might be wealthy.
3 Even though Liz is a millionaire, she's very frugal. In other words, she's careful about how she spends her money.
4 When I was growing up, my family was economically disadvantaged. To put it another way, we didn't have much money.

9 **Complete the second sentence or clause so that it paraphrases the first. Then compare your answers with a partner.**

1 I'd like to get better at following a budget – that is, *being in control of how much money I have and how I spend it.*
2 I hope I never get into debt and have to take out a loan, or to put it another way, ______________________.
3 Understanding basic finance can stop you getting into financial difficulties. In other words, ______________________.
4 One of the most important life skills is developing good financial habits. To put it another way, ______________________.

PRONUNCIATION FOR LISTENING

Silent letters

Some English words include letters which are not pronounced. This is because the pronunciation of the words has changed over time, but the spelling has stayed the same. For example, the letter *w* is not pronounced in *write* and the letter *b* is not pronounced in *comb*. There aren't any rules about which letters are silent and which are not. These words need to be learned individually.

SKILLS

10 8.3 **Listen to the sentences. Pay attention to the pronunciation of the words in bold. Circle the letters which are not pronounced.**

1 Most people think that rich people live lavish lifestyles, that is they drive very expensive cars, eat in expensive restaurants, own a **yacht** or live in big houses.
2 In other words, having expensive things is not always a **sign** that somebody is rich.
3 On the other hand, people who look rich – the people who drive the latest Ferrari or only wear **designer** clothes – may not actually be rich at all.
4 As a result, they don't spend too much and they don't get into **debt**.
5 There is no **doubt** that it's more difficult to save money if you are single.
6 So, what can we learn from the wealthy? The **answer** is surprisingly simple.

11 **Work with a partner. Create new sentences using the words in bold from Exercise 10. Then practise saying them to each other. Check that your partner's pronunciation is correct.**

DISCUSSION

12 Work alone. Decide if you agree with the points below from the podcast. Make notes to explain why / why not. Use examples from your own life.

1 Know how much money you have. *I totally agree. I think it's a good idea to …*
2 Know how much you spend. *I agree, but it can be difficult to …*
3 Don't get into debt. *Of course, that's what you should do, but …*
4 It's easier to save if you are part of a couple. *I don't agree with this. It's much harder …*
5 Be happy with what you have. *I always try to …*

13 Work in small groups and share your ideas. Decide together which point you think is the most important and why.

Knowing how much money you have is great advice, but …

This is very good advice, because …

Maybe, but I think it's okay if …

LANGUAGE DEVELOPMENT

COLLOCATIONS WITH *PAY* AND *MONEY*

1 Read the definitions. Complete the questions with the correct form of the words in bold.

borrow money (v phr) to take money and promise to pay it back later
lose money (v phr) to have less money than you had before
make money (v phr) to earn money from a job or an investment
owe money (v phr) to have to pay somebody money you borrowed
pay a fine (v phr) to pay money for not obeying a rule or law
pay in cash (v phr) to pay for something with money (not a bank card)
invest money (v phr) to put money into something to try and earn more money
raise money (v phr) to collect money from other people, often for charity
save money (v phr) to keep money for use in the future
spend money (v phr) to give money as a payment for something

1 Have you ever ________ by selling something over the internet?
2 Do you prefer to pay by card or to ________ ?
3 Is it a good idea to ________ in a new business?
4 Have you ever ________ for not having the correct ticket for a train or bus?
5 Have you ever ________ by accidentally buying something you didn't want?
6 Is it better to ________ from a family member or from a bank?
7 What are you planning for in the next few years that you might need to ________ for?
8 How long is it acceptable to ________ to a friend without paying them back?
9 Have you ever done anything to help ________ for a charity?
10 Do you prefer to ________ on yourself, or on other people?

2 Work with a partner and answer the questions in Exercise 1.

CONDITIONAL SENTENCES

GRAMMAR

Use *zero conditionals* to talk about general facts, truths and habits. Use *if* + present simple in the *if*-clause. Use the present simple in the main clause.

if + present simple
*If people **have** a lot of money, they **are** happier.*
present simple

Use *first conditional* sentences to talk about things which are possible now or in the future and their likely results. Use *if* + present simple in the *if*-clause and a future verb form in the main clause.

if + present simple
*If we **save** a little money each month, we'**ll be able to** afford a holiday in the summer.*
future verb form

Use *second conditional* sentences to talk about the possible result of an imagined situation in the present or future. Use *if* + past simple in the *if*-clause and a modal verb form in the main clause.

if + past simple
*If I **earned** more money, I **would invest** in a new business.*
modal verb clause

if + past simple
*If you **didn't run** your own business, **would** you **enjoy** your working life as much?*
modal verb clause

You can also use conditional sentences to give advice and suggestions. These are formed with *if you* … in the *if*-clause and an imperative in the main clause.

*If you want to be rich, **don't spend** a lot of money!* *If you want to retire early, **start** saving now.*
imperative imperative

3 Read the statements. Decide which letter best describes each one: *A* for advice or suggestions, *T* for things that are generally true, *P* for things that are possible now or in the future, or *I* for imagined things that might be possible now or in the future.

1 __A__ If you want to be a millionaire, don't spend a lot on your house.
2 ____ If you don't have to worry about monthly credit card payments, you're less likely to buy things to make you feel better.
3 ____ If I end up with a good degree, I will be able to get a job that pays well.
4 ____ If you invested all your money in just one company, you might regret it.
5 ____ If you move house a lot, it is impossible to save money.
6 ____ If people weren't so focused on earning money, the world would have fewer problems.

4 These sentences include mistakes. Delete, change or add one word in each sentence and write it correctly on the line.

1 If you want to save money, you don't buy lots of expensive things.

____

2 If I have money, I always bought new clothes.

____

3 If you will pay off all your debts, you will be happier.

____

4 If I would lost my job, I would look for a new one.

____

5 Work with a partner. Complete the sentences with a pair of verbs from the box in the most likely form. In the brackets, write whether each sentence is a zero (0), first (1) or second (2) conditional.

can / be	finish / be able to	need / ask	spend / deserve	want / find

1 If you __________ to be happy in the long term, __________ a job you love. (____)
2 If I __________ afford to take a flight into space, it __________ the best moment of my life. (____)
3 If you __________ more than you can afford, you __________ to get into debt. (____)
4 If I __________ my homework before Friday evening, I __________ to enjoy the weekend more. (____)
5 If I suddenly __________ a lot of money, I __________ my parents for a loan, but that's never going to happen. (____)

6 Complete the sentences with your own ideas. Then work with a partner and discuss your sentences. Give reasons for your answers. Ask each other follow-up questions.

1 If you put aside money every week, ______________________ .
2 If you want to be happy, ______________________ .
3 If I couldn't afford to pay my university fees, ______________________ .

7 Work in small groups. Think of ideas to complete the sentences below. Share your sentences with the other students. Respond to what they say with another conditional sentence.

If I get a better job, …
If I end up doing a job I love, …
If we learned to speak perfect English, …
Student A: *If I get a better job, I'll make a lot more money.*
Student B: *If you make a lot more money, you'll buy an expensive car.*
Student C: *If you buy an expensive car, you'll …*

LISTENING 2

PREPARING TO LISTEN

USING YOUR KNOWLEDGE

1 8.4 Listen to the introduction to a programme about how some universities are trying to motivate students. In your notebook, write down the key words and phrases you hear.

2 Work with a partner. Use your notes from Exercise 1 to reconstruct the programme introduction. Write a short paragraph. Then check it against the audio script for Track 8.4 on page 222 of your Student's Book.

UNDERSTANDING KEY VOCABULARY

3 Match the words (1–6) to the definitions (a–f). Then compare your answers with a partner.

1 **sense**
2 **services**
3 **minimum wage**
4 **responsible**
5 **encourage**
6 **decision**

a a general feeling or understanding
b make somebody more likely to do something
c types of support connected to education or facilities
d a choice you make after thinking about several possibilities
e having the ability to act correctly and make decisions on your own
f the smallest amount of money that employers are legally allowed to pay workers

4 Work with a partner. Complete the sentences with the words from Exercise 3 in the correct form.

1 My teacher ____________ me to apply to university. I followed her advice and I'm going to graduate next month!
2 Meg works at a restaurant for ____________ . She doesn't make a lot of money, but it pays her rent.
3 She is a hardworking and ____________ student. She always does her homework and gets to class on time.
4 Many young people make the ____________ to work rather than go to university.
5 Going to university while working part-time requires a strong ____________ of responsibility.
6 My school provides many ____________ , including financial and career advice.

5 Work in small groups to complete the sentences with the correct form of the words from Exercise 3. Then discuss the questions.

1 'Choosing what to study at university is one of the most important life ____________ you will make.' Is this true? Why / Why not?
2 Do you think paying students for good grades would ____________ them to finish their education? Why / Why not?
3 What are the most important ____________ a university should provide to students? Why?
4 Do you think university students are generally ____________ and can manage their time well? Why?
5 What can teachers do to increase their students' ____________ of responsibility for studying hard?
6 In many countries, students have to take ____________ jobs to pay for their studies. Is it common for students in your country to work part-time while they study? Why / Why not?

I'm not sure this is always true because ...
I think that if students were paid for good grades, they would ...
There's no doubt that the most important services ...
In my country, students often have to ...

LISTENING FOR OPINION

6 8.5 Listen to the discussion in the programme. Which of the three main speakers is in favour of paying students: Dr Burns, Dr Hassan or Mrs Thorne?

LISTENING FOR DETAIL

7 8.5 Read the opinions expressed by the three main speakers: Dr Burns, Dr Hassan and Mrs Thorne. Write the name of the speaker next to the opinion expressed. Then listen and check.

1 ________________ is concerned about the plan to pay students.
2 ________________ thinks some students get bad studying habits from their parents.
3 ________________ is not confident that paying students will work.
4 ________________ thinks paying students sends them the wrong message.
5 ________________ thinks it would be better to spend the money on improving student services.
6 ________________ thinks paying students will help them get better jobs.
7 ________________ thinks students will take easy courses just to get the money.
8 ________________ thinks paying students will hide the problem, not solve it.
9 ________________ thinks it will make students feel more responsible for their studies.
10 ________________ thinks money should be given to teachers and universities instead.

POST-LISTENING DISCUSSION

SYNTHESIZING

8 Work in small groups. Use ideas from Listening 1 and Listening 2 to answer the following questions.

1 When are people best able to develop good financial habits: at school, at university or at work?
2 How might teaching money management at a young age help when students go to university?
3 Do you think students should be paid to go to university? Why / Why not?
4 Do you think that being paid to get good grades would persuade a wealthy person to stay in university and work hard? Why / Why not?
5 Should universities be responsible for students who can no longer afford to pay for their course? Why / Why not?

9 Complete the email to the programme producer. Express your own opinion about the idea of paying students for good grades.

To:
Date:
Subject:

Dear Producer,
I'm writing in response to yesterday's programme. It mentioned the idea of paying students for good grades. I'd like to say that ________
____.
In my opinion, ________________________________
____
____
____
____
____.
Kind regards,

SPEAKING

CRITICAL THINKING

At the end of this unit, you will do the speaking task below.

Take part in a discussion about whether young people should be allowed to have credit cards.

Evaluating arguments

SKILLS

When you think about a topic, it can be helpful to evaluate the various arguments and categorize them according to whether they are for or against a position. Then you can add supporting details.

UNDERSTAND

1 Complete the table with arguments from Listening 2. Use information and the notes you made on page 181, and read audio scripts 8.4 and 8.5 on page 222.

Position: University students should be paid for good grades.

arguments which support the position	arguments which oppose the position
Argument 1: Supporting details:	Argument 1: Supporting details:
Argument 2: Supporting details:	Argument 2: Supporting details:

2 Work with a partner. Read the news story and answer the questions on page 184.

With the financial difficulties faced by many countries around the world, more and more banks are reaching out to teenagers and university-age students. Many young people are sent advertisements for free credit cards as soon as they become old enough. As a result, many of them get into debt and start their adult lives owing money. This situation has started a public discussion about whether young people should be allowed to have credit cards.

1 Do you have a credit card? If yes, at what age did you get it?
2 If you don't have a credit card, would you like to have one? Why?
3 What are some of the problems with credit cards?

I do have a credit card. I got it when …

I don't have a credit card and I'm happy that way because …

EVALUATE

3 Work alone. Make a list of the advantages and disadvantages of allowing young people to have credit cards.

advantages

1 ______________________________
2 ______________________________
3 ______________________________

disadvantages

1 ______________________________
2 ______________________________
3 ______________________________

4 Work with a partner and discuss your ideas from Exercise 3. Then work with another pair to compare your ideas.

APPLY

5 Work alone. Decide which side of the argument you support. Complete the table with your three best arguments and supporting details. Then think of counter-arguments somebody who supports the other side might use. How would you respond to these?

my position: ______________	possible counter-arguments
Argument 1: Supporting details:	Counter-argument 1: Response:
Argument 2: Supporting details:	Counter-argument 2: Response:
Argument 3: Supporting details:	Counter-argument 3: Response:

PREPARATION FOR SPEAKING

USING GERUNDS AS SUBJECTS TO TALK ABOUT ACTIONS

LANGUAGE

The gerund is the *-ing* form of a verb. It functions as a noun and can act as the subject of a sentence.

To focus on an action, use a gerund in a noun phrase at the start of a sentence. Make this noun phrase the subject of the sentence and put it before the main verb. The main verb is in the singular form.

Doing small jobs for money ***teaches*** *children how to be responsible.*
gerund

Make a sentence negative by adding *not* before the gerund.

Not teaching children about money is a disadvantage in later life.
gerund

1 Underline the subject in each sentence.

1 Learning should be about studying new things and improving yourself.
2 Saving money is not easy if you have bills to pay.
3 Reading books about millionaires is not a good way to get rich.
4 Teaching children about money should start at an early age.

2 Rewrite the sentences to focus more on the actions in bold.

1 It is not a good idea to **pay children for housework**.
Paying children for housework is not a good idea.
2 It is very important to **teach children to save money**.
____
3 You can encourage children to study if you **pay them**.
____
4 You can spoil children at an early age if you **give them money**.
____
5 It's difficult to **learn about money** when you're a child.
____
6 If you **don't have much money** it makes it difficult to start a family.
____

3 Work with a partner. Complete the sentences with your own ideas. Then discuss your opinions and ideas with another pair.

1 Teaching children about money is ______________________________ .
2 Giving money to charity is ______________________________ .
3 Being a millionaire is ______________________________ .
4 Not saving money is ______________________________ .
5 Spending money on luxury cars is ______________________________ .

PRESENTING REASONS AND EVIDENCE TO SUPPORT AN ARGUMENT

SKILLS

Speakers use reasons and evidence to make their argument stronger and persuade listeners to agree with them. You can use these phrases to introduce reasons and evidence:

One effect / result / consequence of *being a couple is that it's easier to save money. If there are two of you, it's easier to pay attention to how much money you have and what you're spending.*

However, will paying students really encourage them to continue?

In my experience*, it won't.*

Advisors can help students learn to manage their time better.

As a consequence / As a result / Because of that*, students will do better at university and will be more likely to graduate.*

Because of / Due to *the high cost of living, we had to move out of the city.*

Note:

One effect / result / consequence of is usually followed by a gerund (like ***being** a couple*) or *this* or *that* to link back to a previous idea.

Because of / Due to is followed by a noun phrase, for example, *the high cost of living*.

4 Circle the correct phrase in each sentence.

1 Around 75% of millionaires know exactly how much money they have and they know exactly how much they spend on food, bills, clothes, etc. *As a result / In my experience*, they don't get into debt.
2 *One effect of / As a result of* paying university students would be that more students would finish their education.
3 *Due to / As a consequence* the huge sales of the app he designed, he became a millionaire almost overnight.
4 *One consequence of / In my experience*, treating students like adults makes them more responsible.
5 *As a consequence of / Because of that* saving money, they can plan for their future.

USING PARAPHRASES

SKILLS

To make your arguments clearer, use paraphrases. Paraphrases can help you explain or summarize something you think your audience might not understand very well. Paraphrases also help your listeners remember the information by letting them hear it a second time.

The first important thing is that millionaires always have a good handle on their budget. ***In other words****, they know how much they're spending.*

In John Holm's opinion, being 'wealthy' is a feeling. ***That is****, it doesn't mean being rich or having millions. It means being happy with what you have.*

They don't spend too much and they don't get into debt. They can plan for the future and save their money. ***To sum up****, the lesson here is that you should never spend more money than you have!*

5 Complete the paraphrases. Then read your paraphrases to a partner. Did your partner understand what you were saying?

1 I can't afford to buy a new car right now. In other words, ________ ____.

2 Millionaires often have simple lifestyles. That is, ________ ____.

3 So, what can we learn from the wealthy? The answer is surprisingly simple. To sum up, ____.

4 Students need encouragement to stay at university. To put it another way, ____.

5 We've talked a lot about the effects of paying students to attend university. To sum up, ____.

6 When young adults have the choice between going to university or making money, they often make the wrong decision. That is, ____.

SPEAKING TASK

Take part in a discussion about whether young people should be allowed to have credit cards.

PREPARE

1 Look at the table you created in Exercise 5 in the Critical thinking section. Review your notes and add any new information.

2 Refer to the Task checklist below as you prepare your points for the discussion.

TASK CHECKLIST	✔
Use collocations with *pay* and *money* correctly when appropriate.	
Used conditional sentences when appropriate.	
Use gerunds to talk about actions clearly.	
Present reasons and evidence to support your argument.	
Use paraphrases.	

PRACTISE

3 Work in small groups. Discuss your opinions about whether young people should be allowed to have credit cards. Give your reasons and evidence.

4 Discuss the questions in your group.

1 Was your point of view strong and well-presented?
2 What could you improve about your arguments?

DISCUSS

5 Work in different groups. Each group should have some students who agree with the topic and some who disagree. Discuss the topic.

OBJECTIVES REVIEW

1 Check your learning objectives for this unit. Write *3*, *2* or *1* for each objective.

3 = very well   2 = well   1 = not so well

I can …

watch and understand a video about money management.	____
understand paraphrases.	____
evaluate arguments.	____
use conditional sentences.	____
use gerunds as subjects to talk about actions.	____
present reasons and evidence to support an argument.	____
use paraphrases.	____
take part in a discussion about whether young people should be allowed to have credit cards.	____

2 Use the *Unlock* Digital Workbook for more practice with this unit's learning objectives.

UNLOCK DIGITAL WORKBOOK

WORDLIST

afford (v) ⊙	lose money (v phr)	put aside (phr v)
borrow money (v phr)	make money (v phr)	raise money (v phr)
come up with (phr v)	millionaire (n)	responsible (adj) ⊙
debt (n) ⊙	minimum wage (n)	save money (v phr)
decision (n) ⊙	owe money (v phr)	savings (n pl) ⊙
encourage (v) ⊙	pay a fine (v phr)	sense (n) ⊙
get into (phr v)	pay in cash (v phr)	service (n) ⊙
invest money (v phr)	pay off (phr v)	spend money (v phr)
loan (n) ⊙	payment (n) ⊙	take out (phr v)

⊙ = high-frequency words in the Cambridge Academic Corpus

GLOSSARY

⊙ = high-frequency words in the Cambridge Academic Corpus

Vocabulary	Pronunciation	Part of speech	Definition
UNIT 1			
abandon ⊙	/ə'bændən/	(v)	to leave somebody or something somewhere, sometimes not returning to get them
abuse ⊙	/ə'bjuːs/	(n)	violent or unfair treatment of somebody
abuse ⊙	/ə'bjuːz/	(v)	to treat somebody violently or unfairly
analyze ⊙	/'ænəlaɪz/	(v)	to study or examine something in detail, in order to discover more about it
communicate ⊙	/kə'mjuːnɪkeɪt/	(v)	to share information with others by speaking, writing, moving your body or using other signals
conditions ⊙	/kən'dɪʃəns/	(n pl)	the situation in which somebody lives or works
connect ⊙	/kə'nekt/	(v)	to join two things or places together
critically ⊙	/'krɪt.ɪ.kli/	(adj)	in a way that is very bad or serious
cruel	/'kruːəl/	(adj)	not kind
damage ⊙	/'dæmɪdʒ/	(v)	to hurt
debate ⊙	/dɪ'beɪt/	(v)	to discuss a subject in a formal way
depend on	/dɪ'pend ɒn/	(phr v)	to need
endangered	/ɪn'deɪndʒəd/	(adj)	at risk of no longer existing
environment ⊙	/ɪn'vaɪərənmənt/	(n)	the air, land and water where people, animals and plants live
extinct	/ɪk'stɪŋkt/	(adj)	If a type of animal is extinct, it does not now exist.
habitat ⊙	/'hæbɪtæt/	(n)	the natural environment of an animal or plant
illegal ⊙	/ɪ'liːgəl/	(adj)	not allowed by law

Vocabulary	Pronunciation	Part of speech	Definition
involve	/ɪn'vɒlv/	(v)	if a situation or activity involves something, that thing is a necessary part of it
issue	/'ɪʃuː/	(n)	a topic or problem which causes concern and discussion
loss	/lɒs/	(n)	the fact of not having somebody or something that you had before, or of having less of something than before
poacher	/'pəʊ.tʃər/	(n)	somebody who catches and kills animals illegally
protect	/prə'tekt/	(v)	to keep safe from danger
species	/'spiːʃiːz/	(n)	a group of plants or animals which share similar features
suffer	/'sʌfə/	(v)	to feel pain or unhappiness
support	/sə'pɔːt/	(v)	to agree with an idea, group or person
survive	/sə'vaɪv/	(v)	to continue to live, in spite of danger and difficulty
threat	/θret/	(n)	the possibility of trouble, danger or disaster
welfare	/'welfeə/	(n)	somebody's or something's health and happiness

UNIT 2

Vocabulary	Pronunciation	Part of speech	Definition
affordable	/ə'fɔːdəbl/	(adj)	not expensive
alternative	/ɔːl'tɜːnətɪv/	(adj)	different from what is usual or traditional
benefit	/'benɪfɪt/	(n)	advantage
crisis	/'kraɪsɪs/	(n)	a very dangerous or difficult situation
disaster	/dɪ'zɑːstə/	(n)	a terrible accident which causes a lot of damage
environmental	/ɪnvaɪərən'mentəl/	(adj)	relating to the air, water and land
limited	/'lɪmɪtɪd/	(adj)	small in amount or number

Vocabulary	Pronunciation	Part of speech	Definition
long-term	/lɒŋ'tɜːm/	(adj)	continuing for a long time
opponent	/ə'pəʊnənt/	(n)	somebody who disagrees with an idea
pollute	/pə'luːt/	(v)	to make something, like air or water, dirty or harmful
provide	/prə'vaɪd/	(v)	to give something
resource	/rɪ'zɔːs/	(n)	something you have and can use
risk	/rɪsk/	(n)	the possibility of something bad happening
solution	/sə'luːʃən/	(n)	a way of solving a problem
system	/'sɪstəm/	(n)	a way of doing things

UNIT 3

avoid	/ə'vɔɪd/	(v)	to stay away from something or not allow yourself to do something
block	/blɒk/	(v)	to prevent movement through or past something
break the law	/breɪk ðə lɔː/	(v phr)	to fail to obey the rules of a country, state or city
control	/kən'trəʊl/	(v)	to limit something
convenient	/kən'viːniənt/	(adj)	easy to use or suiting your plans well
cope	/kəʊp/	(v)	deal successfully with a difficult situation
crash	/kræʃ/	(n)	an accident in which a vehicle hits something
extreme	/ɪk'striːm/	(adj)	very severe or bad
figure out	/fɪgər 'aʊt/	(phr v)	to think about a problem until you know the answer
fine	/faɪn/	(n)	money which has to be paid as a punishment for not obeying a law
fixed	/fɪkst/	(adj)	not able to be changed
impact	/'ɪmpækt/	(n)	effect

Vocabulary	Pronunciation	Part of speech	Definition
influence	/'ɪnfluəns/	(v)	to affect how somebody acts or thinks
injure	/'ɪndʒə/	(v)	to hurt or cause physical harm
management	/'mænɪdʒmənt/	(n)	the control and organization of something
measure	/'meʒər/	(v)	to discover the exact amount or size of something
method	/'meθəd/	(n)	a way of doing something
pass	/pɑːs/	(v)	to go past something or somebody
prevent	/prɪ'vent/	(v)	to stop something from happening
primary	/'praɪməri/	(adj)	more important than anything else
respect	/rɪ'spekt/	(n)	polite behaviour towards somebody
safety	/'seɪfti/	(n)	the condition of not being in danger
serious	/'sɪəriəs/	(adj)	important; bad
solve	/sɒlv/	(v)	to find a way to fix a problem
trouble	/'trʌbl/	(n)	problems

UNIT 4

acceptable	/ək'septəbəl/	(adj)	satisfactory and able to be agreed to or approved of; good enough
agreement	/ə'griːmənt/	(n)	the situation in which people have the same opinion, or in which they approve of or accept something
anniversary	/ænɪ'vɜːsəri/	(n)	the day on which an important event happened in a previous year
behaviour	/bɪ'heɪvjər/	(n)	a particular way of acting
celebration	/selə'breɪʃən/	(n)	doing something to mark a special day or event
commercial	/kə'mɜːʃəl/	(adj)	relating to buying and selling things
development	/dɪ'vel.əp.mənt/	(n)	the process in which somebody or something grows or changes and becomes more advanced

Vocabulary	Pronunciation	Part of speech	Definition
die out	/daɪ aʊt/	(phr v)	to become rare and then disappear
endless	/'endlɪs/	(adj)	continuing for a long time and never finishing, or never seeming to finish
event ⊙	/ɪ'vent/	(n)	anything which happens, especially something important or unusual
generation	/dʒenə'reɪʃən/	(n)	all the people of about the same age within a society or a family
graduate	/'grædʒueɪt/	(v)	to complete university or college successfully
helpful ⊙	/'helpfʊl/	(adj)	willing to help
interact	/ɪntər'ækt/	(v)	to communicate and do things with somebody or something
modernize	/'mɒdənaɪz/	(v)	to make something more modern
multicultural	/mʌlti'kʌltʃərəl/	(adj)	including people who have many different customs and beliefs
obligation ⊙	/ɒblɪ'geɪʃən/	(n)	something which you have to do
occasion ⊙	/ə'keɪʒən/	(n)	a special event or ceremony
personal ⊙	/'pɜːsənəl/	(adj)	relating to an individual person and not anybody else
political ⊙	/pə'lɪtɪkəl/	(adj)	relating to the activities of the government
prevention ⊙	/prɪ'venʃən/	(n)	ways of stopping something happening or stopping somebody doing something
social ⊙	/'səʊʃəl/	(adj)	relating to a large group of people who live together in an organized way
specialize	/'speʃəlaɪz/	(v)	to spend most of your time studying one particular subject or doing one type of business
strengthen ⊙	/'streŋθən/	(v)	to become stronger or make something become stronger
thoughtful	/'θɔːtfəl/	(adj)	showing care and consideration in how you treat other people

Vocabulary	Pronunciation	Part of speech	Definition
traditional	/trə'dɪʃənəl/	(adj)	following the customs or ways of behaving that have continued in a group of people or society for a long time
useless	/'juːsləs/	(adj)	not useful

UNIT 5

Vocabulary	Pronunciation	Part of speech	Definition
come down with	/kʌm 'daʊn wɪð/	(phr v)	to get an illness, especially one which is not serious
concentration	/kɒnsən'treɪʃən/	(n)	the ability to give your whole attention to one thing
cultural	/'kʌltʃərəl/	(adj)	relating to the habits, traditions and beliefs of a society
cut down on	/kʌt 'daʊn ɒn/	(phr v)	to eat or drink less of something
educational	/edʒʊ'keɪʃənəl/	(adj)	relating to learning
emotional	/ɪ'məʊʃənəl/	(adj)	relating to feelings
get over	/get 'əʊvə/	(phr v)	to become healthy again after having an illness
give up	/gɪv 'ʌp/	(phr v)	to stop a habit, often because it is unhealthy
habit	/'hæbɪt/	(n)	something which you do regularly
illness	/'ɪlnəs/	(n)	a disease of the body or mind
in shape	/ɪn ʃeɪp/	(adj)	physically fit, strong and healthy
intellectual	/ɪntəl'ektʃuəl/	(adj)	relating to your ability to think and understand things, especially complicated ideas
join in	/dʒɔɪn 'ɪn/	(phr v)	to agree to become involved in an organized activity
mental	/'mentəl/	(adj)	relating to the mind
overweight	/əʊvə'weɪt/	(adj)	being heavier than you want or than is good for you
participate	/pɑː'tɪsɪpeɪt/	(v)	to be involved in an activity
performance	/pə'fɔːməns/	(n)	how well a person does an activity

Vocabulary	Pronunciation	Part of speech	Definition
personal	/'pɜːsənəl/	(adj)	relating to a single person rather than to a group
physical	/'fɪzɪkəl/	(adj)	relating to the body
prove	/pruːv/	(v)	to show that something is true
reduce	/rɪ'djuːs/	(v)	to make (something) less in size, amount, etc.
relax	/rɪ'læks/	(v)	to become less tense or worried
ridiculous	/rɪ'dɪkjələs/	(adj)	stupid or unbelievable and deserving to be laughed at
sign up	/saɪn 'ʌp/	(phr v)	to become involved in an activity with other people
social	/'səʊʃəl/	(adj)	relating to activities in which you meet and spend time with other people
stress	/stress/	(n)	worry caused by a difficult situation
take up	/teɪk 'ʌp/	(phr v)	to start doing a particular job or activity
treatment	/'triːtmənt/	(n)	a way to cure an illness or injury
try out	/traɪ 'aʊt/	(phr v)	to compete for a position on a sports team or a part in a play
unhealthy	/ʌn'helθi/	(adj)	not good for your health; not strong and well
work out	/wɜːk 'aʊt/	(phr v)	to exercise in order to make your body stronger

UNIT 6

Vocabulary	Pronunciation	Part of speech	Definition
access	/'ækses/	(v)	to be able to enter or use something
allow	/ə'laʊ/	(v)	to make it possible for somebody to do something
app	/æp/	(n)	(abbreviation for *application*) software designed for a particular purpose which you can download onto a smartphone or other mobile device

Vocabulary	Pronunciation	Part of speech	Definition
contribution ⊙	/ˌkɒntrɪˈbjuːʃən/	(n)	something that you do to help produce or develop something, or to help make something successful
create ⊙	/kriˈeɪt/	(v)	to make something new or invent something
device ⊙	/dɪˈvaɪs/	(n)	a piece of equipment which is used for a particular purpose
diagram ⊙	/ˈdaɪəgræm/	(n)	a simple picture which shows how something works or what it looks like
discovery ⊙	/dɪˈskʌvərɪ/	(n)	an occasion when somebody discovers something
industry ⊙	/ˈɪndəstri/	(n)	the companies and activities involved in the process of producing goods for sale
install	/ɪnˈstɔːl/	(v)	to put new software onto a computer or mobile device
make a comparison	/meɪk ə kəmˈpærɪsən/	(v phr)	to consider the similarities between two things
make a contribution	/meɪk ə kɒntrɪˈbjuːʃən/	(v phr)	to help to make something successful
make a decision	/meɪk ə dɪˈsɪʒən/	(v phr)	to choose
make a difference	/meɪk ə ˈdɪfərəns/	(v phr)	to change something
make an investment	/meɪk ən ɪnˈvestmənt/	(v phr)	to put money into something to make a profit
make attempts	/meɪk əˈtempts/	(v phr)	to try
make improvements	/meɪk ɪmˈpruːvmənts/	(v phr)	to make something better
make public	/meɪk ˈpʌblɪk/	(v phr)	to share information about something
outcome ⊙	/ˈaʊtkʌm/	(n)	the final result of an activity or a process
product ⊙	/ˈprɒdʌkt/	(n)	something which is made to be sold

Vocabulary	Pronunciation	Part of speech	Definition
scholar ⊙	/ˈskɒlə/	(n)	somebody who has studied a subject and knows a lot about it
technology ⊙	/tekˈnɒlədʒi/	(n)	knowledge, equipment and methods used in science and industry
user ⊙	/ˈjuːzə/	(n)	somebody who uses a product, machine or service
weapon ⊙	/ˈwepən/	(n)	an object used in fighting

UNIT 7

Vocabulary	Pronunciation	Part of speech	Definition
admire	/ədˈmaɪə/	(v)	to respect or approve of something
collaborate ⊙	/kəˈlæbəreɪt/	(v)	to work together or with somebody else for a special purpose
collection ⊙	/kəˈlekʃən/	(n)	a selection of clothing designs which are sold at particular times of the year
combine ⊙	/kəmˈbaɪn/	(v)	to mix or join things together
confidence ⊙	/ˈkɒnfɪdəns/	(n)	a feeling of being certain about yourself and your abilities
convert ⊙	/kənˈvɜːt/	(v)	to change something into something else
copyright	/ˈkɒpiraɪt/	(n)	the legal right to control the use of a design, an artwork, a piece of music, etc.
criticize ⊙	/ˈkrɪtɪsaɪz/	(v)	to express that you believe something or somebody is bad
design ⊙	/dɪˈzaɪn/	(n)	the way in which something is arranged or shaped
ethical ⊙	/ˈeθɪkəl/	(adj)	relating to what is right or wrong
focus on	/ˈfəʊkəs ɒn/	(phr v)	to give a lot of attention to one subject or thing
image	/ˈɪmɪdʒ/	(n)	a picture or photograph, especially one shown on a computer or television screen
individual ⊙	/ɪndɪˈvɪdʒuəl/	(adj)	considered as one thing, not part of a group

Vocabulary	Pronunciation	Part of speech	Definition
modest	/'mɒdɪst/	(adj)	not showing too much of a person's body
practical	/'præktɪkəl/	(adj)	suitable for the situation in which something is used
smart	/smɑːt/	(adj)	operated by computer or digital technology
style	/staɪl/	(n)	a way of designing hair, clothes, furniture, etc.
unique	/juː'niːk/	(adj)	different from everybody or everything else

UNIT 8

Vocabulary	Pronunciation	Part of speech	Definition
afford	/ə'fɔːd/	(v)	to have enough money to buy or do something
borrow money	/bɒrəʊ 'mʌni/	(v phr)	to take money and promise to pay it back later
come up with	/kʌm ʌp wɪð/	(phr v)	to find and produce something that is needed, usually money
debt	/det/	(n)	money which is owed to somebody else
decision	/dɪ'sɪʒən/	(n)	a choice that somebody makes after thinking about the options
encourage	/ɪn'kʌrɪdʒ/	(v)	to make somebody more likely to do something
get into	/get 'ɪn.tuː/	(phr v)	to become involved in something
invest money	/ɪn'vest 'mʌn.i/	(v phr)	to put money into something to try and earn more money
loan	/ləʊn/	(n)	an amount of money which you borrow and have to pay back
lose money	/luːz mʌni/	(v phr)	to have less money than you had before
make money	/meɪk mʌni/	(v phr)	to earn money

Vocabulary	Pronunciation	Part of speech	Definition
millionaire	/mɪljə'neə/	(n)	a person who has more than one million dollars, pounds, etc.
minimum wage	/mɪnɪməm 'weɪdʒ/	(n)	the lowest pay for an hour's work which a worker can legally be paid
owe money	/əʊ mʌni/	(v phr)	to have to pay somebody money which you borrowed
pay a fine	/peɪ ə faɪn/	(v phr)	to pay money as a punishment for not obeying a rule or law
pay in cash	/peɪ ɪn kæʃ/	(v phr)	to pay for something with money (not a credit card)
pay off	/peɪ ɒf/	(phr v)	to pay the money that you owe
payment	/'peɪmənt/	(n)	an amount of money paid
put aside	/pʊt ə'saɪd/	(phr v)	to save something, usually money, for a special purpose
raise money	/reɪz mʌni/	(v phr)	to collect money from other people, often for charity
responsible	/rɪ'spɒnsəbl/	(adj)	showing good judgement and able to be trusted
save money	/seɪv mʌni/	(v phr)	to keep money for use in the future
savings	/'seɪvɪŋz/	(n pl)	money you keep, usually in a bank
sense	/sens/	(n)	a quality of being or feeling loyal, responsible, etc.
service	/'sɜːvɪs/	(n)	a system which supplies things that people need
spend money	/spend mʌni/	(v phr)	to give money as a payment for something
take out	/teɪk aʊt/	(phr v)	to arrange to get something from a bank or company

VIDEO AND AUDIO SCRIPTS

UNIT 1

The mental skills of chimpanzees

Narrator: For 30 years, scientists at Georgia State University have been studying the mental skills of chimpanzees. They're finding out if chimpanzees can plan ahead and how much they plan ahead.

Man: OK, I'm going to set up the computer, right here.

Narrator: They use a computer maze to find out about the chimpanzee's ability. In the wild, chimpanzees have to find food and protect themselves, so they probably need to make plans.

But how good are they at planning?

One of the chimpanzees, named Panzee, is excellent. She can often complete difficult mazes that she's never seen before better than humans.

Man: Tell me what you want.

Narrator: This is an amazing discovery! Panzee doesn't make many mistakes and she can sometimes see the solution to the maze faster than a human can.

The ability to look ahead and find the way from the beginning to the end of the maze means she's very smart.

And it means that planning before acting is not just a human skill.

Scientist: Chimpanzees do plan ahead. I don't believe that they can plan ahead nearly so far as we can. I think also that they reflect upon the past but not to the degree that we do. I would suggest that chimpanzees are able to plan ahead over the course of several days, whereas we can plan ahead for years or centuries if we wish.

1.1

Host: Hello and welcome. Today's debate is on using animals for work. The first animal that was domesticated by humans is the dog. Even now, dogs are still used to **protect** our houses and keep us safe. Other domesticated animals – used for food – include sheep, cows and goats. The first donkeys were used by humans approximately 6,000 years ago in Egypt. Horses were domesticated 5,000 years ago in Europe and Asia. All these animals have been used to help human beings **survive**, either by providing food or by working for us. Horses, camels, elephants – they have all helped humans explore their land and transport goods from one place to another. But is this fair? What about animal rights? To argue for this **issue** today we have Amy Johnson, an animal rights activist and writer. To argue against the issue is Dr Jacob Kuryan. Dr Kuryan is a professor of zoology, which is the scientific study of animals, and a writer of several books on animal **welfare**. You both have two minutes to introduce your point of view. Ms Johnson, would you like to begin?

Ms Johnson: Thank you for inviting me to this debate. It's well known that animals have worked side by side with humans for thousands of years. In fact, they helped us develop our civilization and helped humans survive. Animals like elephants and horses were used to build amazing structures, like the pyramids in Egypt. Yet their hard work and suffering are hardly ever recognized. For example, horses, camels and elephants were used to transport armies and soldiers during wars and many of these animals died in these wars. And there are other examples. Even now, dogs are used to pull sleds in cold climates and elephants are used for logging. These animals work long hours and live in difficult **conditions**. However, they get very little reward. Humans just use them to their advantage. My main argument is that in the modern world, there is no longer any need to use animals for work. We have technology that can replace them. It's similar to using children to work in factories. Two hundred years ago, factory owners got rich by using children. Nowadays, people still get rich by using animals to do work for them. The problem is that the animals have no one to represent them and protect their rights. Even though animals work hard for us, they are often abandoned when they get sick or too old to work. They **suffer**. In short, I strongly believe that using animals for work is an old-fashioned and **cruel** practice.

Host: Thank you, Ms Johnson. Dr Kuryan – your introduction, please.

Dr Kuryan: Thank you. It's true that animals have helped our civilization develop. Camels and horses helped us carry goods across huge distances. Dogs helped us hunt and protected us from wild animals. Humans don't have the skills or strength to do these jobs. I want to argue that, in many low-income countries, people still need animals to survive. These are people who can't afford cars, house alarms or expensive machines. Another point is that not all animal use is **abuse**. On the contrary, without humans, these domesticated animals would not have been able to survive. They need us to take care of them. There are many animal lovers around the world who work in animal shelters and help animals. There are laws that stop animal suffering. And people give a lot of money to animal charities and organizations that help save wildlife. At the same time, there are still millions of children in the world who don't get this kind of treatment. They go without food or clothing. I strongly believe that, in a modern society, people often care more about animals than they do about people in low-income countries.

Host: Thank you both for your arguments! Now, let's hear from our listeners …

1.2

Hello, and thank you all for coming. I know you're all busy students and I appreciate that you're here today. As we all know, there are many animals which are disappearing from our planet: rhinos, orangutans, sea turtles ... the list is shocking.

Now, what do you think of when you hear 'African elephant'? Perhaps something like: intelligent, majestic, powerful. Now, even though these words describe these creatures perfectly, those three qualities may not be enough to save them. A century ago, there were around five million elephants across Africa. Today, it is believed that there are less than 500,000. In fact, both **species** of African elephants are **endangered**. While people are generally more familiar with the Savanna elephant, I'm here today to talk about the African forest elephant, which is smaller, less well-known, and it's **critically** endangered because of the **threat** that it faces from humans.

The main human threat to forest elephants comes from **poachers**, who hunt them for their long, white, beautiful tusks. It's widely known that these tusks are made of ivory, a material that poachers sell to make a lot of money, even though it's **illegal**. The international trade of ivory was banned in 1989, yet several countries still allow ivory to be bought and sold across their borders. This has actually increased over recent years.

The second threat is the loss of the elephants' **habitat**, which happens when humans destroy rainforest areas to make the land suitable for farming. This means the elephants have less space to live in, so the food they **depend on** for survival, such as fruit, grasses and leaves, not only becomes less available, but also has to be shared between the same number of elephants.

A third threat is contact between humans and elephants. Habitat loss sometimes forces elephants to leave the rainforest and go into villages, where they damage crops growing in farmers' fields. Because of this, local people sometimes kill the elephants ... they see this as the only way to protect themselves, their families, their food and their homes.

However, there is good news: it may not be too late to save the African forest elephant, but there are several things that really **ought to** happen first.

First, there **needs to** be an increase in the number of specially trained guards who work in the rainforests to catch the poachers.

Second, governments **must** introduce an immediate and complete ban on anyone buying or selling ivory, even between countries sharing a border.

Third, we **have to** find ways of reducing contact between humans and elephants. For instance, local communities **should** be helped to build suitable fences that can protect their land.

So, to summarize, as well as habitat loss and human contact, the main threat to forest elephants comes from poaching – we'**ve got to** end the illegal trade of ivory. The governments and environmental organizations who can do this **must not** delay for a moment longer. Without a ban, the African forest elephant may soon become **extinct**.

1.3

1 First, there needs to be an increase in the number of specially trained guards who work in the rainforests to catch the poachers.
2 Second, governments must introduce an immediate and complete ban on anyone buying or selling ivory, even between countries sharing a border.
3 So, to summarize, as well as habitat loss and human contact, the main threat to forest elephants comes from poaching.

1.4

… they see this as the only way to protect themselves, their families, their food and their homes.

Perhaps words like: intelligent, majestic, powerful.

1.5

As we all know, there are many animals which are disappearing from our planet: rhinos, orangutans, sea turtles …

1.6

1 large, white, strong
2 pandas, sea turtles, chimpanzees, tigers
3 poachers, loss of habitat, human contact
4 more guards, a ban on selling ivory, building fences

1.7

It's often said that it's cruel to use animals for entertainment. However, I would like to argue against this idea. I know that many animal lovers would disagree with me, but let me explain my point of view.

First of all, keeping animals in zoos helps protect them. For example, many species, such as the giant panda and the snow leopard, are endangered in the wild, so they are safer in zoos. Another point is that zoos have an important educational role. For instance, children can see animals up close. When I was a child, my father took me to the zoo. I learned about exotic animals and I also learned to care about animals. Modern zoos have improved their conditions. Animals are no longer kept in small cages and zoos have large areas where animals can feel as if they are in their natural habitat.

To summarize, zoos help protect animals and educate us. In short, modern zoos are comfortable, safe places for wild animals. In conclusion, I believe that we should help zoos by visiting them and donating money.

1.8

1 First of all, keeping animals in zoos helps protect them.
2 For example, many species, such as the giant panda and the snow leopard, are endangered in the wild.
3 Another point is that zoos have an important educational role.
4 To summarize, zoos help protect animals and educate us.

UNIT 2

Blowing in the wind: offshore wind farms

Narrator: We humans use a lot of energy and some traditional energy sources are running out. Where can we find alternative energy sources? These days, one popular source is wind.

In 2013 an enormous offshore wind farm opened here in the open sea.

It's called the London Array and it's located about 12 miles from the southeast coast of England.

How was it possible to build this giant wind farm in the water?

This was the answer.

Discovery is a special ship that can rise completely out of the water on giant 'legs'. It made a safe building area in the middle of the sea possible. And it could hold all the parts to build each wind turbine.

These huge pieces of the turbine look like airplane wings. They were designed to get as much energy as possible, even from light winds.

But as you can imagine, they were difficult to assemble, especially in windy weather.

It took a team effort.

Everything had to line up perfectly.

Success!

Each one of these wind turbines is almost 400 feet across. That's 120 metres, about as big as the London Eye. And they built 175 of them.

Every turbine can provide power for 3,000 homes. So now, because of the London Array wind farm, over half a million homes in England have clean electricity.

2.1

1 Today I want to explain some alternative solutions.
2 As we all know, in order to grow plants we need water and sunlight.
3 I think that desert farms might be a very interesting way to farm in the future.
4 If you add the nutrients to water, you can grow fruit and vegetables in water.

2.2

Good morning. Today I want to explain some **alternative solutions** which may help reduce some of the problems related to climate change. The first solution uses solar energy to grow food in the desert. First of all, I'll explain how farming in the desert works. Then, we'll briefly discuss how this type of farming could solve some of the **environmental** problems we are now facing. We'll discuss some possible problems with this **system**.

So, how does it work? As we all know, in order to grow plants we need water and sunlight. There's a lot of sunlight in the desert, but very little water. Scientists have combined solar energy with a farming technology called *hydroponics*. Hydroponics means growing plants in water. Plants don't need to grow in the ground, but they *do* need nutrients to help them grow. Nutrients are like food for the plants. So, if you add the nutrients to water, you can grow fruit and vegetables in water. NASA scientists have been developing this method of growing food because it could allow us to grow food in any climate – in Antarctica, the Sahara desert or even on Mars. You might ask how this method of growing plants helps with the problem of climate change. I mean, after all, it uses fresh water, which is a **limited resource**.

An Australian company, Sundrop Farms, combined hydroponics with solar energy. Traditional farming uses between 60 and 80 percent of our planet's fresh water. However, Sundrop Farms doesn't use fresh water. It uses seawater. Sundrop Farms is only 100 metres from the shore. A line of mirrors reflects heat from the sun onto a pipe which has oil inside. The hot oil in the pipe heats up seawater, which is kept in special containers. When the seawater reaches 160 °C, the steam **provides** electricity. Some of the hot water is used to heat the greenhouse during the cold desert nights. The plants grow in the greenhouse – a building with glass walls and a glass ceiling. The rest of the heated water goes to a desalination plant. Desalination is when we remove the salt from seawater to create drinkable water – that is, water which is clean and safe to drink. The desalination plant can produce up to 10,000 litres of fresh water every day. The farmer adds nutrients to this fresh water and then grows fruit and vegetables.

To summarize, solar energy removes the salt from the seawater and the fresh water is then used inside the greenhouse, where the plants are growing. Many people around the world are really excited about this technology. So far, Australian farms have grown tomatoes, peppers and cucumbers using hydroponics. Many supermarkets are interested in buying these vegetables because they're grown without pesticides or other chemicals. Some people think hydroponics is the perfect solution to the world food **crisis**.

Finally, the desert farms use solar energy and not fossil fuels, thus their negative effect on the environment is minimal. Now, of course, the future of hydroponics is unknown. But I think that desert farms might be a very interesting way to farm in the future. Now let's discuss some of the problems …

2.3

An Australian company, Sundrop Farms, combined hydroponics with solar energy. Traditional farming uses between 60 and 80 percent of our planet's fresh water. However, Sundrop Farms doesn't use fresh water. It uses seawater. Sundrop Farms is only 100 metres from the shore. A line of mirrors reflects heat from the sun onto a pipe which has oil inside. The hot oil in the pipe heats up seawater, which is kept in special containers. When the seawater reaches 160 °C, the steam provides electricity. Some of the hot water is used to heat the greenhouse during the cold desert nights. The plants grow in the greenhouse – a building with glass walls and a glass ceiling. The rest of the heated water goes to a desalination plant. Desalination is when we remove the salt from seawater to create drinkable water

– that is, water which is clean and safe to drink. The desalination plant can produce up to 10,000 litres of fresh water every day. The farmer adds nutrients to this fresh water and then grows fruit and vegetables.

To summarize, solar energy removes the salt from the seawater and the fresh water is then used inside the greenhouse, where the plants are growing. Many people around the world are really excited about this technology. So far, Australian farms have grown tomatoes, peppers and cucumbers using hydroponics. Many supermarkets are interested in buying these vegetables because they're grown without pesticides or other chemicals. Some people think hydroponics is the perfect solution to the world food crisis.

Finally, the desert farms use solar energy and not fossil fuels, thus their negative effect on the environment is minimal. Now, of course, the future of hydroponics is unknown. But I think that desert farms might be a very interesting way to farm in the future. Now let's discuss some of the problems …

2.4

Host: Welcome to today's debate on the advantages and disadvantages of nuclear energy. Some people think that nuclear power is an environmentally friendly source of energy because it creates less pollution than traditional power plants. However, the **opponents** of nuclear energy believe that it has more dangers than **benefits**. Debating this issue today are Emma Martinez and Jack Sullivan. Thank you for joining us today to share your opinions about this important issue.

Emma: Thank you. I want to argue that there are many problems with nuclear power. It may be true that there are very few accidents caused by nuclear plants, but if there is an accident, then it will be huge and it will have **long-term** effects on the environment. For example, after the Fukushima nuclear **disaster** in Japan, the government had to tell people to leave their homes because of the possibility of radiation. The radioactive material spread to water and food, such as tea, milk, beef and fish. For months after the accident, the Fukushima plant was dangerous. People will not be able to live in the nearby area for the next 20 years. This is the big **risk** of building a nuclear power plant. In my opinion, it's irresponsible for governments to allow nuclear power plants to be built near cities. They're just too dangerous.

Jack: I have to disagree. I think we should look at the bigger picture. Some people are worried that nuclear power is a big risk. And yet there are hundreds of nuclear power plants all over the world and there have only been three major nuclear accidents in the last 30 years. In fact, research shows that many more people die while working with coal, natural gas and hydropower – that is, electricity powered by water. On top of that, nuclear power is the most environmentally friendly and the most sustainable source of energy. In other words, it doesn't damage the environment and there will always be enough of it. A nuclear power plant does not **pollute** the air, it's relatively cheap and it can provide a huge amount of electricity to our cities. And of course, our cities are growing …

Emma: I'm sorry, can I interrupt? Some people say that nuclear energy doesn't pollute the air, but that's not completely true. It takes many years to build a nuclear power plant. During this time, hundreds of machines work day and night and pollute the air in the area. I don't think it's necessary to build nuclear power plants when we have safer and more environmentally friendly energy sources, such as solar and wind energy. They're cheaper and they're unlimited sources of energy. Also they're more **affordable** for most countries, when compared with nuclear power. Building a nuclear power plant is not a solution for low-income countries.

Jack: I'm not sure about that. I think that building nuclear power plants is the perfect solution for many low-income countries. Yes, it might be expensive to build the plant, but once the nuclear plant is there, the cost of the production of energy is very low. Plus, the country can sell the electricity to its neighbours and improve its economy. It's a long-term solution. And it makes a country less dependent on oil and gas. At the moment, whenever oil or gas prices go up, it's low-income countries and the people who live in them that suffer. Some people think that solar and wind energy are greener than nuclear energy. But I don't think that's accurate. Wind turbines are not exactly friendly for birds, not to mention that solar panels and wind turbines take up a lot of space. They're also very expensive and don't last as long as a nuclear power plant. In short, wind and solar energy can't solve the problem of climate change and they aren't a good solution for low-income countries.

Host: Thank you both very much. Let's take some questions from the audience …

UNIT 3

Sustainable transport

People spend a lot of time travelling, but our love of travel has a serious disadvantage. Transportation produces a large amount of the carbon emissions that cause climate change around the world. While emissions from planes are particularly high, three quarters of all transportation emissions are actually from road vehicles. Many cars, buses and motorbikes still use fossil fuels, and these produce dangerous pollution, especially in cities. So what's being done to make short journeys cleaner and more sustainable? To make more people use public transportation, some cities charge drivers to enter the city centre, such as in London's congestion zone. Other options include car sharing, and no-drive days. In Mexico City, there is one day per week when drivers are not allowed to use their cars, depending on their registration number. Similar ideas have been introduced in New Delhi, São Paulo, Paris and Dubai. Millions of people now leave their cars at home and use electric scooters to get to work. With mobile phone apps, electric scooters can be rented easily. The most sustainable form of road transportation is cycling. In Amsterdam, more journeys are made by bike than by car. And from Barcelona to Bogotá, many cities have plans to increase the popularity and safety of bike travel. It's easy to cycle in a city if it's flat. Where there are steep hills, like in Batumi, electric cable cars are a useful alternative. This cable car in Medellín uses solar power. Older forms of transportation can be green too. Low-cost tickets encourage passengers to use the tram systems of Prague, Melbourne, and this suspension railway in Wuppertal. It's a challenge to make longer journeys sustainable. Journeys can be greener if we take the train instead of the plane. The power for new trains like the Maglev comes from electromagnets. The Hyperloop is very efficient. It travels inside a tube from which most of the air has been removed. People will always want to travel. And it's up to us to make sure that our ways of travel are as sustainable as possible.

3.1

1 There has been a decrease in the number of bus passengers this year.
2 The traffic will decrease after they have finished repairing the road.
3 Most cities don't permit cyclists to ride on the pavement.
4 You need a special permit to park in the city centre.

3.2

1 The town hall keeps a record of how many vehicles use this road.
2 His mum bought him a new car as a present for passing his exams.
3 I went back to the shop to get a refund on my bus pass.
4 Each year, the taxi company presents an award to its most careful driver.
5 Will you promise me that you'll call as soon as your flight lands?
6 The train company are going to refund the cost of my ticket because of the delays.
7 We want to record the traffic noise around the city to see how high it actually is.
8 This car is the most comfortable you will ever drive. That's a promise!

3.3

Host: Do you live, study or work in a large city? Are the traffic problems so serious they often cause you to be late? If so, you're not alone. Over the past century, there's been a huge increase in the traffic that moves through our cities. And if, as the United Nations predicts, 70% of the world's population will be living in cities by the year 2050, what will we do when the amount of traffic increases even more? How will we **cope**? Can we do anything to control it? With me in today's podcast is Mark Knowling, an expert in transport and traffic **management**. Mark, what's happening in our cities?

Mark: It's a fact that, in a great many cities, the traffic is more **extreme** than ever before. The **primary** cause is that there are so many private vehicles on the roads carrying only one or two people. Compare this to buses, which are by far the most efficient option for reducing traffic, as they can transport huge numbers of passengers at the same time. But people don't seem to want to leave their expensive cars at home and take the bus instead.

Host: What other factors influence how well traffic flows?

Mark: Well, a crash on a busy city centre road can have a huge impact on all the other roads close by. Or someone parking their vehicle so that it **blocks** the traffic, even if only for a minute or so – a delivery driver, for example – can cause trouble for everyone behind them. Even something small like that means everyone's journey suddenly becomes more difficult than they expected. It's the most annoying thing in the world!

Host: Should we blame car drivers for all this, then?

Mark: It's not always their fault. Traditional traffic signals in so many of our cities are years old now. They always change colour after a certain number of seconds. That's not a sensible idea, when we consider the number of vehicles driving today. For instance, a driver might see a green light and continue, but immediately join a long queue of vehicles that isn't moving. Then, when the lights turn back to red, they are parked across a busy junction. That usually leads to all sorts of delays over the day.

3.4

Host: And how can we solve these problems?

Mark: Let's think again about traffic lights. Because of improvements in technology, modern traffic signals can **measure** how quickly the vehicles are moving along the roads, or see whether there's been a **crash**, and send this information back to a control centre.

Host: I've heard about this. It means that the traffic controllers – either human or computer – can check for changes in traffic throughout the day and figure out the best way to organize the signals to keep everything moving.

Mark: Yes. They don't have to follow the same, fixed timings for the lights all day long, like signals used to do. And although it's expensive to put in these signals across a whole city, it's far better than doing nothing.

Host: Technology – where would we be without it?

Mark: Exactly. Which reminds me of another way to reduce traffic – businesses replacing their vehicles with drones.

Host: Okay. Tell me more.

Mark: Some tasks city governments need to do, such as checking electricity lines, don't necessarily need to be carried out by a single person arriving in a big vehicle. A drone with a camera could send this information to engineers, who only need to go out if there is a problem. Think of how many work vans this could take off the roads every day ...

Host: And delivery vans ...

Mark: That's another good example. In some cities, businesses can use drones to deliver small parcels, which is fantastic. It means even fewer vehicles on the roads.

Host: What would you say to people who refuse to give up driving their cars, ever?

Mark: I honestly think people should try to **avoid** driving as much as possible. But, if they can't, they should consider their behaviour. It's not just bad parking that causes traffic issues. Everyone needs to be a lot more responsible as drivers.

Host: In what way?

Mark: When people get behind the steering wheel, they often become less helpful than normal. Like when someone is turning in to a side street – that often means driving across the other lane, past vehicles going in the opposite direction. If no one slows down to let in the person who wants to turn, the traffic gets worse and worse behind them. Even more so if someone stops in traffic with their car across the side street that person wants to turn in to.

Host: Agh! Listeners, if that doesn't annoy you as well, you're a better person than me!

Mark: Me too. Please, everyone, stop and give people enough space to turn in to side streets!

Host: Mark, thanks for joining me.

Mark: Thank you.

3.5

1 The course was a lot more challenging than I expected.

2 We can see that by far the most affordable form of transport is walking.

3 The risks of driving a car are considerably more significant than those of flying.
4 For me, flying is much more comfortable than travelling by train.
5 Taking a train is definitely more relaxing than driving.
6 Using the underground is a lot faster than travelling by bus at rush hour.
7 Driving is considerably more expensive than walking.
8 Cycling is absolutely the healthiest form of transport.

3.6

Hello, everyone. Thank you for being here today. Welcome to the first meeting of Wheels to Work. As you know, the goal of this group is to make our city more bicycle-friendly. Specifically, we'd like to make it easier for people to cycle to work. Cycling to work is good for the environment and it provides great exercise. And personally, I think it's a lot of fun!

I'm hoping that we can work together to **solve** the problems which can make it difficult for city residents to cycle to work. Today I'm going to talk about a few of those problems and share some ideas for solving them.

So, the biggest issue is safety. A lot of people would love to cycle to work, but they're scared – they feel that it's just too dangerous. This is because there's a lot of traffic during rush hour, when most people drive to or from work, and there's very little space for cyclists. Many of the cycle lanes we have are too narrow and some of the busiest streets don't even have cycle lanes. What's more, many drivers don't have **respect** for cyclists. Cars sometimes even drive in the cycle lanes to **pass** other cars. Of course, if a car hits a bicycle, it's going to **injure** or even kill the cyclist.

A second issue is storage. Many people don't have a safe place to put their bicycles while they're at work. They worry that if they leave their bicycle outside, it'll get stolen. Also, it'll get wet when it rains and might get damaged over time.

A third problem is that, for some people, cycling to work isn't **convenient**. Maybe they live far from their job or maybe they sometimes work late and don't want to cycle home in the dark. And a lot of people don't like to cycle in the rain. What if you cycle to work and then later it starts raining? From my own experience, I can tell you that it's pretty terrible to ride home during a storm.

So, those are three of the biggest issues: safety, storage and convenience.

3.7

Now I'd like to share some possible solutions. First, to improve safety, I'd suggest that police officers give big **fines** to drivers who **break the law** by driving in a cycle lane.

Also, I'd like to see wider cycle lanes to allow more bicycles to pass at the same time. We should also add cycle lanes to busy streets which don't have them yet. These proposals would **prevent** cars from hitting cyclists and would save lives.

As for the issue of storage, I think that city parking garages ought to create special parking sections for bicycles. This would keep bicycles safe and dry while people are working.

Finally, convenience. In my opinion, we should make it easier to take bicycles on public transport. For example, we could put cycle racks on the outside of buses. That way, people wouldn't have to cycle at night or in bad weather. And people who live far from work could cycle part of the way to work and take public transport the rest of the way. As a result, more people could cycle to work.

Well, thank you again for listening to my ideas. I hope this is the beginning of a conversation about how we can make this a great city for cyclists!

3.8

A: I'm really surprised by these statistics. I didn't know that eating while driving is dangerous. I don't think the government should do anything about it. Personally, I eat fast food in my car a few times a week and I've never had an accident. And I'm not convinced that driving while eating is a big problem. Have you ever eaten while driving?

B: No, I haven't. We should take this really seriously. I think it would be better if they closed drive-through restaurants. This is because they only encourage drivers to buy food and eat it while they drive. How can you focus on the road if you're holding a big burger in your hand? It seems dangerous to me. What do you think?

C: I completely agree. I think it would be much better if drivers weren't allowed to eat or drink while they drive. From my own experience, I can tell you that it can be very dangerous. Last week, I bought some coffee and something to eat on the way to work. As I was driving, I had to brake suddenly and I spilled hot coffee over my legs. I almost lost control of the car. I think the police should give heavy fines if they see someone doing it.

D: OK, I understand, but it might be very difficult for the police to see drivers eating, especially if they're driving fast. The best thing would be to have more cameras on the roads to record what drivers are doing. The reason for this is the police can check the videos to see who's eating, who's texting and so on. Then, I'd suggest that the police give the drivers points on their licence. If the driver has a lot of points, the police should take their car away for a few months.

UNIT 4

Chinese moon cakes

Narrator: The Mid-Autumn festival is celebrated by Chinese people across the world. It is traditionally a harvest festival, to celebrate the rice and wheat that has been grown that year, and it takes place on the full moon. People get together with family and friends to watch the moon, admire the lights and eat the traditional sweet of this festival – moon cakes. Moon cakes are rarely made at home because the recipe is quite complicated. Most people prefer to buy their moon cakes from a shop or a hotel.

Here at the famous Peninsula Hotel in Hong Kong, chef Yip Wing Wah shows how the cakes are made.

First, he makes the filling for the moon cakes. Here he is mixing butter with sugar. To that he will add other ingredients to make a thick, sweet paste.

Now the chef is taking a yellow ball of filling and wrapping it in a thin layer of pastry. Moon cakes can have a number of different fillings. For example, in more traditional recipes, the filling is made from sweet red beans, and you will find half of a salty duck egg inside that.

Next, the chef takes a special wooden mould and shapes each moon cake, one at a time. Each moon cake has a decoration on top of it. Many different patterns are used on moon cakes, including flower patterns or Chinese letters. The decoration on top is brushed with egg yolk. When baked in the oven this will turn a lovely golden brown.

Then, the moon cakes must be left for a day or two. The butter from the filling will go into the pastry layer and make it soft and delicious.

And here we have it, a sweet treat perfect with a cup of refreshing tea, on the night of the full moon.

4.1

This Sunday on *Book of the Week*, we interview Dr Kevin Lee, the well-known anthropologist and author. In this podcast, he will tell us of his love for Cultural anthropology and we'll discuss whether traditions are adapting to the modern world or dying out.

4.2

Host: Welcome to this week's book review. In the studio with me is Dr Kevin Lee, professor of Anthropology and author of the best-selling book *Changing Traditions in the Modern World*. First of all, could you tell us what anthropologists study and what your own area of interest is?

Dr Lee: That's a good question! Anthropology, in a general sense, is the study of humanity. I know that's not very exact. That's why we have many types of anthropology, like linguistic anthropology and **social** anthropology. My speciality is cultural anthropology. I study different cultures around the world and how social and **political** changes affect these cultures.

Host: And when did you first become interested in anthropology?

Dr Lee: I grew up in a **multicultural** home. My mother is American and my father is Korean. They were both English teachers, so we travelled a lot. As a child, I lived in Japan, Thailand and Egypt. That's why I decided to study anthropology. Growing up in different cultures helps you realize that customs and traditions are often local. Things that are acceptable in one culture can be completely unacceptable in another. However, despite some differences between cultures, I have noticed that there are often more similarities than differences between people.

Host: And do traditions change?

Dr Lee: Absolutely! Customs and traditions change all the time. Some traditions **die out** because our way of life changes, but most traditions adapt.

Host: As I understand it, that's one of the main points of your latest book.

Dr Lee: Yes. My book is about the effect of modern technology on traditions around the world. It's well known that things such as electricity, the telephone and television have changed our lives significantly. The introduction of these inventions into our lives has changed many of our customs. For example, in the past, families spent time playing board games or listening to the radio in the evening. These activities would deepen family relationships. Now, due to developments in technology, people spend more time **interacting** with other people over the internet.

Host: Is that a bad thing?

Dr Lee: I don't think so. There are people who complain about the changes that technology has brought to our lives. Personally, I think these changes are fine. We still spend time interacting with other people, but it's not always face-to-face.

Host: In your book, you discuss how technology has changed the way we celebrate important holidays.

Dr Lee: That's right. A simple example is sending cards or messages. In the past, people sent each other cards to celebrate important events, like an **anniversary** or a new baby. But now, more people send messages through social networking sites or by text or email. Another example of changing customs is holiday food. A few **generations** ago, people spent a lot of time and effort preparing special meals for **celebrations**. It was usually the women who did this. Some dishes could take up to a week to prepare. But now we don't have to work so hard. This is because we have modern kitchens and supermarket food. We don't have to spend endless hours making our own butter or bread any more. Everything is quicker and easier now.

Host: Hmm … I remember my grandmother working for days to make food. She had a huge cookery book which she got from her grandmother. Everything had to be exactly as it was when she was a little girl.

Dr Lee: That's a good example of a tradition which has been replaced by technology. You can find any recipe you want on the internet. This means that many people don't need cookery books any more. Another thing is that many families now go out instead of cooking at home. In India, for example, families hire catering companies to provide food for weddings or special occasions. In the United States, at Thanksgiving, which is one of the biggest celebrations, many families go to restaurants because they don't want to spend their holiday working in the kitchen.

Host: So people do continue their tradition of eating a special meal – they just do it in a different way.

Dr Lee: Yes. Traditions don't always die out – but customs and traditions do change and adapt to the modern world.

4.3

1 Anthropology, in a general sense, is the study of humanity. I know that's not very exact. That's why we have many types of anthropology, like linguistic anthropology and social anthropology.
2 Some traditions die out because our way of life changes.
3 Now, due to developments in technology, people spend more time interacting with other people over the internet.
4 But now we don't have to work so hard. This is because we have modern kitchens and supermarket food.
5 In the United States, at Thanksgiving, which is one of the biggest celebrations, many families go to restaurants because they don't want to spend their holiday working in the kitchen.

4.4

I study different cultures around the world and how social and political changes affect these cultures.

4.5

1 My book is about the effect of modern technology on traditions around the world.
2 People spent a lot of time and effort preparing special meals.
3 Growing up in different cultures helps you realize that customs and traditions are often local.
4 We still spend time interacting with other people, but it's not always face-to-face.

4.6

Gabriela: So, our assignment is to discuss customs which have been changing recently – you know, how modern lifestyles have changed people's **behaviour**. Any ideas?

Yildiz: Hmm … Let me think. Well, holidays are one kind of custom. Can you think of any holidays which have changed?

David: Oh, don't talk about holidays! It reminds me that Mother's Day is in two days and I haven't bought a gift for my mum yet.

Gabriela: Yeah, I haven't either. Who has time for shopping when we have so much work to do?

David: I agree. I get tired of shopping for gifts. I actually don't know why we have to get gifts for every little holiday. Wouldn't our mothers be just as happy if we just spent time with them – you know, made it a special **event**, like taking them out to lunch at a nice restaurant? How did this whole gift-giving for every holiday tradition get started, anyway? It seems silly to me.

Gabriela: That's it! There's our topic! How holidays have become too **commercial**.

4.7

Yildiz: Hold on, too commercial? I disagree. I like giving gifts. I think that it shows that you were thinking of someone.

David: Because you went out and got someone some chocolate or jewellery or a scarf or something at the last minute? Everyone knows that people usually buy gifts because it's an **obligation**, not because they really want to.

Yildiz: Well, you have to spend time thinking about the gift and get something **thoughtful**, you know, **personal**. Like maybe the new book by their favourite author.

Gabriela: I see your point. But I'm not convinced because then you have to spend money … money which could be spent on more important things. Also, all that time you spent shopping you could have instead spent with the person you're shopping for.

David: I couldn't agree more. And it's not just holidays which are a problem – personally, I think we give too many gifts for other special **occasions**, too. Like when my sister **graduated** from university last year, she got lots of gifts. And money, too. The focus was all on opening gifts. I've heard that when people receive more than a few gifts, they usually can't even remember who gave them which gift. Instead, why not write letters of advice for the future? That would be more special.

Gabriela: That's a great idea!

Yildiz: Sorry, I don't agree. I doubt that graduates would be happy if we changed that custom! I think that graduation gifts are practical. Don't young people need some gifts and money for starting their new life? And they can always look at the gift and think of the person who gave it to them. I think it's a nice custom.

Gabriela: I'm still really not convinced. I mean …

4.8

Gabriela: So, our assignment is to discuss customs which have been changing recently – you know, how modern lifestyles have changed people's behaviour. Any ideas?

Yildiz: Hmm … Let me think. Well, holidays are one kind of custom. Can you think of any holidays which have changed?

David: Oh, don't talk about holidays! It reminds me that Mother's Day is in two days and I haven't bought a gift for my mum yet.

Gabriela: Yeah, I haven't either. Who has time for shopping when we have so much work to do?

David: I agree. I get tired of shopping for gifts. I actually don't know why we have to get gifts for every little holiday. Wouldn't our mothers be just as happy if we just spent time with them – you know, made it a special event, like taking them out to lunch at a nice restaurant? How did this whole gift giving for every holiday tradition get started, anyway? It seems silly to me.

Gabriela: That's it! There's our topic! How holidays have become too commercial.

Yildiz: Hold on, too commercial? I disagree. I like giving gifts. I think that it shows that you were thinking of someone.

David: Because you went out and got someone some chocolate or jewellery or a scarf or something at the last minute? Everyone knows that people usually buy gifts because it's an obligation, not because they really want to.

Yildiz: Well, you have to spend time thinking about the gift and get something thoughtful, you know, personal. Like maybe the new book by their favourite author.

Gabriela: I see your point. But I'm not convinced because then you have to spend money … money which could be spent on more important things. Also, all that time you spent shopping you could have instead spent with the person you're shopping for.

David: I couldn't agree more. And it's not just holidays which are a problem – personally, I think we give too many gifts for other special occasions, too. Like when my sister graduated from university last year, she got lots of gifts. And money, too. The focus was all on opening gifts. I've heard that when people receive more than a few gifts, they usually can't even remember who gave them which gift. Instead, why not write letters of advice for the future? That would be more special.

Gabriela: That's a great idea!

Yildiz: Sorry, I don't agree. I doubt that graduates would be happy if we changed that custom! I think that graduation gifts are practical. Don't young people need some gifts and money for starting their new life? And they can always look at the gift and think of the person who gave it to them. I think it's a nice custom.

Gabriela: I'm still really not convinced. I mean …

4.9

1 I couldn't agree more.
2 How did this whole gift-giving for every holiday tradition get started, anyway? It seems silly to me.
3 I agree. I get tired of shopping for gifts.
4 I disagree. I like giving gifts.
5 But I'm not convinced because then you have to spend money … money which could be spent on more important things.
6 Instead, why not write letters of advice for the future? That would be more special.
7 Sorry, I don't agree. I doubt that graduates would be happy if we changed that custom!

4.10

I completely agree that holidays have become too commercial.

I absolutely disagree that we should stop giving gifts on Mother's Day.

I really think that we should give fewer gifts.

UNIT 5

Brain health

Our brain is the most complex part of the human body. The brain contains billions of neurons which send signals to each other. Everything we learn, our memories and feelings, are a result of neurons sending signals which the brain interprets. It's well-known that physical exercise is good for the body, but scientists are learning that it is also good for the brain. Exercise releases proteins in the brain, and neurons need these proteins to grow and stay healthy. Different kinds of exercise help the brain in different ways. Aerobic exercise, like running or cycling, helps the brain to learn new skills. Resistance training, like lifting weights, helps the brain to stay focused. Exercise programmes are most successful when they are personal. We can use fitness trackers and apps to set fitness goals, track our progress and access personal advice. Science is also making us think about what foods are good for our brains. We know that foods with lots of fat and sugar are unhealthy for our bodies, but researchers have found that they also prevent neuron growth. This can cause problems, including headaches and poor memory. Nuts are good for the brain. They contain fatty acids which support the growth of neurons, especially in the brains of young people. Sleep also plays an important role in brain health. Some people think that less sleep gives us more time during the day, so we can be more productive. But few of us work effectively when we're tired. Good sleep is essential for looking after our neurons. Sleep research shows that people who have had the right quality and quantity of sleep experience more positive moods. They are also more able to learn new skills and remember information. Smart devices can measure how long we sleep, and how much of this is deep sleep. Scientific research into brain health – supported by the latest developments in technology – is helping us take care of and make the most of our incredible brains.

5.1

Host: Today we're talking about the key to a long and happy life. Recent studies of people who live to be 100 years old have shown that a healthy diet and exercise may not be enough.

In fact, many of the people who celebrate their hundredth birthday have not eaten a healthy diet and have never exercised regularly. This has led many people to believe that our lifestyles are not important. What's most important is that we have good genes. It seems that if you have the right genes, then you'll live for a long time, whatever you do.

5.2

Host: So, new research shows that having a healthy lifestyle is not the most important thing if you want to live a long life. We asked four people on the street for their reactions to this news.

A: I think it's great news! Most people think that if they eat healthy food and exercise a lot, they'll live forever. These people never drink coffee or sugary drinks. They spend hours **working out** in the gym or doing yoga. And none of this matters if you have the wrong genes. I think that the key to a healthy life is to enjoy yourself. If you focus all your energy on what to do and what not to do, you'll be unhappy eventually. There's no question that happy people live longer. I'd much rather go out and have a pizza with friends than spend time in the gym. I'm really happy about this new research!

B: This research **proves** what I've known for a long time. It's **ridiculous** to get too worried about healthy eating and exercise! My grandfather lived until he was 95, even though he never exercised. He ate lots of sugar and never ate vegetables. He was brought up in a different world. He had different **habits**. He certainly never went to a gym. Yes, I'm sure that genes are more important than our lifestyle. Of course, I'm not going to give up exercising or start eating fast food every day. The research shows I should stay **in shape** because it makes me feel better – but I won't allow fitness to take over my whole life.

C: Well, first of all, I prefer to exercise and eat well. What's wrong with being healthy? I also think that you won't know whether or not you have the right genes until you get sick. So why take the risk and be **unhealthy**? Also, don't forget that you might get the flu or a cold much more easily when you don't eat healthy food or exercise. I'd say that it's always better to have a healthy lifestyle. There's no doubt that bad health habits increase the chances of getting a serious **illness**.

D: Oh, that's great. So now we should all eat fast food and stop exercising? I mean I look around and I see **overweight** children everywhere. No matter how good their genes are, I'm sure that these children won't be able to enjoy a long and healthy life unless they give up crisps, chocolate bars, sugary drinks … Well, it's great that some people can live to be 100 and do whatever they want in their lives, but I prefer to be careful and take care of myself because I don't know if I have good genes!

5.3

I'm really surprised about that.
I'm really surprised about that.
I'm really surprised about that!

5.4

1. I'm really happy about this new research!
2. There's no question that happy people live longer.
3. It's ridiculous to get too worried about healthy eating and exercise!
4. He certainly never went to a gym.
5. There's no doubt that bad health habits increase the chances of getting a serious illness.

5.5

1. I think it's great news!
2. Oh, that's great.
3. What's wrong with being healthy?
4. So now we should all eat fast food and stop exercising?
5. I'd say that it's always better to have a healthy lifestyle.

5.6

Presenter 1: Do you have problems focusing on your work? Are you under a lot of **stress**? Do you want to get more exercise while trying something new and exciting? If so, it's time to take up taekwondo! Taekwondo is great exercise. And as we all know, exercise is good for your health. Taekwondo also has **mental** benefits – it has been shown to improve your **concentration**. In addition, it makes you feel good about yourself. This martial art was developed in Korea, and is now popular around the world. Whether you are looking for physical well-being, increased confidence or a life with less stress, *Black Belt Taekwondo* has it all. **Sign up** now for a free introductory class, starting on January the 15th.

Presenter 2: Would you like to improve your social life, your intellectual **performance**, your physical fitness and your team-building skills? Scientific research has proven that team sports offer all of these benefits. Join us and take advantage of the many benefits of team sports. We're a group of energetic adults of all ages who get together on Sunday afternoons to play football and we're always looking for new players to join in the fun. Whether you've been playing football for years or want to take up a new sport, you're welcome to **participate**. Everyone can play – you don't even need to **try out**! If you're interested in learning more about our group, check out our website at www.footballsundays.cup.com. Sign up today and you can be part of a team as early as this weekend! Hope to see you on the field soon!

Presenter 3: Hi, my name's Angie Stratton and I'm the director of CultureCycle. CultureCycle is a new concept in travel: educational fitness touring! We offer courses all over the world which combine learning with exercise and travel. Each course has an educational theme, such as Brazilian cooking or the history of Türkiye. As a small group, we cycle from place to place, stopping for several days in each location to rest, **relax** and do some hands-on learning. Not only does this trip provide terrific exercise and a fascinating cultural experience, it's the best way to learn. There's no question that physical activity improves our memory and thinking skills – so after a few days of cycling, your brain will be ready to learn. So, be kind to your body and your mind and come with us on an amazing adventure you'll never forget!

Presenter 4: Are you interested in alternative **treatments**? Have you ever wanted to explore the secrets of traditional Chinese medicine? This spring, join our six-month course in acupuncture – a treatment for pain or illness which involves putting needles under the skin at special points on the body. The course covers the theory of acupuncture and practical skills in using needles. Acupuncture is known to **reduce** pain, but it's also a great alternative for people who want to lose weight in an easy way. Learn more about the course and visit us on our open house days on the first Saturday of every month.

UNIT 6

A career as a research scientist

Being a research scientist can be an exciting career. But what skills are needed? Research scientists have a strong interest in their chosen area, normally one of the STEM subjects – Science, Technology, Engineering or Math. Asking why and how things happen, testing ideas and evaluating solutions – or critical thinking – is fundamental to science. Mental flexibility is essential too – the ability to move from one task to another and think of more than one solution to a problem. The inventor of the most popular vacuum cleaner in the UK, James Dyson, made over 5,000 unsuccessful attempts, the first of which were made with just cardboard and sticky tape. But he succeeded in producing a vacuum cleaner that worked differently from all the others on the market at the time. Flexibility helps in adapting to different environments too. Research scientists may work in a laboratory, a lecture hall, underwater, outdoors or even in space. Successful scientists take the initiative, and want to make a real difference to people's lives. The Laserphaco Probe is a device which is used to remove cataracts. It was invented by Dr Patricia Bath who noticed that her African-American patients in New York were more likely to lose their sight. Her invention is now used in many countries. Research scientists also need to be good at teamwork and collaboration. The company BioNTech was started by scientists Özlem Türeci, Uğur Şahin and Christoph Huber to research treatment for cancer. This involved research into the immune system and during the pandemic they were able to partner with the drug company Pfizer to produce a successful vaccine against Covid-19. So if you have a special interest and are keen to develop the skills, among others, of critical thinking, flexibility, taking initiative and collaboration, research science may be the career for you. Who knows what you may invent?

6.1

Welcome to the Museum of Science! The exhibition that we're about to see is called *Discovering Medieval Science*. As some of you may know, the Middle Ages have often been called the 'Dark Ages'. During this tour, you will find out that they were not. The Middle Ages were an interesting time and they were full of scientific **discoveries**. During this time, inventions and **technology** from India, China, North Africa and the Middle East were brought to Europe.

Inventions and machines designed by medieval **scholars** made a great **contribution** to society and many are still in use today. And some of these inventions are very common. For example, the first fountain pen was made in 953 in Africa. Before then, people used bird feathers and ink to write with. This method would often leave your fingers and clothes covered with black ink. So the first fountain pen had a small container with ink inside and did not stain people's clothes or fingers while the user was writing. You can see a model of this fountain pen in Room 11B. In the same room, you'll find early examples of glasses. Glasses were invented in Italy in the thirteenth century. No one knows who invented them. The first glasses were held in front of the eyes or balanced on the nose. They were developed to help people with bad vision to read. But let's now move on to some other inventions.

In rooms 12A and 12B we have works by the great medieval engineer, al-Jazari. Al-Jazari lived in twelfth-century Türkiye. His work *The Book of Knowledge of Ingenious Mechanical Devices* lists one hundred different machines with instructions and **diagrams** explaining how to build them. In this exhibition, you can see models of some of the **devices** which were designed by al-Jazari. Here, you can see his mechanical clocks. Water and weights make the clocks work. However, his most important invention was the crankshaft. The crankshaft is a long arm which allows machines to move in a straight line. It was first used for watering gardens and fields on farms. In more modern times, a crankshaft is used in car engines.

As we move along, you'll find one of the most important inventions of medieval times. This invention has changed the history of the world in ways that we can't even imagine. It's one of the four great inventions of Chinese culture: gunpowder. Gunpowder was invented in the ninth century by Chinese scientists who were trying to create a powder which would make you live forever. They weren't successful, of course, but their attempts led to the invention of fireworks and **weapons**. The first instructions on how to make gunpowder were written in the eleventh century by Zeng Gongliang, Ding Du and Yang Weide. The invention of gunpowder has changed the way we fight wars. It changed the **outcome** of many medieval battles and affected the history of the world. Many people think gunpowder is the most important invention in history. Now, let's move to the next room, which is all about medieval medicine …

6.2

1 Inventions and technology from India, China, North Africa and the Middle East were brought to Europe.
2 The first glasses were held in front of the eyes or balanced on the nose.
3 The crankshaft is a long arm which allows machines to move in a straight line.
4 As we move along, you'll find one of the most important inventions of medieval times.

6.3

1 The Middle Ages were an interesting time and they were full of scientific discoveries.
2 Inventions and machines designed by medieval scholars made a great contribution to society and many are still in use today. And some of these inventions are very common.
3 Many people think gunpowder is the most important invention in history.

6.4

Good morning! In today's lecture I want to discuss an invention which has changed our lives. This **product** has made a huge difference in the way we work, travel, communicate and socialize with friends. Can you guess what it is? I'm talking here about mobile phone apps. The word *app* comes from *application*. Traditionally, applications were used in computers to help them perform better. However, with the invention of smartphones, the word *app* is used to refer to phone applications. In this lecture, we'll start by discussing the very first apps and their development. We will then discuss how apps have changed our lives. Finally, we'll focus on some of the most popular apps used by people today.

6.5

I'd like to start by talking a little bit about the first apps. These were included with each smartphone. These types of apps were placed in the phones to help **users access** the internet, check emails, send texts and so on. The first apps were designed to increase efficiency at work and **allow** people to access important information. However, it was the second generation of apps that really changed things. These were downloadable apps. Users simply downloaded apps from the internet and **installed** them on their phones. Since its introduction, the app market has grown far beyond anyone's expectations. The first app store was opened in 2008. By 2011, it was reporting over 10 billion downloads and people were using apps more than internet browsers on their phones. And by 2017, an estimated 180 billion apps had been downloaded. These numbers have been growing ever since and they give us a good idea about how popular apps are and how quickly they've developed. People from all over the world use apps for entertainment, travel and communication. So, I'm going to briefly talk about how these apps have changed our lives.

It's hard to imagine life before smartphones and mobile phone apps – or, for those of us who are old enough, to remember it. But let's go ahead and make an attempt anyway. So, imagine for a moment that you're taking a road trip in the days before smartphones.

Weeks before the trip, you go to the bookstore or library to get some guidebooks about the places you're going to visit. A few days before you leave, you get some audio books to entertain you during the long trip. You go to a shop and buy some maps – yes, the paper kind. The day before the trip, you sit down at your computer and look up the directions and print them out. Then, you pack some of your favourite CDs to bring along. You also pack your camera – and your torch, in case your car breaks down. And you write down some phone numbers and addresses – of the friends you'll be visiting and the hotels where you'll be staying.

While you're driving, your passenger reads the directions to you and looks for street signs. If you get lost, you stop at a petrol station to ask for directions. You have to write them down on a piece of paper. OK, so I think you get the idea.

Now let's make a comparison with the same trip today. No books, no maps, no CDs, no lists of phone numbers, no friend giving you directions – the smartphone does it all! Think of the apps you'd use just for that one trip. You'd read reviews and book your hotel with a travel app. The GPS would replace the directions and maps and your friend in the front seat. Of course, a music app would replace the CDs and you could listen to podcasts, as well as audio books. And, of course, you wouldn't need to bring a camera or a torch. Yes, we've certainly made a lot of progress since the pre-smartphone days!

So, now I'd like to mention another important effect of the invention of apps. It has **created** a whole new IT sector. It is one of the fastest-growing **industries** and there is a great need for skilled software engineers.

But apps have also had some negative effects. For one thing, people have become more helpless because they're so dependent on their phones for information. For example, if they're in a place with no phone signal, they're not very good at asking for and following directions. And apps have made people less patient because they expect to have information immediately. In fact, a recent study found that 87 percent of smartphone users leave a web page if it doesn't load in two seconds. OK, in the next part of the lecture, I'll discuss some of the most common apps in more detail …

6.6

I would like to present an invention which has made the way we organize our work easier. It's a simple invention and most of you have used it. It's a small yellow piece of paper which is known all over the world. It's the Post-it® note. A Post-it® note is a piece of paper with special glue on the back. Modern Post-it® notes can be any colour or shape. Post-it® notes are simple to use. You can stick them on anything and the note will stay in place. The notes can be easily removed from any surface. First, I am going to talk about the history of this invention. Then, I will explain how it has made a difference in our lives.

UNIT 7

Interview with College of Art graduate Christopher Raeburn

Narrator: Christopher Raeburn is a fashion designer with a difference. His clothes are both extremely fashionable and good for the environment, too. He started making recycled fashion items from old military uniforms when he was at university. These days, his recycled brand, *Remade*, is a fashion success, and he is now making clothes from other spare military materials, such as parachute material.

Christopher Raeburn: I'm based here in London in the East End, Hackney Wick, but err … originally I'm from Kent in southeast England.

I … I never really set out to um to create an ethical or sustainable brand. For me it's just more about intelligent use of materials, it's about um the fact that I knew I wanted to do my production here in England and because I … I love the fabrics and I recycle the fabrics. Inherently, you've already got a very sustainable brand you know because you are recycling, because you are doing your production because you are employing local people.

This season we're actually splitting the collection into three sections. We have the *Remade* that hopefully everyone knows and loves before, we've got our lightweight fabrics, you know the parachute and, erm … waterproof fabrics, but this season we're also working in a new British erm … section of the collection and that's very much focused on, erm … incredibly good quality British milled wools.

We're actually doing my London Fashion Week presentation at Aldwych Tube Station. It hasn't actually been used for proper underground, err … trains for 10 to 15 years now and so we'll be getting in and doing a very different event, erm … it'll be multimedia, I'll be presenting my new film. And for the first time I'll also be working with um models as well presenting the garments, erm … both men's- and womenswear.

Narrator: The ideas for Christopher's designs come firstly from the old fabric or piece of clothing he's recycling. Then he adds ideas he gets from other places. He's particularly interested in the military, adventure, outdoor activities and cultures that come from cold places, like the Inuit. He connects all these ideas in the different garments in each collection.

7.1

Yoriko: So, Hamed, shall we continue working on our group presentation?

Hamed: Good idea, Yoriko. Now, Danial and Samia are **focusing on** the environmental issues of fast fashion – so we'll be talking about **copyright** infringement.

Yoriko: Danial said they've already written their part of the presentation, you know …

Hamed: Wow, really? We've only just got started on ours! Anyway, we're focusing on the way that fast fashion companies lift unknown artists' designs and put them onto their products, which they then sell in huge numbers.

Yoriko: That's right. So, first, I think we should talk about what happened to Vanessa Bowman.

Hamed: The artist from the south of England who paints the world around her?

Yoriko: Yes, views out onto her garden, natural scenes, that sort of thing. A fast fashion company lifted **images** of her paintings they found on her website, and used them on a clothing range. I'm sure they made a lot of money, and I don't think she got anything in return.

Hamed: No, she didn't get anything. No payment, no credit for her work, nothing. She's not alone, though.

Yoriko: No. We should also use the example of Kirstie Moran. She creates interesting, unusual designs of animals. Her artwork was also used by a fast fashion company and again, she got nothing from them.

Hamed: I mean, this is a perfect example of a company taking an artist's designs without permission and using them to sell clothes and make a profit. What can anyone do?

Yoriko: Some large fashion companies take legal action when their designs are copied, but it takes money and power to do that. It's just not **practical** for an independent artist like Kirstie Moran to say, 'if you don't pay me for my hard work and talent, I'll be contacting my lawyer'.

Hamed: Well, I *have* seen some examples of artists defending their intellectual property, but not many. Elora Pautrat, for example.

Yoriko: I haven't read about her yet.

Hamed: She *did* do something about it, after she discovered that a fast fashion company was **converting** her designs into images and putting them on clothing and bags. At first, Elora decided it wasn't worth complaining to them by email, so she tried a different approach. She posted her complaint on social media, and it went viral. Thousands of people from all over the world **criticized** the company and promised never to buy anything from them again. Finally, the company wrote to her offering an apology. They actually paid her something for using her work and promised it would never happen again.

Yoriko: That's one happy ending, at least.

Hamed: Not quite. The same company's lifted her work several times since then and used it on all sorts of products. Although they've accepted it was their fault again, she still hasn't received a second payment. She's going to be disappointed this time, I imagine.

Yoriko: The thing is, these companies *do* have the ability and the resources to **collaborate** with artists, pay them for their designs and still make a lot of money – but they choose not to.

Hamed: I know. It's plagiarism, basically. And it's not **ethical**.

Yoriko: Oh, I *do* agree. Imagine doing that sort of thing at our university! Can you see the situation changing any time soon?

Hamed: No, I don't think it *will* change. In a few years, these companies will be ignoring copyright law just like they do now, and artists still won't be getting anything.

7.2

Hamed: I've seen some examples of artists defending their intellectual property, but not many. I *have* seen some examples of artists defending their intellectual property, but not many.

Yoriko: Can you see the situation changing any time soon?

Hamed: No, I don't think it *will* change.

Yoriko: I agree. I *do* agree.

Hamed: She did something about it. She *did* do something about it.

Yoriko: These companies have the ability and the resources to collaborate with artists. These companies *do* have the ability and the resources to collaborate with artists.

7.3

1 a That's amazing.
b That *is* amazing

2 a You've asked me that before, you know.
b You *have* asked me that before, you know.

3 a I agree that it's not very practical.
b I *do* agree that it's not very practical.

4 a I think it'll be interesting.
b I *do* think it'll be interesting. / I think it *will* be interesting.

5 a I know I look tired, but I've been working very hard.
b I know I look tired, but I *have* been working very hard. / I *do* know I look tired, but I've been working very hard.

7.4

Narrator: One

Yoriko: She creates **interesting**, unusual designs of animals.

Narrator: Two

Hamed: It's plagiarism, **basically**.

Narrator: Three

Hamed: The company's lifted her work **several** times since then.

Narrator: Four

Hamed: She tried a **different** approach.

Narrator: Five

Hamed: **Finally**, the company wrote to her offering an apology.

7.5

Host: In today's show, we'll be interviewing the talented fashion designer Aysha Al-Husaini. Hot on the heels of her fashion week show, Aysha's new **collection** is very popular in Doha. She got the attention of the fashion world with her **unique** designs, which **combine** traditional Muslim fashion with French chic. Aysha, thank you for coming to the studio.

Aysha: Thank you for having me.

Host: First of all, can you tell me where you get your ideas from?

Aysha: Well, I come from a Muslim family. My parents are both from Qatar. I was born there, but then we travelled a lot. I went to school in New York and I went to a design school there.

These days, I spend my time travelling between Qatar and the United States.

7.6

Host: How did you feel about growing up in New York?

Aysha: Well, as a teenager in New York, I had a lot of problems trying to dress in a **modest** way. For example, when you look at summer fashion in New York, the trend is always to wear skirts, shorts and sleeveless shirts. I didn't feel comfortable wearing them, but at the same time my friends thought it was strange to wear long sleeves and jeans in the summer. So I've always tried to combine my culture with fashion. As a teenager, I would make my own clothes, like colourful skirts and scarves. I wanted my designs to be **individual**. They were unique and, eventually, people **admired** my clothes rather than laughed at me.

Host: I see. So, do you know what ideas most people have about Muslim clothes?

Aysha: Well, I think there's a lot of misunderstanding about Muslim clothes. The thing is that when you say *Muslim fashion*, people in New York think of a *burka*. You know, like the blue or black cloaks which cover women from head to toe.

Host: And could you explain what you think Muslim fashion is?

Aysha: Let me give you an example. When I first started at design school, my teachers would ask me strange questions, such as how I was going to stay in the fashion business if I'm not going to design miniskirts or sleeveless shirts. But as far as I'm concerned, there is much more to fashion than showing your body. There are millions of Muslim women who live in the United States and Europe who want to wear fashionable clothes. There are also women who simply like to dress in a modest way.

Host: So, are you saying that there is a need for fashionable clothes for Muslim women?

Aysha: Absolutely. We want to be fashionable and be ourselves at the same time. My feeling is this: I want to create clothes which are modest, but at the same time, give women **confidence** – clothes which allow women to be themselves.

Host: I see what you mean. So, how would you describe your **style**?

Aysha: Well, many reviewers have described my style as 'traditional chic', and I guess I'd agree with them. What I think is that combining traditional with chic is a huge area in fashion. I keep my eye on the fashion trends in other countries. When you look at the works of other designers in China and India, you can see that many traditional styles are being reused by young designers. Above all, people like to be individuals and show their cultural roots – they like to show where they come from.

Host: As I understand it, your designs are must-haves for Muslim women outside the United States as well. Could you tell me more about that?

Aysha: Yes. In addition to New York and Paris, I sell my collection in big cities like Doha, Dubai and Abu Dhabi. Another thing is that I also receive requests for my clothes from women in Pakistan, Indonesia, Singapore and Malaysia, so someday I might open stores there.

Host: Well, I hope you decide to go for it! That would make a lot of women around the world very happy. So, Aysha, thank you for coming to the studio today.

Aysha: It was my pleasure. Anytime!

7.7

Host: In today's show, we'll be interviewing the talented fashion designer Aysha Al-Husaini. Hot on the heels of her fashion week show, Aysha's new **collection** is very popular in Doha. She got the attention of the fashion world with her **unique** designs, which **combine** traditional Muslim fashion with French chic. Aysha, thank you for coming to the studio.

Aysha: Thank you for having me.

Host: First of all, can you tell me where you get your ideas from?

Aysha: Well, I come from a Muslim family. My parents are both from Qatar. I was born there, but then we travelled a lot. I went to school in New York and I went to a design school there. These days, I spend my time travelling between Qatar and the United States.

Host: How did you feel about growing up in New York?

Aysha: Well, as a teenager in New York, I had a lot of problems trying to dress in a **modest** way. For example, when you look at summer fashion in New York, the trend is always to wear skirts, shorts and sleeveless shirts. I didn't feel comfortable wearing them, but at the same time my friends thought it was strange to wear long sleeves and jeans in the summer. So I've always tried to combine my culture with fashion. As a teenager, I would make my own clothes, like colourful skirts and scarves. I wanted my designs to be **individual**. They were unique and eventually people **admired** my clothes rather than laughed at me.

Host: I see. So, do you know what ideas most people have about Muslim clothes?

Aysha: Well, I think there's a lot of misunderstanding about Muslim clothes. The thing is that when you say *Muslim fashion*, people in New York think of a *burka*. You know, like the blue or black cloaks which cover women from head to toe.

Host: And could you explain what you think Muslim fashion is?

Aysha: Let me give you an example. When I first started at design school, my teachers would ask me strange questions, such as how I was going to stay in the fashion business if I'm not going to design miniskirts or sleeveless shirts. But as far as I'm concerned, there is much more to fashion than showing your body. There are millions of Muslim women who live in the United States and Europe who want to wear fashionable clothes. There are also women who simply like to dress in a modest way.

Host: So, are you saying that there is a need for fashionable clothes for Muslim women?

Aysha: Absolutely. We want to be fashionable and be ourselves at the same time. My feeling is this: I want to create clothes which are modest, but at the same time, give women **confidence** – clothes which allow women to be themselves.

Host: I see what you mean. So, how would you describe your **style**?

Aysha: Well, many reviewers have described my style as 'traditional chic', and I guess I'd agree with them. What I think is that combining traditional with chic is a huge area in fashion. I keep my eye on the fashion trends in other countries. When you look at the works of other designers in China and India, you can see that many traditional styles are being reused by young designers. Above all, people like to be individuals and show their cultural roots – they like to show where they come from.

Host: As I understand it, your designs are must-haves for Muslim women outside the United States as well. Could you tell me more about that?

Aysha: Yes. In addition to New York and Paris, I sell my collection in big cities like Doha, Dubai and Abu Dhabi. Another thing is that I also receive requests for my clothes from women in Pakistan, Indonesia, Singapore and Malaysia, so someday I might open stores there.

Host: Well, I hope you decide to go for it! That would make a lot of women around the world very happy. So, Aysha, thank you for coming to the studio today.

Aysha: It was my pleasure. Anytime!

UNIT 8

Money management

The average person spends about one third of their life earning money. People work hard to be able to support themselves and others. So you might expect that earning more money increases a person's life satisfaction. But psychologists testing this idea found something slightly different. It's actually spending more money, rather than earning more, that increases people's life satisfaction. One study found that British people go shopping over 300 times per year. While many of these hours are spent on essential food shopping, researchers have found that shopping in stores or receiving an online delivery releases dopamine in the brain – the chemical that makes us feel good. Studies show that for some people, the reason behind a big purchase is to appear successful. But we don't just spend on ourselves, we also spend money on others, whether it's buying presents or helping people in need. And this makes us feel good about ourselves. It's important, however, not to forget the impact of spending too much. Good financial habits, such as saving money and reducing spending, aren't always easy. Many people admit that they find managing money complicated. But good financial habits are essential life skills. Some skills, such as setting and following a budget, or choosing the best deal, can be taught at a young age. Some would argue that finance should be on the school curriculum: research has found that children who learn to do these things manage their money more successfully and have fewer money problems as adults. It's often only adults with an interest in working in money who actually study finance. But knowledge of basic finance can help with life decisions such as choosing a credit card or a savings account, or buying a car or house. It also reduces our chances of getting into financial difficulty. Money is not just about numbers. It's about psychology and it's about education, too. The evidence shows that good financial habits are worth learning. After all, we spend so much of our lives earning and spending money.

8.1

In this week's programme, I'd like to talk about a book that has changed the way I think about money. It's called *The Secret of Being Wealthy*. It was written by a business school graduate named John Holm who decided to study the behaviour of wealthy people. He paid close attention to what rich people do: checking where they eat, what they buy, how they live and so on. The results of his study were pretty surprising.

8.2

When you think of someone who is very rich, what comes to mind? Most people think that rich people live lavish lifestyles – that is, they drive very expensive cars, eat in expensive restaurants, own a yacht or live in big houses. But, as John Holm discovered, people who have money don't actually do these things. Most **millionaires** actually seem to have ordinary lifestyles. In other words, they have normal cars, average houses and so on. On the other hand, people who *look* rich – the people who drive the latest Ferrari or only wear designer clothes – may not actually be rich at all. Instead, they have spent all their money trying to show off – showing other people that they might be wealthy. In other words, having expensive things is not always a sign that someone is rich.

So, what do millionaires do and what can we learn from them? Well, millionaires are often financially savvy. To put it another way, they're smart about how to save and spend money. The first important thing is that millionaires always have a good handle on their budget. In other words, they know how much they're spending. According to Holm, around 75 percent of millionaires know exactly how much money they have and they know exactly how much they spend on food, bills, clothes, etc. As a result, they don't spend too much and they don't get into **debt**. They can plan for the future and save their money. To sum up, the lesson here is that you should never spend more money than you have!

Another surprising fact is that millionaires usually have simple lifestyles. They have nice houses and nice cars, but they don't spend all their money on these things. In fact, most rich people stay in the same place for a very long time and don't live in big, expensive palaces. Indeed, according to John Holm, half of millionaires have lived in the same house for 20 years. Also, around 65 percent of millionaires live in homes which cost around the national average. Again, the important lesson here is to live within your means – that is, don't spend more money than you have. If you spend all your **savings** on a luxury BMW, then you probably aren't rich – you just want to look rich. In fact, the study reveals that 86 percent of luxury cars are bought by people who can't **afford** them. Most rich people don't have bank **loans** – they only spend a small percentage of what they have and they save or invest the rest.

Now here is an interesting fact. The study shows that most millionaires have very happy relationships. Not only are they married, but they stay married for a long time. In John Holm's opinion, this is very important because of the golden rule about **saving money**. There is no doubt that it's more difficult to save money if you are single. One effect of being a couple is that it's easier to save money. If there are two of you, it's easier to pay attention to what money you have and what you're spending.

And of course, people who don't have huge bank loans and debts are happier. If you don't have to worry about the monthly credit card **payments**, you're less likely to buy things to make you feel better. People with debt often spend more time shopping just to make themselves feel happier, but real millionaires don't need to do this.

So, what can we learn from the wealthy? The answer is surprisingly simple. Don't spend more money than you have. Don't get into debt or take out bank loans. Pay close attention to your money and don't spend time trying to show other people that you're rich. In John Holm's opinion, being 'wealthy' is a feeling. That is, it doesn't mean being rich or having millions. It means being happy with what you have.

8.3

1 Most people think that rich people live lavish lifestyles, that is they drive very expensive cars, eat in expensive restaurants, own a yacht or live in big houses.

2 In other words, having expensive things is not always a sign that someone is rich.

3 On the other hand, people who look rich – the people who drive the latest Ferrari or only wear designer clothes – may not actually be rich at all.

4 As a result, they don't spend too much and they don't get into debt.

5 There is no doubt that it's more difficult to save money if you are single.

6 So, what can we learn from the wealthy? The answer is surprisingly simple.

8.4

Host: In today's programme, we discuss the recent **decision** made by several universities to give students money in return for good grades. Students will be paid by the hour to take additional Maths and Science classes. The students who improve their grades and keep their grade average high will be given cash rewards at the end of each term. To discuss this new project, we have invited education expert Dr Michael Burns and we welcome your calls during the programme. We'd like to hear your opinion: Do you think university students should be paid for good grades?

8.5

Host: Dr Burns, thank you for coming today. Can you tell us more about the project? Where does this idea come from?

Dr Burns: Thank you. Well, the idea of paying students for their work isn't new. For example, students in Denmark are paid about €760 a month to attend university. They receive the payments for a maximum of six years, starting at the age of 18. The goal of paying students is to **encourage** them to finish their education and be able to get a good job in the future.

Host: I see. Let's hear from our first caller. Mariam Hassan is the president of a medium-sized university. Dr Hassan?

Dr Hassan: Hello. Yes, I recently read about this new programme and I really don't think it's a good idea. I understand that many students drop out of university because of financial problems. At my university alone, the dropout rate is over 25 percent. However, will paying students really encourage them to continue? In my experience, it won't. Of course, the statistics are terrible, but I'm not confident that this programme will solve the real problems – it may just cover them up. I think the money would be better spent on student **services**, like hiring additional professors and advisors. Two of the reasons why students drop out are stress and poor time management. Advisors can help students learn to manage their time better. As a consequence, students will do better at university and will be more likely to graduate.

Dr Burns: I can see your point, but we have already spent a lot on student services. I think that paying students to study will show them that we treat them like adults. It will give them a **sense** of responsibility. University students are young adults and so, when they have a choice between staying at university and studying or going to work and making money, they often make the wrong choice. They want to have money so that they can buy things for themselves. Besides, we don't want to pay them a lot. I think we're simply giving them an option: stay at university and be paid or get a **minimum wage** job.

Host: Christine Thorne is a parent with two children at university.

Mrs Thorne: Hello. I was very worried when I heard about this new programme. I realize that students need encouragement to stay at university, but are we going in the right direction? First of all, I feel that we're sending the students the wrong message. Learning should be about studying new things and being **responsible**. Personally, I think the students who aren't interested in studying will simply take the easy courses to keep their average grade high and get the cash. I believe that we should focus more on rewarding excellent universities and teachers and not on students who might be lazy.

Dr Burns: These are all good points, but I don't think that this view applies to all students. Not all parents are educated or interested in studying. They pass this bad attitude on to their own children. Then the children don't see the benefits of learning. To change this image, we need to show them a good reason for studying.

Host: Thank you. Let's have a look now at some of the comments we've received during the programme.

THANKS AND ACKNOWLEDGEMENTS

The authors and publishers acknowledge the following sources of copyright material and are grateful for the permissions granted. While every effort has been made, it has not always been possible to identify the sources of all the material used, or to trace all copyright holders. If any omissions are brought to our notice, we will be happy to include the appropriate acknowledgements on reprinting and in the next update to the digital edition, as applicable.

Key: U = Unit.

Photography
All the photographs are sourced from Getty Images.

U1: Michael S.Lewis/Corbis Documentary; Anadolu/Contributor/Anadolu; Phynart Studio/E+; Sasacvetkovic33/E+; Jason Edwards/The Image Bank; Somnuk Krobkum/Moment; **U2:** Kaicheng Xu,Landscape And Architecture Photographer/Moment; James O'Neil/The Image Bank; Hhakim/E+; Tanukiphoto/E+; Wilatlak Villette/Moment; Weiquan Lin/Moment; Huangyifei/iStock/Getty Images Plus; Lorado/E+; Mischa Keijser/Image Source; John Harper/Stone; **U3:** Wachirawit Jenlohakit/Moment; Bernie Dechant/The Image Bank; Aire Images/Moment; Hugh Threlfall/Photodisc; Shen Wei/Moment; Olaser/E+; Maskot; **U4:** a.v.Photography/Moment; Kilito Chan/Moment; Rifka Hayati/E+; Barry Austin Photography/The Image Bank; **U5:** Dan Porges/Photodisc; Mint Images; Justin Paget/Digitalvision; Charday Penn/E+; Miodrag Ignjatovic/E+; Aldomurillo/E+; Pipat Wongsawang/Moment; Bojanstory/E+; Image Source; Gbh007/iStock/Getty Images Plus; Fangxianuo/E+; **U6:** Archive Photos/Stringer; Smith Collection/Gado/Archive Photos; Roberto Machado Noa/Lightrocket; Adyna/iStock/Getty Images Plus; Voren1/iStock/Getty Images Plus; Kevinjeon00/E+; Tetra Images; 200mm/iStock/Getty Images Plus; Markfgd/iStock/Getty Images Plus; Simonen/iStock/Getty Images Plus; Viewstock; Dragos Condrea/iStock/Getty Images Plus; Stocknroll/E+; Albert_Karimov/iStock/Getty Images Plus; Witthaya Prasongsin/Moment; archives/E+; **U7:** Tongpool Piasupun/iStock/Getty Images Plus; Aleksandargeorgiev/E+; Lilly Roadstones/Stone; Ishii Koji/Digitalvision; **U8:** Sam Bassett/The Image Bank; Captured Blinks Photography/Moment; Edwin Tan/E+; Ljubaphoto/E+; Blackcat/E+; Emilija Manevska/Moment.

Front cover photography by Giacomo Augugliaro/Moment/Getty Images.

Illustrations
U1, U4: Szilvia Szakall/Beehive Illustration; **U2:** Fiona Gowen.

Videos
The following videos are sourced from Getty Images:

U3: vichie81/Creatas Video; tawattiw/Creatas Video; simonkr/Vetta; PassionStudio/Vetta; Schroptschop/Creatas Video; abdul7amid/Creatas Video; AerialPerspective Works/Creatas Video; SolStock/Vetta; Easy_Company/Creatas Video; Blimp Tele Inc/DigitalVision; Wengen Ling/Creatas Video; mgost/Creatas Video; thisnight/Creatas Video; korudirect/Creatas Video; SolStock/Creatas Video; Richard Newstead/Moment Video RF; abalcazar/Creatas Video; f11photo/Vetta; FernandoPodolski/Creatas Video; John_Lamb/Creatas Video; Emanuel M. Schwermer/DigitalVision; whitebalance.oatt/Creatas Video; Krisada tepkulmanont/Creatas Video; fivepointsix/Creatas Video; SVPhilon/Creatas Video; piola666/Creatas Video; andresr/Creatas Video; serefozdemir/Creatas Video; staticnak1983/Vetta; Sergey Alimov/Moment Video RF; holgs/Creatas Video; Jorg Greuel/Verve; Craig McCourry/Verve+; Dkosig/Creatas Video; Devrimb/Creatas Video; Dorian Weber/DigitalVision; MStudioImages/Creatas Video; AerialPerspective Works/Vetta; Mehmet Hilmi Barcin/Creatas Video; **U4:** AFPTV; kickimages/Creatas Video+/Getty Images Plus; Faithfulshot; topnatthapon/Creatas Video; **U5:** OlgaGroza/Vetta; DKosig/Creatas Video; nmlfd/Vetta; Vasyl Shulga/Vetta; SolStock/Creatas Video; Alistair Berg/DigitalVision; Dean Mitchell/Vetta; simonkr/Creatas Video; staticnak1983/Creatas Video; simonkr/Vetta; Kobus Louw/Creatas Video; Trevor Williams/DigitalVision; tawattiw/Creatas Video; PeopleImages/Vetta; Caiafilm/Vetta; valentinrussanov/Creatas Video; khanoglu/Creatas Video; Picture Palace/DigitalVision; LumiNola/Creatas Video; Ashley Cooper/Corbis Video; gerenme/Creatas Video; helovi/Creatas Video; lovestock/Creatas Video; hoozone/Creatas Video; Peresmeh/Vetta; andreswd/Vetta; FG Trade/Creatas Video; xavierarnau/Creatas Video; tawattiw/Vetta; robyvannucci/Creatas Video; commandoXphoto/Creatas Video; Filmstax/Creatas Video; FilmColoratStudio/Vetta; nopparit/Creatas Video; **U6:** Laurence Dutton/Vetta; SolStock/Creatas Video; Caiafilm/Creatas Video; tawattiw/Creatas Video; kontekbrothers/Creatas Video; Red Stock Studio/Vetta; 2021 Leader Graphic Studio/Vetta; Sean Anthony Eddy/Creatas Video; Red Stock Studio/Creatas Video; South_agency/Vetta; Снимаю, обрабатываю и выставляю свои фото только сам/Creatas Video+/Getty Images Plus; zokov/Creatas Video+/Getty Images Plus; janiecbros/Vetta; Caiafilm/Vetta; Placebo365/Creatas Video; simonkr/Vetta; Edwin Tan/Creatas Video; SDI Productions/Creatas Video; FG Trade/Vetta; Serg Myshkovsky/Digital Vision; alvarez/Creatas Video; Hispanolistic/Vetta; nopparit/Creatas Video; janiecbros/Creatas Video; onuroner/Vetta; leventince/Vetta; Michael H/DigitalVision; Portra/Creatas Video; **U7:** Crane.tv - Footage/Getty Images Editorial Footage; **U8:** alice-photo/Vetta; pictafolio/Vetta; simonkr/Creatas Video; Pekic/Creatas Video; Laurence Dutton/Vetta; FG Trade/Creatas Video; SolStock/Creatas Video; John_Lamb/Creatas Video; Pavitra Srital-on/Creatas Video; SDI Productions/Creatas Video; Treedeo/Creatas Video; ReeldealHD Ltd./Verve+; SimonSkafar/Creatas Video; SolStock/Vetta; patcharin saenlakon/Creatas Video; FG Trade/Vetta; somboon kaeoboonsong/Vetta; tawattiw/Creatas Video; pixdeluxe/Creatas Video; ATHVisions/Vetta; travelism/Creatas Video; Alistair Berg/DigitalVision; PonyWang/Creatas Video; commandoXphoto/Creatas Video; OneForAll/Creatas Video; OneForAll/Vetta; Schroptschop/Creatas Video.

The following video stills are sourced from Getty Images:

U3: abdul7amid/Creatas Video; SVPhilon/Creatas Video; holgs/Creatas Video; Dorian Weber/DigitalVision; **U4:** AFPTV; topnatthapon/Creatas Video; **U5:** OlgaGroza/Vetta; Trevor Williams/DigitalVision; Picture Palace/DigitalVision; tawattiw/Vetta; **U6:** Red Stock Studio/Creatas Video; simonkr/Vetta; FG Trade/Vetta; janiecbros/Vetta; **U7:** Crane.tv - Footage/Getty Images Editorial Footage; **U8:** SolStock/Vetta; pixdeluxe/Creatas Video; travelism/Creatas Video; OneForAll/Vetta.

The following videos and stills are sourced from other source:

U1, U2: BBC Worldwide Learning.

Audio
U3, U5, U6, U8: Epidemic Sound via Getty Images.

Audio Production by John Marshall Media.

Typeset
Typesetting by emc design ltd.

Corpus
Development of this publication has made use of the Cambridge English Corpus (CEC). The CEC is a multi-billion word computer database of contemporary spoken and written English. It includes British English, American English and other varieties of English. It also includes the Cambridge Learner Corpus, developed in collaboration with Cambridge English Language Assessment. Cambridge University Press has built up the CEC to provide evidence about language use that helps to produce better language teaching materials.

Cambridge Dictionaries
Cambridge dictionaries are the world's most widely used dictionaries for learners of English. The dictionaries are available in print and online at dictionary.cambridge.org. Copyright © Cambridge University Press, reproduced with permission.

UNLOCK ADVISORY PANEL

We would like to thank the following ELT professionals all around the world who contributed their expertise to *Unlock* Second Edition. Their insights then have continued to inform the development of *Unlock* Third Edition:

Adnan Abu Ayyash, Birzeit University, Palestine	Takayuki Hara, Kagoshima University, Japan	Megan Putney, Dhofar University, Oman
Bradley Adrain, University of Queensland, Australia	Esengül Hasdemir, Atilim University, Türkiye	Wayne Rimmer, United Kingdom
Sarah Ali, Nottingham Trent International College (NTIC), United Kingdom	Irina Idilova, Moscow Institute of Physics and Technology, Russia	Sana Salam, TED University, Türkiye
Ana Maria Astiazaran, Colegio Regis La Salle, Mexico	Meena Inguva, Sultan Qaboos University, Oman	Setenay Şekercioğlu, Işık University, Türkiye
Asmaa Awad, University of Sharjah, United Arab Emirates	Vasilios Konstantinidis, Prince Sultan University, Kingdom of Saudi Arabia	Robert B. Staehlin, Morioka University, Japan
Jesse Balanyk, Zayed University, United Arab Emirates	Andrew Leichsenring, Tamagawa University, Japan	Yizhi Tang, Xueersi English, TAL Group, China
Lenise Butler, Universidad del Valle de México, Mexico	Alexsandra Minic, Modern College of Business and Science, Oman	Valeria Thomson, Muscat College, Oman
Esin Çağlayan, Izmir University of Economics, Türkiye	Daniel Newbury, Fuji University, Japan	Amira Traish, University of Sharjah, United Arab Emirates
Matthew Carey, Qatar University, Qatar	Güliz Özgürel, Yaşar University, Türkiye	Poh Leng Wendelkin, INTO City, University of London, United Kingdom
Eileen Dickens, Universidad de las Américas, Mexico	Özlem Perks, Istanbul Ticaret University, Türkiye	Yoee Yang, The Affiliated High School of SCNU, China
Mireille Bassam Farah, United Arab Emirates	Claudia Piccoli, Harmon Hall, Mexico	Rola Youhia, University of Adelaide College, Australia
Adriana Ghoul, Arab American University, Palestine	Tom Pritchard, University of Edinburgh, United Kingdom	Long Zhao, Xueersi English, TAL Group, China
Burçin Gönülsen, Işık University, Türkiye		